FINDING DAD

A novel by Joseph Lynch

ISBN: 1517035961
ISBN 13: 9781517035969
Library of Congress Control Number: 2015913900
CreateSpace Independent Publishing Platform
North Charleston, South Carolina

Cover photo credit to CRMP Archive

For Ann, Avery, Barrett & Delaney - I love you and hope you never have to find me.

Prologue

Sunday—12 a.m.
December 7, 1941
Pearl Harbor, Hawaii

In a two-story apartment overlooking Pearl Harbor, a man rotated the dial on his shortwave radio. He made out the code phrase, "East wind, rain." Instantly his heart started to race. This was it. The surprise attack was happening. Immediately, he began destroying all his notes and paperwork he'd compiled over the last three months. He broke his hollow reed—they'd know what it was for. He used it as a breathing device to swim undetected around the harbor collecting information on the battleships, aircraft carriers, destroyers and cruisers for months now. Sure, they'd seen him on the streets but no one had any reason to question him. Now that was about to change. As soon as the first bomb dropped they could be at his door. All he could do was clean his apartment as quickly as possible and make his way to the rendezvous point, hoping the rubber raft from the submarine would be there on time.

Three hundred miles northwest of Oahu, six Japanese aircraft carriers readied 420 torpedo planes, divers and bombers. Crews were busy attaching the bombs and aerial torpedoes, making sure the delicate firing mechanisms were operable. Each torpedo was specially adapted for shallow water and was capable of sinking an entire ship all at once. All the pilots had to do was line their planes up and pull the trigger. It was that simple.

Captain Hasegawa of the carrier Akagi looked at the sheet of paper in front him, then glanced up at the clock. When he nodded, a young Japanese sailor turned, slid down the narrow stairs, and ran through the hall. It was time to wake the pilots.

Sunday—6 a.m.
December 7, 1941
5,000 miles to the east, in Greenwich, Connecticut

"*Get up*! You're not sleeping the day away while you're under my roof."

The figure in bed lifted his head, looked at the black window and rolled away from the disturbance.

"Oh no you don't. You're gettin' up now!" The man grabbed the blankets and threw them off the bed revealing a twenty-year-old male curled up in a fetal position.

Rubbing sleep from his eyes, he croaked out, "Wh-what? Sleeping the day away? Dad, it's not even light out."

"Don't talk back to me. Now get up!"

Vince staggered out of bed clad only in his underwear and stumbled down the hall to the sole bathroom where he splashed some cold water on his face and tried to focus. His father stood there watching to make sure his son didn't turn around and go back to sleep. It'd happened before.

Once Vince had dried the water off his face, he squeezed some toothpaste out on a toothbrush. "What are we going to do this early?"

"Gene needs a workout and you're gonna work on your left. You embarrassed the hell out of me in that match against Harvard last month. It's not gonna happen again!"

Vince spat in the sink. "Dad, that guy outweighed me by twenty pounds and I still got the best of him."

The man standing over him crossed his arms in disgust. "You had two inches of reach on that kid and it still had to come down to a decision. That ref is an old friend of mine and I wouldn't be surprised if he gave you the nod just because he felt sorry for you. That match should've been over by the second round."

Vince shook his head and spat out the last of the toothpaste. He followed it up by drinking an entire glass of water. He needed it. It'd been a late night—or morning—one that involved a good friend's wedding, a reception with an open bar and well, he wasn't sure what else. Now he was hung over, close to throwing up, and looking anxiously at the commode.

When his father was satisfied the boy wouldn't go back to bed, he went to finish off a cup of coffee. Vince combed his hair and made his way back to the bedroom. He closed his eyes before flipping on the light—he knew it'd be painful. It was. Of course it was nothing compared to the pain he was about to receive. Gene Tunney—the Fighting Marine—had once been the heavyweight champion of the world. He'd beaten Jack Dempsey twice—one of the most famous heavyweight fighters ever. Over 120,000 people had watched the first fight with the iron-fisted Tunney, and it was won on points alone. The rematch took place in 1927 and brought in $2 million at the gate. Tunney was paid $1 million just to show up. It was a thrilling fight—both fighters knocked the other down at least once before Tunney won a unanimous decision. And now, in an hour or so, because his father thought he was soft, Vince would spar with this man and likely come out the worse for it.

If only I hadn't drank so much.

It was bitterly cold as they quietly exited the house and began the short walk to the gym. No words were spoken, and in fact, not many words were ever spoken between these two men. Frank was a hard man who constantly worried his son was growing up soft. He wouldn't have it—couldn't have it. Life was hard and a man had to be harder if he was to conquer it in a respectable manner.

Frank's parents had been Irish immigrants who barely had enough money to feed him when he was growing up in Connecticut. Still, he'd managed to attend Yale, working at a shipyard in New Haven to pay for it. When World War I broke out, he joined the newly formed First

Yale unit—the famous Millionaires' Unit—and became one the country's first naval aviators. During the war, he'd been awarded the distinguished Navy Cross for his countless excursions into enemy territory, taking out a number of German U-boats. After the war, with a degree from Yale and a sterling military track record in hand, Frank was prepared for greatness but greatness never arrived. Instead, The Great Depression came in the war's wake, stripping clean almost everything he had. Like so many men of his generation, he felt like a failure despite the fact that he had little control over world events. Even so, he never complained.

Vince was the oldest of Frank's four children. It was his job to be a role model for his two brothers and one sister and so far he'd done well. His hard work at Philips Exeter Academy had earned him a spot at Yale University, where he played football, baseball, ran track and boxed. Boxing was something he did for his father, but football was his first love. He loved baseball and track too but his primary reason for participating was to keep him in shape throughout the spring. He was tall, muscular, and very fast. Unfortunately he was never tough enough for his demanding father. As an example, during the Yale-Harvard game in 1940, after catching a pass Vince received a jarring blow that broke his upper jaw. He staggered to the sidelines and was being worked on by the team trainer when his father came bursting out of the stands. "Quit whining and get back in the game!" Vince knew there was no point in arguing so he put on his thin leather helmet, swallowed as much blood as he could and finished the game. When the contest was over his father berated him for coming out of the game at all. Vince politely listened while he sipped food through a straw for the next six weeks.

As the gym came into view they could see only one car in the parking lot, a beautiful new Chrysler New Yorker. This was Gene's car. Frank turned to Vince and said, "Don't embarrass me."

When they entered the gym Vince saw his dad's best friend warming up by doing some pushups next to the ring. The only other person around was a crusty, old, unshaven man named Charlie, sitting in a glassed-in office.

Charlie had run the gym for as long as Vince could remember. If Charlie had a last name, Vince had never heard it. Charlie looked up briefly when he saw Frank and Vince cross the gym, giving them a quick wave before returning to his newspaper. Frank yelled out, "Hey Charlie, wanna jump in with my son when Gene's done with him?"

Charlie didn't take his eyes off the paper but said, "I could whup him, I shore could."

Frank smiled. "I know, that's the problem."

When Gene heard the commotion he jumped to his feet and walked over to the two men giving Frank a firm handshake. "Frank, it's great to see you old man. You're looking well."

"Thanks Gene, and you look like you could make another run at the title."

Gene laughed. "No, unfortunately those days are over. This is about as close as I'm gonna get to another big fight."

"Well then," Frank said sarcastically. "I guess your glory days really are over."

With that, Gene turned towards Vince and extended his hand. "How's it going Vince? Are you ready for some sparring?" They had been sparring since Vince was in high school and Vince hated every session. He was always way overmatched.

Vince shook his hand and said, "Hello, Uncle Gene." He looked Gene over. In front of him was a forty-four-year-old man well past his prime, but in great physical condition.

Suddenly Gene pulled the boy close to him, flared his nostrils and inhaled. "Jeez Vince, did you drink the whole bottle?"

Vince gave a half smile. "I tried, Uncle Gene. I might've gone a little easier if I'd a known we were gonna be sparring at 6 a.m."

Gene raised his eyebrows and looked at Frank. "You're a heartless old bird, Frank, considering we planned this little workout a week ago. You could've at least warned the lad." Like Vince, Gene knew a "workout" against a hung-over college kid would end the same way each previous workout had ended—with Vince in a bloody heap on the floor.

Frank waved his hand at Gene. "The boy doesn't need a warning. He needs a left hook."

"Well," said Gene, "we'll see what we can do about that. Go get yourself ready kid and I'll see you in the ring in fifteen minutes."

Vince headed to the wet area of the gym, while Frank and Gene walked off to talk about boxing. Once he was alone, Vince found the nearest stall and threw up. He was happy there wasn't anyone else around because that would've embarrassed him tremendously. They'd correctly assume Vince was throwing up because of both alcohol and nerves. If they told his father about it, the beating would be worse—it would further prove to Frank that Vince needed a stronger constitution.

When he was through in the stall he walked over to the shower, turned on the cold water, and let it run freely over his head. He needed to shake out the cobwebs, and fast. The water made him feel better, but he was still feeling lightheaded and a bit nauseous. He donned his boxing trunks and shirt and began warming up by running in place. He thought about how he was scheduled to take the train back to New Haven later that day to wrap up things at school before the long Christmas vacation. How would he look on the train with a swollen face? For a few minutes more he continued shaking away the fog that seemed to cling to his eyelids, before finally heading out to the gym for some quick work on the punching bag.

After fifteen minutes Frank called out to his son, "Vince, it's time. Gene's ready."

"What about me?" Vince murmured to himself.

The brief warm-up had made Vince feel better, but he knew it wouldn't help him a great deal. Gene loved Vince like a son, even giving him a tiny pair of boxing gloves when he was born. But deep inside was a fierce competitor—one that had beaten Jack Dempsey—twice. Once the bell rang he only knew one speed. For his part, Vince had no good options. He had to try his hardest with his father watching or else he'd be torn apart for being weak. Yet when he tried hard, Gene would respond in kind and the match would quickly escalate. That's when Vince would be in serious trouble because Gene was a professional, with tremendous skills, despite his age. Like telling a pit-bull to barely bite, taking it easy was not something he could easily do.

The two men climbed into the ring, while Frank took a seat in front of the bell. Gene walked over to Vince and in a hushed voice said, "Okay my boy, your father thinks you need some help with your left hook. The last time we sparred I thought it was pretty good, but who am I to argue with your old man?"

Vince grinned and said, "Former heavyweight champion of the world."

Gene smiled and winked at Vince. "You know Vince, that may be true, but I swear to God your old man's as stubborn as a mule. If he thinks you need a better left, then no one—not even I—can convince him otherwise." Vince nodded; he knew it was the truth. They headed back to their corners where each man slipped in a rubber mouth guard.

Frank called out, "Okay, you two ready?" Both men nodded and Frank rang the bell.

With fists up Vince and Gene met at center ring. They danced around for a few seconds and then Vince began to throw some tentative right jabs, all which Gene easily deflected. Gene responded connecting a few minor blows, which made Vince's already aching head pound harder. Halfway through the first round Vince saw an opportunity and threw a sweeping left hook. To his surprise it connected squarely with Gene's right eye and cheek. The sound of the glove striking flesh echoed through the otherwise quiet gym. Vince felt the force radiate up his arm and knew he'd landed a solid hit. Gene took a wobbly step back, but stayed on his feet. Then Vince saw his opponent's eyes change. The beast deep inside Gene was now awake. There'd be no turning back.

Gene came in hard to Vince and started in on the body. The blows—delivered with unbelievable speed—felt like sledgehammers. Vince did his best, protecting himself for the remainder of the round, but as he headed back to his corner he found it difficult to stand up straight. His stomach and ribs were already so sore he wished he could call the match right now. He took a swig of water and tried to stretch, glancing at the dour look on his father's face.

The bell sounded. Vince and Gene met in the middle of the ring again, and this time Gene worked in a few left hooks of his own. Vince dodged and ducked, but the near misses were terrifying. He knew if Gene made solid contact he'd be down. Seemingly frustrated by his younger opponent's ability to quickly move away from his flurry of punches, Gene went back to the body and attempted to force Vince into the corner. The tactic worked and as the second round drew to a close, Vince was once again hammered with body blows. Just when he thought he couldn't take another hit, the bell rang.

As the two boxers regrouped in their corners, Charlie left his office and walked over to Frank. "Your kid's good Frank."

Frank nodded and said, "He has his moments."

Charlie continued, "Gene took out Dempsey—twice—and your son just survived two rounds with him. I'd say he's doing pretty well for a twenty-year-old college kid. Give the boy some credit."

Frank didn't like Charlie telling him how to act towards his son. He simply said, "Gene's an old man." Then he rang the bell for the third round.

Vince's body ached as he made his way to the center of the ring. He was pleased to see Gene looking tired and bruised as well. Vince wondered if maybe he could wear down Gene and finish with some degree of respect from his father. This thought gave him a quick shot of adrenalin and an idea. If he could land another left and stun his opponent, it might end the fight. He didn't want to hurt Gene, but he did want the respect of his father and he desperately wanted the match to end. He tried to distract Gene with a few right jabs. Then, when he saw an opening, he swept his left hand towards Gene's head just like before. This time Gene saw it coming and unleashed his own savage left hook. Gene's punch landed a split second before Vince's. It was a solid shot that connected with the right side of Vince's face instantly sending him to the mat. He was out cold.

A few minutes later Vince woke up to a fuzzy image. Charlie was kneeling over him holding smelling salts under his nose. Vince twisted his head at the sharp smell while slowly coming out of it. There was his father discussing the match with Gene in the casual tone of two old friends discussing the weather. Neither had any concern for the wellbeing of the young man lying on his back, barely five feet away. Charlie put his hand on Vince's chest to ensure he didn't try to get up too quickly. As he surveyed Vince's eyes and head, he said, "You did good kid. You did real good."

When he arrived back home, he showered and quickly crawled back into bed. The pain was intense but somehow, he faded out. Sometime later he awoke to the radio blaring. Vince slowly made his way to the living room to find his mom and dad along with his only sister sitting next to the radio with the volume turned way up. Both wore serious looks.

"What's going on?" he said.

"The Japs just bombed Pearl Harbor," his dad spit out. "Got us good too. It's war now, Vince. "

Vince sat down and processed this news. It was hard to believe and even harder to understand. After listening to the news reports, he began to question boarding the train back to New Haven.

An hour later his two brothers came bursting into the house and the entire family sat spellbound in the living room. The huge loss of life. The ships destroyed. The entire nation stunned. At 6:00 p.m. Vince's mother, Helen, got up to finish dinner preparations. Just then, the phone rang. She answered it with a concerned look on her face. "Frank, it's Walter."

"Walter" was Rear Admiral Walter North, Commander of the Pacific Fleet, and another old friend of Frank's from the Navy. Frank had initiated the call to Walter the moment he learned of the attacks. He wanted to know more about what would happen next. Frank took the phone from his wife, "Hello Walter. Helluva day at Pearl. What's happening and what can I do to help out?"

Walter sighed and said, "Frank, it's a mess and we're going to need every man we can find. This is a courtesy call—nothing official yet—but you'd better start planning for the worst."

"I'll do anything. Where do you need me?"

There was a brief pause on the other end of the line. "Frank, war's for young men. You're an experienced pilot. We all know what you did in the Great War, but that was a long time ago. This war will be fought by men half our age. When I said prepare for the worst I was referring to Vince. Boys like him will be doing all of the heavy fighting."

Frank had never thought of himself as being old and he'd certainly never thought of his son as being old enough to do anything worthwhile. The suggestion that men Vince's age would be the ones to fight and die was jarring, and sent a chill down his spine.

He stammered a moment then said, "I can help. I want to help. Surely there must be something I can do."

"Well, if I were to guess I'd say that you may be needed running patrols out in the Pacific Northwest. We just don't know where these damn Japs plan on hitting us next."

Frank recoiled a bit and said, "You want your most experienced men running patrols? I want to be where I can do the most good—where the action is."

"I understand how you feel, but running patrols is an important job. We're going to need experienced reservists like you protecting the mainland."

Frank was still reeling from the thought of his firstborn son going into battle, but he pushed the thought out of his head then said. "Tell me when and where you need me. I'll be there."

"Thanks Frank, I'll let you know something as soon as I can."

Frank hung up the phone and sat quietly for a moment. Then he stood up and entered the dining room to join his family seated around the table. Vince could see his dad's stunned demeanor and said, "Hey Dad, what did Admiral North tell you?"

Frank thought carefully about his next words. "Not much son. Just what a mess this is." He stared at Vince's young face for several seconds. "Okay, let's eat."

The next day President Roosevelt asked for a formal declaration of war before a joint session of Congress, and within an hour, he got it. America was in another world war. Two days after the attack on Pearl Harbor Vince woke up early to go to the local recruiting station. As he opened the door to leave, Frank called out his name. Vince turned to see his father standing in the dimly lit kitchen. The two men looked at each other for a moment before Frank said, "Son, make sure you're flying over it and not running through it."

Vince smiled because he knew what his father was saying. "Don't worry dad, I've always wanted to be a pilot. I'll be joining the Navy. . . if they'll have me."

His father smiled. "Oh, they'll have you alright and they'll be better for it. Good luck, son."

"Thanks Dad," then he turned and left.

After the door closed and Vince was gone, Frank whispered, "God Speed, son. I love you." Then he sat down at the kitchen table and for the first time in his adult life, he put his hands over his face and cried.

Friday—8 p.m.
November 7, 1986
University of Mississippi at Oxford, Mississippi

He slammed the car door shut and looked at the fraternity house.

These guys! Again!

Abernathy hated making these trips, but every time he got the campus police involved, students got arrested, parents were called, lawyers fired off nasty letters, and his world went from a peaceful academic utopia to a living hell. It was better to keep giving verbal warnings until . . . well, he really didn't have a breaking point. Yet wherever the line was going to be drawn, the young men of Kappa Sigma fraternity were right next to it.

Turning up his collar against the cold, biting wind, he started walking. He could hear the deep thumping of the music even from here and through the stiff breeze blowing towards the frat house—the same music neighbors had just complained about.

Crossing the street, he climbed up onto the back porch and saw students spilling out of every opening in the house. There was no doubt that this was a rocking party, the kind that brought back memories of his own college days. But those days were long gone and he was now the Dean of Students. It was his job to get these guys in line, either that or the campus police would start breaking out the silver bracelets. If they hadn't called him first to see if he wanted to handle it, these kids would be getting fingerprinted and booked right then.

"Dean Abernathy! Can I get you a beer?"

He turned to see a student with flushed cheeks in a thin sweater standing out in the cold. Three other students were next to him, wearing the same sweaty red cheeks. They weren't five feet away from monster speakers blasting the Gap Band. "Where's your *leader*?!" he yelled through the music.

"*Peter's* inside. Want me to get him?"

Dean Abernathy shook his head. "No! Your leader. I mean—*president*!"

"Oh! I don't know. He's around here somewhere."

Dean Abernathy waved off the kid and opened the sliding door to let himself in. Now the music was almost humanly intolerable as four louder speakers faced him. His hearing had deteriorated as he'd aged, and he was sure this little trip would send it down another notch.

Looking for his target, Dean Abernathy picked his way through the mass of bodies and the debris of the frat house party. Not finding him amongst the sea of humanity on the first floor, he came to the stairs and began climbing just as a song—"What I Like About You"—from The Romantics began blaring away. When he made it to the landing, there were kids everywhere. They ignored him for the most part, almost as if he belonged there. Slowly, he squirmed his way through the masses and stood before the first door. Part of him didn't want to see what was behind it. Yet the only other option was to leave and let the campus police handle it.

He sighed, then knocked on the door. Someone from inside opened it up and let him in. Three students stood around drinking whiskey shots.

"Where's your president?!" he yelled.

The kid pointed with his drink, "Next room over."

As he left the room, six more kids blocked his path, making him work to reach the next door. Raising his fist he knocked on the door.

"Onn-*tray!*"

He opened the door and saw four young men lounging around the room, each with a beer in hand. They were all staring at the TV, which was tuned to ESPN, but couldn't be clearly heard over the loud music. The sudden appearance of the Dean of Students in their doorway, brought no reaction from the boys. Not one of them moved a muscle or said a word. Dean Abernathy looked at the faces until he saw the one he wanted. "Joe, can I speak with you in private?"

The fraternity's president looked his way and said, "Sure, what's up Johnny?" But neither he nor the other young men moved.

Dean Abernathy was now agitated. He didn't expect the boys to snap to attention in his presence, but this was ridiculous. "Okay, you three out! NOW!" The three boys began to move, albeit very slowly. When they'd finally left the room, Dean Abernathy closed the door and turned toward the only young man left.

"Joe, we've talked about these impromptu parties that keep materializing at your house before. I want them to stop!"

Joe was now paying attention, but his posture was somewhat defiant. "Are we breaking any rules by having some friends over on a Friday night? I mean, c'mon."

"We've been over this before. The world's changing. This university is under tremendous pressure to lessen its liability. If the lawyers get their way, alcohol is going to be banned on campus very soon."

"That'll never happen."

Dean Abernathy shook his head and sat down so that he was directly facing Joe. "Look, you're a twenty-year-old kid. How in the hell would you know what will or won't happen? Let's talk about the bigger issue here. You're a junior—a campus leader—a fraternity president—yet you still haven't declared a major. What're you going to do with your life, Joe? When I leave here, the campus police are coming to begin your criminal record, which could drastically limit your choices. "

Joe sat upright. "Okay, okay, I'll get it quiet. We don't need the police. But as far as my major is concerned, I just plain don't know."

"Look, you're a smart kid. Your parents are great people. You actually *could* have a future, which is more than I can say for some of these other liquored up derelicts. Have you considered insurance or real estate? Both are great industries. You could do well."

Joe sniffed the air. "Insurance? Real estate? What do I know about those?"

Dean Abernathy leaned in closer. "Nothing. That's why you declare a major."

"Oh, I guess we're back to that."

"Yeah, we're back to that. What about healthcare?"

"What?" Joe said.

"Healthcare. By the time you get into the real world all these baby boomers are going to need care. It's a future growth industry. Think about it."

"*Healthcare.* Don't I have to be a doctor for that?"

"No, you don't. But you do have to have a clean criminal record," Dean Abernathy said his voice rising unexpectedly, "Which for you is about to change if this party doesn't stop NOW!"

Joe sprang to his feet spilling his beer as he ran to door, leaving behind the Dean of Students with a sly grin on his face.

August, 1988
Dallas, Texas

The moment I walked in the door of my parent's north Dallas home, my nostrils were overwhelmed with the heady aroma of bacon wrapped chicken in mushroom sauce. It was one of my Mom's go-to recipes because she was so good at making it, one taste could almost make you cry.

"There you are. I was just telling your father the best way to make you show up over here is to cook a meal."

"Gee thanks, Mom. I just happened to be in the area finishing up an interview and thought I'd drop in." It was true that I just had an interview, but it was also true that, being out of college and unemployed, I tried to time my visits around meal times.

Mom kissed me on the cheek. "We're glad to have you any time of day. Why don't you go talk to your dad while I get things ready."

"How's he doin' today?"

"It's an okay day. Not too grouchy."

I left Mom in the kitchen and found Dad in the living room, sitting in his favorite chair watching the evening news. The chair had deep impressions in the armrests because he rarely left it. "Hey Dad, how ya doin'?"

Dad glanced at me with a flat look. "What're you going to do with your life?"

I stopped in front of him. "Hey good to see you, too." It was like this every time. In fact, if I was in the area, sometimes I just kept on going because I didn't want to hear these exact words—the same words I'd been hearing since I was a kid.

"You need to get a job. That's what you need to do." I could tell he was teetering between grouchy and angry.

"I know Dad, I'm trying. I'll figure it out."

Now he got angry. "Dammit Joe, it's your life, you *need* to figure it out! Your older brothers went to Ivy League schools and then on to Wall Street, your sister went to Harvard and is now the president of a public corporation. Did you know that?" I nodded. "They have drive and determination. You *need* to figure this out on your own."

"Okay, okay," I said trying to calm him down as red splotches appeared on his neck and cheeks. With his condition, this sometimes happened when he got agitated.

"I need a *drink*!" he spat out lifting himself out of his chair and walking over to the bar. There he fished out ice cubes from an ice bucket that was shaped like a cowboy hat—a "Welcome to Texas" gift from one of his friends on the east coast years ago.

Dad was now sixty-seven years old and already suffering through the early stages of dementia. He looked a bit frail for him, even though he was still a large man of six foot four inches, and I guessed he weighed about 230 pounds. This stressed out version of his former self had now irretrievably replaced the active, athletic man of his youth. With his physical condition and the oil crash three years ago, he was on blood pressure medication which I knew didn't mix well with alcohol. But who was I to stop him? There was enough anger in the room without wading into those deep waters.

When the drink was fixed to his satisfaction, he gathered it up and made his way back to his chair. Plopping down he took a long sip and set it on the table. I was just about to attempt redirecting the conversation when he started in on me again.

"Have you looked into the insurance business? Your brother says a real hustler can make some money there."

Now he sounded like Dean Abernathy three years ago in my frat house, trying to push me into something. And as the youngest of six children, I hated hearing how great everyone else was doing. It just didn't motivate me. I needed to shift the conversation somehow, but I didn't really know how to do that. The dementia had clouded his brain at a time when I needed him most. I felt a little lost professionally, and I wanted Dad to help me find my way. At the same time I needed to find Dad, find out who he was. Growing up, he was so busy trying to build his small empire that I guess I got lost in the five other siblings. I'd never really sat down and talked with him, got to know him. He was in his world and I was in mine, and the two didn't often meet. Now, when I needed to move the conversation to something else, I was out of bullets.

When I had left for college, Dad was doing great both physically and in his business. I had always assumed that when I returned we'd strike up an adult relationship and become good friends. But a lot had changed with him while I was away. I'd matured but Dad's condition had caused him to regress, making him less communicative. Now that I needed his advice I was going to have to be creative to get it.

I stared at a news report on the TV and asked him an innocuous question. "Dad, what do you think about Bush's chances to beat Dukakis? Think he can do it?"

Dad's demeanor changed. "Bush? Did you know I grew up with him?"

"What?! You and George Bush? The guy that's running for president?"

"Yes, him. And he was involved in *my* first job."

"Really," I was hoping he wouldn't go back to berating me so I ran with it. "What was that?"

"Gene Tunney had been the heavyweight champion of the world in the twenties after he beat that monster Jack Dempsey in two big fights. My dad and Gene were old friends and Dad thought some sparring sessions with him would toughen me up. I didn't like getting my butt whipped by Gene, but I'd never openly question my father—just wouldn't do that. We had one of those sparring sessions early in the morning on December 7, 1941—Pearl Harbor Day. I remember it as if it were yesterday. I left my parents' house early one morning a few days later to pay a visit to our local recruiting station. Bush, and thousands of other young men like us did the same thing. We were in different units but I crossed paths with George many times while we were in the service. My first job was as a member of one of the greatest fighting forces this world has ever seen. I saw a lot of horrible things during my time in the Navy, but I'd never trade a single moment of that time. I'm proud of my service to this great nation. So my first real job was a sailor, fighting for freedom, for the man next to me, for you even though you weren't born yet, and for my country."

I just sat there listening, hoping he'd go on, and I was intrigued by his comment about remembering Pearl Harbor Day "as if it were yesterday."

"So see if you can top that!" Suddenly, Dad looked away and stopped talking. It was odd.

Mom served dinner, and I left without any more incidents. In the car, driving to my tiny apartment, I started thinking about a career in something, anything. Then I thought back to Dean Abernathy and the one industry he mentioned that I'd been interested in: healthcare. Perhaps I should explore this some more. After all, I liked the idea of helping others and, as the Dean had said, the demographic trends pointed towards a very high demand for quality healthcare in the years ahead. And I could work with doctors, hospitals, and patients. That would be cool. The more I thought about it, the more excited I got. One day me: a healthcare executive. It had a nice ring to it.

So a few days later, I took my first job: a salesman for a wholesale paper business. One day me, a wholesale paper executive. It had a nice ring to it.

Three Years Later

I sat in front of my boss watching him fix coffee at his desk. He had a large mug filled with black coffee from our machine—a machine that likely hadn't been cleaned in the year and a half I had been there. Each morning this was a ritual I had to go through. Five times a week.

I waited while he blew on the coffee, then he reached for the special sugar box in his lower left drawer. Carefully placing the box on his desk as if it were a priceless work of art, he undid the metal spout with a fingernail that also hadn't been cleaned since I'd been here. Once the sugar was ready, he poured it vigorously into his mug making it seem like a magician's trick—there was no end to either the sugar being poured or the amount the cup would hold. Finally, when he'd poured in enough, he stirred it, took a sip, and was ready for our sales meeting.

"Joe, what're you going to do today to be a champion?"

Gee, I don't know. Enter the U.S. Open and win?

"I'm going to get an order from each one of my appointments today, then I'm going to cold call and pick up another five orders. That's what I'm going to do to be a champion today!" The words left my mouth in an enthusiastic but rehearsed manner. I wondered if this was how folks in communist countries sounded when reciting their oath each morning. As far as my sales were concerned, I'd never picked up more than two orders in one day. And out of my four appointments today, two of them were job interviews. Of course, my boss didn't know that last bit.

"Excellent! Let me have your orders from yesterday, please."

This was another part of the ritual, one where he used assumptive language to essentially shame me. "Dwight, I failed in my quest to be a champion yesterday and have no orders to turn in. But, today will be different."

Dwight Paxton deliberately smoothed back his thinning, unwashed rusty-colored hair, leaned back in his chair to give me the . . . *here it comes* . . . sad, grimacing look of disappointment. Because he was 150 pounds overweight, the first time I saw this particular face I was absolutely sure he was having a heart attack. I'd immediately jumped up from my chair to call for help. I didn't know CPR, but I was desperate to keep my new boss alive, especially since he'd convinced me to quit my last job. (He'd promised me I'd be making six figures in no time.) When he saw me jump up, he leaned forward in his chair and became agitated. That's when I knew it was all part of his act. I had to cover it up by saying I had a cramp in my leg. I was sure he thought I was a little bit off. From that point, it had all been uphill, especially when I learned a few months later that I really could make six figures so long as the two of them were to the right of the decimal point. That's when I knew I had made a big mistake.

"Joe, this is Tuesday and you have four days to get your act together. Now I want you to bring in six orders tomorrow morning and be the champion I know you are!" This was my signal to leave, so I nodded and rose to my feet. "Oh, and send in Clarence."

Clarence, the tiny, sneaky assistant sales manager, was sitting next to Dwight's door waiting to be called in just like he was every day. I didn't even have a chance to say a word as he rushed right by me. All this would be hilarious if it wasn't my life.

My life was being chained to The American Coupon Company, a direct mail company. We mailed out coupon booklets to households in the Dallas/Ft. Worth area, and it was my job to convince small business owners to place advertisements with us. I had quit a worthless job at a printing business and before that, my first job with a wholesale paper distributor. Now I found myself with a career going nowhere. It was depressing if I stopped to think about it, which I tried not to.

Two months ago I'd reached the final straw with my boss, Dwight. With my sales dropping, he ordered me to dress in work clothes and help out in the warehouse, moving around rolls of paper and other supplies. Even though he had explained we were shorthanded, I knew it was punishment for my low sales numbers. It was not only humiliating, but exhausting work, especially since I carried a college degree in my hip pocket. Sadly, his tactic worked. My sales increased to ensure I didn't have to go through that sweaty ordeal again. But the whole thing made me angry, pushing me to begin interviewing for a new job. I'd been trying hard for the last two months to no avail. Someone with little experience and three jobs in three years wasn't particularly appealing to most employers. Now I was stuck with the Boob, as I called him, due more to his ineptitude as a sales manager than his appearance. (Though I have to admit, with each sugar pour he was rounding out nicely.)

Now that the daily morning interview with Dwight was over, I was free to go to my desk to get organized for the day. It was 8:06 a.m. and I had my first sales call at 9:00 a.m. My interview was at 10:30 a.m. In no more than fifteen minutes I was out the door and on my way to my first appointment. It was a tailor located in a rundown strip center. They'd advertised with us a year ago and stopped—probably because our coupons produced dismal results. Now, it was my job to get them back and extract some of their hard earned cash for the fantasy of picking up more customers. I looked at my watch and saw I was ten minutes early. This gave me time to go over my sales presentation.

Mailings went out once a month. In Dallas there were four mailing areas: North, South, East, and West. Whoever thought up that scheme was brilliant, I'm sure. These areas alternated monthly since they couldn't all be sold at once. To me, this meant I had three weeks to call on every business in my assigned area. When I was through selling, I had one week to ensure the production department issued the correct proofs, printed each ad in the correct colors, and placed it in the appropriate order in the mailing. It was a logistical nightmare that rarely worked. When the company made a mistake—and we made a lot—we were required to give the customer a 25% discount on the current ad as well as a 25% discount on the customer's next mailing. These discounts came directly out of the salesman's commissions which meant with The American Coupon Company, I was a special kind of business partner: I shared in all the losses, but none of the profits. I barely made twenty grand a year. So much for checking out a job beforehand.

I put my sales materials away and left the car hoping for a quick sale. Checking my look in the glass door reflection, I opened it up and heard a bell ding.

"Good Morning," I said loudly to an empty counter. "Is Patel here?" I had learned to speak like this in case they thought I was there to rob the place. Suddenly I felt my pager vibrating and quickly glanced at the number. It was no one I recognized.

Eventually a woman came from behind a curtain. "Yes, may I help you?"

"Hi, I'm Joe Lynch with The American Coupon Company. I have an appointment at nine with Patel. Is he available?"

"Oh no, he's sick today. No idea when he'll be back."

I heard some rummaging behind the curtain. "I see. Are you the manager?" I had to try and be a champion today, the Boob was counting on me.

"No, I have no authority. Sorry. Goodbye." With that she disappeared behind the curtain. This happened a lot. No doubt Patel was in the back and had decided against placing an ad. It was her job to get rid of me. I decided to leave before they filed for a restraining order. At least I still had my dignity.

On the way to the car, my pager vibrated again with the same strange number. With my meeting a bust, I had time to stop somewhere and return it but decided instead to head to my job interview so I could have plenty of time to prepare.

It was 11:30 a.m. when I finally made it back to the office. My job interview was nothing earth shattering. It was a quasi-government agency that needed salespeople to get rid of all the assets they were taking back in Texas from the oil industry bankruptcies and S&L closings. It was maybe a two-year temporary job with no upward mobility. Still, it looked like winning the lottery compared to working another day for the Boob.

I walked into our lobby and approached Kelly, the receptionist, and saw my message slot was unusually full. "Your fiancé called a few minutes ago to see how your meeting went this morning." Of course what my fiancé was interested in was my job interview. Even though I knew Lisa would never incriminate me, I was somewhat annoyed she'd called. "She's such a sweetie, Joe. You should really hang on to her."

My sour attitude affected my answer. "Yes Kelly, that was the intention when I proposed to her." She handed me a wad full of messages two of which were from Patel telling me he was sick and not to waste my time driving out to see him. He had called minutes after I'd left the office. Nice!

I was just about to turn and walk to my office when Kelly said, "Oh and some girl named Robin Webster called no less than ten times. She said she tried to page you but got no response."

Robin! So that's who's paging me.

"Yeah I got the pages but didn't have time to call her back. Thanks Kelly."

As I went to my office—or actually cubicle—I thumbed through the messages from her. Each one said, "Call me!" The Urgent box was checked too. I wondered what it could be.

I looked around the cubicle farm and all the salespeople were gone, out in the field making calls like I should have been doing. When I strolled over to fill up my cup with water, I saw the Boob was also gone. Clarence, his ever-present assistant was also gone. Because he always echoed every word that came out of the Boob's mouth, I started calling him the Bra since he provided lots of support.

With no one in the office, I felt safe making a personal call from my desk. These were basically forbidden since champions have no personal life and are always smiling and dialing for prospects.

I sat down, picked up the receiver, and carefully dialed the number. Robin was an old friend, but not someone I saw with great regularity—she always seemed to have a boyfriend who occupied most of her time. We'd been high school friends, but not romantically linked. Robin came from a wealthy family and although she was always very nice to me, I'd felt as if she had some other place she'd rather be. Maybe that's why I never pursued her. When she went to a college in North Carolina, that left me seeing her only during holidays and a couple of times each the summer.

After graduating from college, she worked in Dallas for a year before becoming bored. Then she moved to Chicago to trade commodities on the floor of the Mercantile Exchange. During her year in Dallas, she'd invited me and several other friends to her family's lake house to cool off during the blistering summer months. The place became a regular hangout on the weekends and we had a lot of fun. Then, with spending so much time together, the dynamic of our friendship changed. We became much closer, though still without the romantic part. It's not that she wasn't pretty, she was. Robin had long brown hair and dark, exotic eyes. Since my days were filled working with large jackasses like The Boob, what intrigued me the most about her was how smart she was. She could actually engage in a conversation without annoying the crap out of me. When that summer ended we drifted apart again, but when we did see each other, we jumped right back into that summer frame of mind, like we'd never been apart.

I'd last seen Robin at a Fourth of July party four months ago. At this point I couldn't imagine why she'd be so desperate to talk to me. I wondered if a friend of ours had died. My thoughts were suddenly interrupted by a chipper but very professional voice. "UHI, this is Jackie. How can I help you today?"

"Uh . . . yes I'm looking for Robin Webster?"

"May I tell her who's calling?"

"Yes, this is Joe Lynch."

"Thank you Mr. Lynch. One moment while I connect you."

Almost as quickly as the receptionist put me on hold, Robin picked up the phone. "Heeeeyyyyy!"

"Heeeeyyyyy back! How are you?"

"Great Joe. Everything's just great!"

"That's wonderful. I'm happy for you. So who is he? Will I like him? Am I in the wedding?"

She laughed. "Very funny. Believe it or not I'm not seeing anyone right now."

This was interesting. "What gives? How could the queen of heartbreak be so happy when she doesn't have a man's neck on her chopping block?"

"Aren't you the sarcastic ass today?"

Touché. "Sorry, it's been a rough morning." I thought of telling her about it but knew someone might overhear me. Then I looked at the stack of messages from her. "By the way, why did you need to talk to me so desperately?"

"Well, I heard a rumor you might be interested in a career change. Is that true?"

My heart started racing. "Why yes, that's true," I said trying to sound cool. "Do you have a lead for me?"

Without hesitation Robin replied, "No, I don't have a lead for you. I have a job . . . if you want it. It's an excellent opportunity and if I were you I wouldn't pass it up."

Instantly, every ounce of pride in my body evaporated along with my ability to negotiate or be cool. "I'll take it!"

"Great! I thought so. Now do you want to know what kind of job it is? Or what industry it's in?"

"No. I'd clean sewer pipes if it got me out of here." I was serious and seriously ready to quit that very instant.

"Okay, it's not that. But first, I don't know if I told you, but I moved back from Chicago over a month ago."

"What?! Thanks for calling."

"Wait a minute," she said. "Let me finish. My stuff arrived here a month ago, but I started a new job which has me traveling constantly and as a result I just got back last night and . . . "

"Wow! That sounds like fun. Did you become a flight attendant?"

"No, I did not. And if you don't quit interrupting me I'll take this fantastic opportunity to another friend."

That gave me an instant attitude adjustment. "Okay, okay. I'm sorry. I'll shut up."

"Great. Now here's the deal. I work for a company called United Health International. It's a hospital corporation based out of Atlanta, Georgia. We own seventy-six hospitals throughout the continental United States. The part of the company I work for is United Health Initiatives. We oversee all home healthcare operations. We're not formally a division yet, but Harvey says it's just a matter of time."

"Whoa, you lost me. What's home healthcare?"

"Home healthcare is the business of sending nurses, therapists, aides, and social workers into a patient's home to care for them there and keep them out of the hospital. Or after a hospital stay, get them home as soon as possible and help them recover. Every one of our hospitals will eventually have its own home health agency due to the work we're doing at UHI, but until that happens they're losing money."

"Why?" I asked.

"Because a certain percentage of all patients leaving a hospital will need home healthcare, and if they're not going to the hospital's own agency then they're going to someone else. That means the hospital is giving away a fairly large source of revenue."

I was a bit calmer now, so I was able to ask professional questions. "Alright, that makes sense. How many agencies do you have so far?"

Robin sounded exhausted. "Currently we have five agencies fully operational."

"Well, with seventy-six hospitals and only five agencies it seems to me you guys have a lot of work to do."

"Exactly. And since UHI is acquiring new hospitals all the time, that number will climb. The future looks bright for our little division."

I was properly excited now. "Great. So where do I fit in?"

"Oh yeah, I almost forgot. The very first United Home Health Agency is located in Mesquite, Texas and is in need of a Marketing Director. I talked to my boss, Harvey Waller, about you and he thought you sounded perfect for the position."

"I'll take it! By the way, what does a home healthcare marketing director do?"

Robin laughed, "Man it must be bad at that place."

"You'll never know," I said.

"Basically, you'd have to call on physician's offices to try and get them to refer their patients to the Mesquite agency. There are other responsibilities, but I don't know exactly what they are. I thought of you because of your sales experience."

Sales Experience?! I almost blurted out. There was no possible way my current job could actually have given me experience for another, even better job. Was there?

Robin continued, "Your first step should be to contact the agency administrator. Her name is Diane North, and by the way, I've already taken the liberty of telling her what a stellar person you are and that you have Harvey Waller's endorsement. He's my boss. Unless you REALLY screw up the interview, the job is yours. All you need to do is call and make an appointment to see her. And I'd do it soon, before she interviews anyone else."

I took down all of the pertinent information and thanked Robin sincerely for her help. When I hung up the phone I was off-the-charts excited! I looked at my schedule for the rest of the day. A sales call at 1:30 p.m. followed by another job interview at 3 p.m., which I hoped, would soon be a moot point. My afternoon was pretty full. That meant I needed to get home now for lunch and call Diane from there—I certainly couldn't do it from here or from a pay phone with cars rushing by. I started packing up my stuff when a thought hit me.

Dean Abernathy. Who'd a thunk? And he'd mentioned healthcare. Maybe this is the break I need. Good 'ole Dean Abernathy.

"Who's Dean Abernathy?"

My heart stopped. "W-what?" The Bra was draped over my cubicle.

"You were babbling about Dean Abernathy. Is he someone you signed up this morning? I sure hope so!"

Crap! How much did he hear? Did he just come in?

"Uh, yeah, I mean . . . no, he's a prospect. I haven't signed him up yet." I was having trouble breathing.

"Oh. Dwight would like to have a word with you over lunch today."

I blinked several times trying to get my heart started, maybe some oxygen back in to my lungs and my mind working. "Yeah . . . well . . . see that's going to be a problem. I have something else to do at lunch."

The Bra took a step back allowing the Boob's fat head to appear. "Something else? Mr. Lynch, I suggest you go with me to lunch."

I was panicked. No way I was going to wait to call Diane. "Well . . . uh . . . actually I have to run home for lunch, but thanks for the offer."

Dwight raised his voice and leaned over me, "Look, I want to talk to you about your declining sales over the last two months. I suggest you put off whatever you have to do at home until tonight. A champion would."

I looked straight ahead into the wall of my cubicle wishing the man leaning over me would suffer a massive, long, painful, heart attack. Then, just before he took his last breath, I could bend down and yell at his face, "Are you going to be a champion today?!"

Instead of standing up and telling this idiot to go straight to hell, I simply glanced towards him, nodded, "Okay sure. What time?"

As anticipated, lunch was long and miserable. It was a blur of berating comments, Zig Ziglar style sales instruction, and war stories from when The Boob was a young sales executive setting the world on fire. When the Boob said, " . . . and that's how we sell at The American Coupon Company," The Bra nodded and said, " . . . and that's how we sell at The American Coupon Company," in case I'd missed it. Then I got a front row seat as they shoveled in endless pizza slices from the all-you-can-eat buffet. The entire time I glanced at my watch hoping the meeting would end and give me enough time to get home. Unfortunately, there was barely a ten-minute window that I figured was too slim to fit in a trip. The only choice I had was to go to my 1:30 p.m. appointment and pray they canceled too.

My 1:30 p.m. appointment didn't cancel and incredibly, they decided to book an ad. Unfortunately, this took a lot of time as I waded through everything they wanted it to say. As I wrote up the order, the only thing on my mind was finishing quickly so that I could rush to my interview then race home and call Dianne, the woman now holding my golden ticket out of mediocrity.

With five minutes to spare, I reached my three o'clock job interview. I entered the room with determination and focus knowing I had something better waiting for me if I could just get to the phone. As minute by excruciating minute ticked away, I mentally mapped out the route I'd soon take to get to my house all while these potential employers probed every microbe of my prior existence. I thought of using a payphone in the lobby of this building when I was done here, but knew the sound of people rushing by would cause an echo in the large lobby making me sound unprofessional, like I was calling from a bus station or jail.

Eventually, they finished analyzing me and I raced to my car. The strange thing was that I actually felt I had aced the interview and that they'd likely offer me a job. Perhaps having options made me more candid and thus more appealing. Whatever it was, I was quickly past it and focused on a new goal. This caused me to exceed the speed limit multiple times and perhaps ignore a few traffic control devices.

My watch said 4:45 p.m. as I raced up the stairs to my apartment slipping twice in ironically comedic ways and raking my shins hard, once on each leg. The pain was intense but nothing was going to stop me from making this call—except the phone number. I'd left it in the car in my briefcase, which was lying on my front seat. So, I headed back down, grabbed it, and raced back up being careful not to slip again. By the time I dialed the number, it was 4:51 p.m. I sure hoped she hadn't left early.

I took a deep breath and tried to relax as I asked the receptionist if she could connect me with Diane North. A few seconds later she was on the line.

"Hello, this is Diane."

I took another deep breath. "Diane, this is Joe Lynch. Robin Webster told me to call you about a position with your company."

"Yes, I've been expecting your call." That was exactly what I wanted to hear. "How about we set up an interview for . . . say Friday at three o'clock?"

That was in three days. It flashed through my mind to suggest an earlier day but then I didn't want to seem too anxious. Of course I didn't want her interviewing anyone else either. In a split second I decided to just go with it. "Sure, that's great."

She gave me the address and that was that. When I hung up, I was exuberant. Diane sounded professional and courteous, nothing like I was used to at The American Coupon Company. And she actually sounded like she was looking forward to interviewing me. The lift this call gave me was enough to get me through both Wednesday and Thursday as I learned the customer I had sold Tuesday afternoon had canceled their order and the folks from the job interview I had that same day had rejected me. That probably surprised me most of all.

With this great job dangling in front of me, I found I was less motivated. As such, The Boob was hammering me for lack of sales. That's why I was angry but not shocked when The Bra called my apartment Thursday night and informed me 'the boys' needed help in the warehouse the next day and to show up dressed and ready to work. I had been doing some last minute research to prep for my interview with Diane, and now I was pissed. Man I couldn't wait to quit this company!

I showed up the next morning wearing work clothes and carrying a plan in my hip pocket. I knew I'd be sweating and looking terrible so I had arranged for Lisa to call the office at 2:00 p.m. and say that she was the wife of one of my actual customers—an air conditioning business—and they needed to meet with me promptly at 3:00 p.m. to discuss the layout of their upcoming ad. I figured this would give me enough time to wipe off my face and arms with a damp cloth and change into my dress clothes, which were now lying flat in my trunk. Because Diane was located thirty minutes from my office, I figured I could make it with time to spare. I soon learned this was good plan, but not a great one.

First, Lisa called the office ten minutes late. Then, she said she was from some nonexistent pizza restaurant, not the air conditioning customer I actually had. Next, Kelly, the receptionist, took another ten minutes to give me the message. And when she did, I was in the process of carrying one end of a roll of paper so I couldn't just drop it and run to the phone. Then I had to help them with two more rolls before I could realistically break away. Now, my time window had shrunk. The only good thing was that neither Clarence nor Dwight was around so I didn't have to ask for permission to leave. I just cleaned up, dressed and ran out the door.

Through a sheer miracle, I arrived with one minute to spare. Wiping off some extra sweat from my forehead and trying to smooth out my clothes one more time, I entered the UHI offices and told myself I was getting this job. Nothing was getting in my way!

Instantly I noticed the offices were neat and extremely organized. When I met Diane North, I found she was both professional and personable. The first words out of her mouth were, "Joe, you come highly recommended by the corporate office and that gives you an edge over the other applicants." Of course I just smiled and nodded knowing she had no idea that Robin and I were good friends. So I just relaxed and let her sell the job to me.

"Joe, I need someone to organize the office, entertain the physicians, and be a business manager for some of the in-office issues that occasionally pop up. You see I'm a small town girl with a high school education. I just can't relate to these physicians. By the way, do you play golf?"

I made a mental note to buy Robin a dozen roses. "Why yes I play golf. Will that help?"

Dianne looked relieved. "Absolutely. You'll probably need to entertain two or three doctors a month on the course. And then treat them to some food and drinks afterwards." I smiled as I made a mental note to buy Robin a nice watch too.

"Oh, and are you good at handling money? Have you ever had an expense account?" The American Coupon Company gave me five dollars in quarters for calls I needed to make from pay phones when I was out on the road. The Boob had made a huge production about how this was an expense account and each quarter needed to be accounted for. This made it easy to be truthful.

"Yes, I currently have an expense account with my current company and my records are immaculate!"

"Great! You'll need money to entertain and for *incidentals*."

When we finished talking, Diane looked me up and down as if she were studying a stock animal. Then she said, "You know, I feel as if you're the right person for this job."

That's it! I had done it.

Then she continued, "But I'd like to take the weekend to think it over. I'll call you on Monday to give you my decision."

I nodded, thanking her for the time and said I looked forward to hearing from her. When I left UHI and made it to my car, I was on cloud eleven, having passed up nine and ten. Then I looked at my watch. Somehow, we'd been talking for almost two hours. That made me even more confident.

Yet on my way home, I made a mental note not to get overly excited about the interview in front of Lisa. If I got her hopes up too much and the job offer didn't come through, she might be even more upset than me. She was fragile like that.

Lisa was a simple but complex person. I had met her shortly after my crazy summer with Robin. She was a nice person and very pretty. Her long blonde hair and blue eyes are what had initially drawn me to her. Since then, she'd been the only stable part of my life considering my shaky career path, lack of expendable income, and mood swings from the rough days I spent with The Boob. She worked for a PR firm making less than me and unfortunately her chosen field didn't have much of an upside in regards to income potential. So, in our upcoming marriage, she'd be counting on me to bring home the bacon and right now, it was more like crumbled bits.

I had to admit though that over the last few years Lisa had definitely seen the best and worst I had to offer. When things got bad enough at The American Coupon Company, she threatened to leave me if I didn't look for a more suitable place of employment. This scared me because she was one of the few constants in my life. Even though my friends disliked Lisa because of the way she attempted to monopolize my time, I immediately began looking for a new job and proposed, all at the same time. I had always figured I would be deep in love, financially secure with a great job, and own my own house before I proposed to my future wife. Sadly, I learned that in real life, things never work out the way you think they should. Now, I just wanted to do the right thing with Lisa and begin a real career.

As anticipated and despite my attempts to minimize the situation, she was beside herself with excitement demanding to know every detail. Once we got past that, we had a nice weekend and for the first time, we both actually looked forward to Monday morning.

When Monday finally arrived I had my plan mapped out. I'd wait for a call from Diane until 2:00 p.m. If I hadn't heard anything by then I'd take the initiative and place a call to UHI. I didn't want to do this because again, I didn't want to look desperate. But I simply had to have this job.

By ten o'clock I hadn't heard anything and was beginning to panic although for some reason both Clarence and Dwight had not yet shown up for work. I wanted to stay in the office and near a phone since I'd given her my numbers to both the office and my pager. Still, I didn't want to be around when The Boob showed up with the Bra hanging around him. I knew Dwight felt that Monday's were a good day to be out in the field because he believed the business owners of Dallas wouldn't have had a chance to review their finances for the week and this would make them more receptive to buying from us. For this reason, I was the only sales rep in the office and it left me in a bit of a predicament. At 10:15 a.m., I decided to leave.

Just as I was gathering my things, Clarence approached me. "Dwight would like to see you."

Crap! They were back. I should've left five minutes ago.

I stood up and began walking to Dwight's office as Clarence scurried ahead of me to get a good seat for the fireworks. The Boob was waiting for me with his hands folded in front of him as he leaned forward in his chair. He immediately cut into me. "What don't you get about this process? You're supposed to be salesman. Do you know how low yours sales are for this month? And where's the paperwork for that new pizza restaurant?"

It was then that I realized my initial plan was not a good plan at all but a bad plan. Now I had some problems. "Uh . . . Dwight, the owner still has all the paperwork and is supposed to call me when he's ready to go. He wants to the get the design just right."

"And you didn't convince him it's our job to make him happy? Why would you leave the paperwork there? That's in-*sane!*"

"Yes, I realize that now but I'll go back out there now and see if I can pick it up and close the deal."

The Boob shook his head, "This isn't the mark of a champion. And hey, where is the initial order for this restaurant? You haven't given it to me."

That's because my fiancé was suppose to say she was with an air conditioning company which would match the paperwork I've already turned in.

"Uh . . . I thought he'd approve the design and I could turn it in, all in one shot. I was wrong Dwight. I'm sorry but I'll fix it now. Let me go out to there and turn this all around." I sat there trying to look weak and subservient as I studied the Glamour Shot of his plump wife and wished I was anywhere but here.

He rubbed his chin while he looked me over then said, "Since you apparently don't have any calls to make, I'm going to put you back in the warehouse for the day. That way, you can be here when this mythical pizza company calls."

I sensed the jig was up. I had one last move to make. "Uh Dwight, my clothes aren't really suited for that kind of work." He could see I was wearing slacks, a button-down shirt, and loafers.

The Boob grinned and said, "That's your problem."

I wanted to say a lot of things at that moment but instead I said, "Okay," and stood up to leave. As I was leaving I could hear The Bra snickering. But Dwight was right, at least now I'd be close to a phone when the call came in.

Unfortunately the call didn't come in. As I was working and sweating in the warehouse that day, my mind kept wandering back to Diane. What was going on? Why wasn't she calling? Was she interviewing other people? In my current predicament I couldn't initiate a call to her even if I wanted to. I began torturing myself as the day progressed. Maybe this is what I deserved. Maybe this was going to be my life from this point on . . . working in a warehouse for a fat jerk and his stupid sidekick with a college degree sticking uselessly out of my back pocket.

At about the time I had worked myself into a complete mental frenzy, a voice echoed over the speakers, "Call for Joe Lynch on line seven." My heart clenched and I almost crashed the forklift I was driving in an attempt to park it so I could run to the phone.

I took one deep breath and tried to calm my voice as I answered, "Hello, this is Joe Lynch."

"Joe, this is Diane North from UHI."

"Diane! What a pleasure, how are you doing?" My stomach was performing summersaults and my hands were shaking, I knew I was about to burst.

"I'm doing fine. Let me cut to the chase, I'm going to offer you the position. It's yours as soon as you can start. Your initial salary will be $45,000 per year plus a potential bonus."

I tried to not sound desperate as I blurted out, "I'll take it. Just let me give notice and see if they want me to stay the full two weeks. I'll let you know about my start date as soon as I can." This was important because I didn't want Diane to think I was the kind that burned bridges, although I had some serious thoughts about burning two particular people in my life.

As anticipated, The Boob wanted me to serve out my final two weeks. I didn't mind at first since two weeks would be just enough time to inform my customers of my impending departure from The American Coupon Company. The Boob tried to make me work in the warehouse a few more times, but I flat declined stating I needed to be out meeting with my customers. Dwight responded by excluding me from all office activities. On my last day Dwight asked me to join the Friday morning sales meeting, then when the meeting began, he made a big production about having me leave since, "We're gonna be discussing confidential customer information and we can't have you hearing any of it."

Top-secret coupon information?

And after he had asked me to sit in on the meeting? That was all I could take.

I left the meeting and began cleaning out my cubicle and packing up my car. During one of my trips to the car, I was in the lobby when Dwight tapped me on the shoulder and said, "Mr. Lynch, I hope you're not planning on leaving us early as you're obligated to this company until five o'clock."

I put my hand out to shake his hand and with as much sincerity as possible, I said, "I've enjoyed working with you Dwight, but there are a few things I need to do today in preparation for my new job." The Boob refused to shake my hand, nor did he respond in any way. He simply turned on his heels and walked away. The Bra looked at me and said. "How disrespectful." Then he clasped his hands, turned and walked briskly after Dwight. As Clarence was walking away I noticed his pants were ripped in the seat.

"What a fitting end," I mumbled to myself, not realizing the pun. I heard Kelly laughing as I headed back to my desk to collect the last of my belongings.

I quickly finished packing, said my goodbyes, and left The American Coupon Company for the last time. After all, I was going to need a few things before I started my new job—some nice business clothes, a new briefcase, and some golf balls. In fact I was going to have to stop off at the golf course for a while. I figured my game could use a little work.

2

After running my errands I drove to my parent's house to announce that I had 'succeeded' in landing a job in the health care industry. My father, sitting in his easy chair with his usual stern pensive face, greeted me with the comment, "You haven't succeeded at anything yet!" It was a deflating comment and made me wonder if he knew what being in a good mood was like. Dad followed up his comment by asking me, "Why do you want to be in the healthcare business anyway?"

I responded with a sugary tone, "Well, because I like the idea of helping other people." I left out the part about leaving a worthless job and making more money and generally being happy for once.

He scrunched his face up, his bushy eyebrows covering his eyes completely, and said flatly, "You aren't a doctor."

These types of comments grated on me like fingernails on a chalkboard. I thought about dropping my jaw and shouting, "REALLY!!! I thought my undergraduate degree in Business Administration qualified me to be an M.D. Damn! Sure had the wool pulled over my eyes there. Thanks Pop!" Of course this would've been very disrespectful so I stored that thought away for later, like if I needed therapy down the road. Instead I just said, "Yes Dad, I know that," and then I redirected the conversation to my mother who was beaming about my new career.

"I'm so proud of you," she said. "It sounds like a great job!"

"Thanks Mom. I appreciate it."

Mom and I made it through a few minutes of uninterrupted conversation before Dad interjected, "What are you going to be doing anyway?"

I turned to address him, because I hadn't heard his question since he had interrupted us. "I'm sorry, I didn't hear the question."

Frustrated, he put his drink down so he could use his hands to repeat the question. "I just wanted to know what you're going to be doing in this new job of yours?"

"Oh," I said. "I'll be working in a home healthcare agency. It's basically a medical staffing business."

Mom got up to check on dinner and gave me a look as if to say, "Watch it with him."

"Staffing?!" he said. "I didn't know you were getting into the staffing business. Do you really want to do that? Wasn't there some other type of business that interested you . . . uh, healthcare? Didn't you want to be in healthcare?"

"I am in healthcare!" I almost shouted, feeling my face redden by the minute.

"Don't you raise your voice at me," Dad said as he began angrily mumbling to himself.

I didn't feel like jousting with my father when I should be celebrating my new job, then I remembered our last conversation and decided to redirect him. "I'm sorry Dad. I think I forgot to tell you that I'm going to be working with my old friend Robin, do you remember her?"

"No," he barked.

"Well, I was wondering, you said your first real job was in the Navy. Did you join the Navy with any of your old friends?"

In an instant, the look on his face changed from anger to innocent pondering. "Hmm, let's see. I volunteered in 1941 after Pearl but since I was already in the middle of a school year the recruiter suggested I earn more college credits and get to a logical stopping point before my service started. When I actually entered the Navy I didn't know any of the other men, but I made a lot of friends in basic training. It wasn't hard to make friends because we were all scared to death and needed each other. Later in flight training and in the fleet, I met up with some great men—men I'll never forget.

I smiled because I'd got him on a roll. Leaning back in my chair I relaxed and let him take me along for the ride. I could see the dark cloud of anger dissipate and watched as a shining sun replaced it.

"After basic training I was sent to Corpus Christi, Texas for basic flight training where I started with classroom work. The classes were long and tedious. One day after classes, an athletic-looking lieutenant approached me and asked if it was true that I'd been a baseball player at Yale. I told him 'Yes sir' and he then asked if I'd be interested in playing for the Navy team. It sounded like fun, so I said I'd be happy to play.

"On the first day of practice I was introduced to the other men on the team. Among them was Red Sox great, Ted Williams. Ted and I became good friends during the time we played together. It wasn't a long term friendship but one of two men thrust together during difficult times doing the best we could to cope with the hand we'd been dealt."

"Wait," I said. "You were friends with Ted Williams?"

"Yes I was. And obviously after the war our lives took us in very different directions, but while we were together we had a fun and easygoing friendship. It's always been important to me that I befriended and competed with one of the best baseball players of all time, even though it's not something that I've talked about over the years. Playing baseball in the military was a coping mechanism. I attacked it with gusto because it helped me deal with the tediousness of military life. It also gave me a taste of regular life back home and took my mind off the awful things I knew I'd soon face."

He took another sip of his drink and then continued. I shook my head amazed at how little I knew about my dad and of the circumstances with which this conversation had started.

"I started my flight training in the Boeing Stearman and advanced to the Vultee BT-13 Valiant. The last phase of my training took place in Pensacola, Florida where I advanced to the Beechcraft T-6 Texan. Once I was deemed a competent pilot, I began the final phase of training in the plane that I would fly in combat: the Grumman F6F Hellcat. This plane proved to be one of my favorites because it was powerful, maneuverable and very fun to fly. I was carrier qualified on the U.S.S Sable and then became an official Naval Aviator.

"Once they got me combat ready, I was sent to Norfolk where I received orders to join my squadron VF-80 on the U.S.S. Ticonderoga. Since the Ticonderoga was already in the South Pacific, I boarded the U.S.S. Hornet so I could be ferried to my squadron. And among the shipmates was my old friend George Bush.

"George had already spent time in the South Pacific and had just enjoyed some R&R. He was headed back to the U.S.S. San Jacinto where he would rejoin his squadron, VT-51. I remember one night out on the flight deck on our way to the South Pacific, George and I talked about our past and of events to come.

"Bush said, 'Hey Vince, do you remember that baseball game we played against each other in high school?'

"I said, 'Sure, you were at Andover and I was at Exeter. We played hard that day and I thought we had you boys, but I think you beat us in the last inning. Right?'

"He said, 'We did, but that's not what I remember the most from that game.'

"I was intrigued so I let him talk as we both looked out at the moon reflecting off of the ocean. George went on. 'I was happy back then because life was so simple, at least for a seventeen-year-old kid. Sure, I wanted to win badly but even if we'd lost the game, I still enjoyed playing a great game against good friends. It was just a special time.'

"I chuckled a bit and said, 'You really are a thinker. I imagine the rest of us were too wrapped up in the game to look at anything else.'

"He laughed as well. 'Now, I just can't help comparing that day to this war. I guess it's silly to compare a baseball game to a world war, huh?'

"I said, 'Yeah a little, so how does one compare those two events?'

"George turned and faced me. 'Think about it Vince, many of us are old friends and we all have our individual jobs which, when performed correctly, make us an important part of a team. If we work together—like we did on the field that day—this victory can be ours.'

" 'I guess, but the stakes are a little higher than a baseball game.'

" 'Sure they are, but can't you just feel the conviction in the men you've met so far?'

" 'Sure,' I said. 'There's no questioning that. I have no doubt that we'll win this war. Our men are just too determined.'

" 'That's what I mean Vince. We're *determined*. Yes, we're all scared to death but no one I've talked to would rather be doing anything else right now, including me. Despite the risks, I'm proud to be a part of all this and I intend to make the best of it. That's all I am saying.'

"I remember looking at George and thinking how much I admired his passion. I too was proud to be a part of that great American fighting force but my friend had a way with words and did a better job of explaining his feelings. I said to him, 'You know George, you're damned right. There are times when it's just great to be in the mix. I guess this really is one of those times. I just hope when it's all over we can get together again and toast a victory.'

"He smiled, considered my comment, and said, 'We will surely have that toast with the gritty guys around us. We just need to keep our eyes wide open and watch our backs. We're good pilots and we'll be fine but the fellows on the other side can shoot too. Still, we're gonna win this game.'

" 'I hope you're right,' I said. 'I hope you're right.'"

Dad looked content as he contemplated what he'd just told me. George Herbert Walker Bush was at that time the 41st President of the United States. Even in his condition, Dad knew conversations with a man like that were something to be cherished.

At that moment I made a mental note to ask Dad some more about his past. His long-term memory didn't seem to be affected by the dementia the way his short term memory was. Who knows what else was rattling around in his brain, just waiting for someone who cares to let it out.

I had a nice dinner and left early because I needed to prep for my new life at UHI. I wanted to be as prepared as I could as I would now be working with real professionals, and I was determined to become one myself.

My first day of work at UHI was, as anticipated, quite a change from The American Coupon Company. Diane introduced me to everyone in the office and showed me the files of some of the agency's typical clients. There was ninety-two-year-old Vera Johnson. She had a long history of circulatory problems and was recently admitted to the hospital for chest pains. Upon her discharge her physician had ordered home healthcare as a precautionary measure.

Another client was Mabel Lee, a diabetic/triple amputee who was essentially a vegetable. Her deceased husband's insurance had been enough to keep a full-time sitter and a part-time home health nurse employed for the past four years. There was enough money to continue at this pace for about two more years. At that point, the family would have to come up with a new plan.

"Are all these patients so bad off?" I asked.

"No, I'm just showing you some of the more difficult cases so that you can fully appreciate what our nurses do. You're going to be distributing payroll every other Friday, so if the staff sometimes give you a hard time just try to keep in mind what they see on a day-to-day basis." It was obvious that Diane was trying to make a point. She held the upmost pride for her agency and wanted her nurses and workers to be respected. I could see that I'd have to prove myself to her before I fully gained her support.

"By the way," Diane said. "Robin called a little while ago and said she and Harvey would be by around noon to take you to lunch. Your first day at work and you're already being taken to lunch by the folks from corporate. Not a bad start Joe!"

"Harvey . . . that's Robin's boss, isn't it?"

"Yes, Harvey Waller is responsible for all home health operations for United Health International. So, he's actually everyone's boss."

I flashed a smile and straightened my tie. "Well then, I'll try to be as impressive as possible to show him what a wise choice you've made."

"Great, just don't impress him too much, I'd hate to lose you to Harvey too quickly."

This thought hadn't even occurred to me, and I was surprised that Diane mentioned it. What a great company. I was barely two hours into my first day and already there was talk of a promotion.

As I talked with Diane, I learned that she had entered the world of home care as a clerk when she was just sixteen. She was from Mesquite and had a high school degree, but no college. She was married, had two little boys, and seemed like a genuinely nice person. Harvey had recently put her in charge of this hospital-based home care agency before he moved onto corporate. It was a fast-moving company.

Diane felt strongly that I needed to go out into the field with one of our clinical staff and see firsthand what the agency dealt with. The field was where our patients were located and she thought it was important for me to see for myself whom we took care of and how they lived. Diane was going to set that up for later in the week and encouraged me to take some time before lunch to interview the other folks in the office and learn what they did. I agreed and started right on that.

After a hand full of interviews and some shuffling through papers, at 12:30 p.m. Robin entered my office to pick me up for lunch. "You're late," I said jokingly, since there was no way I could ever be mad at her for landing me this plum job.

"Actually, we've been at the restaurant for an hour, so technically *you're* late," Robin said before she burst out laughing. Her cheeks were flushed and her hair was frizzed, I'd seen her like this before.

"By chance have you been drinking?" I said in a hushed voice leaning closer to her.

"By chance . . . yes," she said followed by more hysterical laughter.

I smiled politely, hiding my utter confusion. "So what's the occasion? Someone's birthday?"

Diane leaned in close and in a conspiratorial manor said "We're going to corporate today and Harvey doesn't like to go to corporate sober."

This was disturbing. "Where's Harvey?"

Diane grabbed my shoulder to steady herself, "He's at the restaurant waiting on us, so come on mister."

I grabbed my jacket and since Diane was out to lunch, I left a written message on her desk telling her I'd be back in one hour. Then I left with Robin.

When we arrived at the bar, I was introduced to Harvey who was sitting at the bar talking with the bartender. He was not at all what I had expected. He was short, round, and his skin was as white as sheet. His eyes were sunken into his head and had large black circles under them. He had large flecks of dandruff on his shoulders and, except for his heft, had the general appearance of a zombie straight from a central casting. I tried not to stare, but he had this weird comb over hairdo that looked ridiculous. He walked like Charlie Chaplin, bobbing and weaving everywhere. He had no fashion sense, wearing his polyester leisure suit proudly as if it were Versace. It was a bizarre contradiction to what I'd seen so far at UHI. Could this all be some sick joke? I wondered.

"Hi, I'm Harvey Waller," the circus of a man said, shaking my hand only after he scratched himself. *Of course.* As he stood several beer nuts fell from his clothing. "You must be the pretty boy Robin has told me *sooo* much about." I winced at the slurry comment, but managed to smile politely and introduce myself. I would find out later that to Harvey, any male that appeared more attractive than him was labeled a pretty boy.

"What'll you have Joe?"

"Iced tea please," I said to the bartender.

Harvey interrupted. "Oh come on, you can do better than that. Don't you drink?"

"Yes, but Diane expects me back in . . . "

"Screw her!" Harvey boasted. "She works for me. I'm corporate and as long as you're with me, there's not a damned thing she can do to you." He paused and took a sip from his drink. "You are with me Joe, right?"

I felt unsure as to how to react as this was bizarre behavior, yet there was no way I was going back to work for the Boob. "Uh, yeah, I'm with you. For sure."

Harvey turned to the bartender and said, "He'll have a beer." Then, turning toward me he said, "Let me guess, a *light* beer?"

With this he chuckled and motioned for me to sit down. He then began rambling about all things healthcare. At first I tried to keep up but then it occurred to me he was just repeating himself, and half of the words coming out of his mouth were gibberish. The ramblings went on for an hour and a half with an occasional question or two tossed my way but with no effort to actually hear my response. Finally, the guilt I felt by abandoning Diane was too much for me so I excused myself to call her.

Diane was very understanding and told me this was standard behavior for our 'fearless' leader. She told me to not worry about being away from the office and said to have fun and get back when I could. What kind of job was this turning out to be? Not even getting a slap on the hand for an almost two hour lunch break, drinks provided. I had certainly hit the jackpot. But things were *too* good, there had to be some catch about this job, other than the grotesque boss.

When I arrived back at the table, Harvey and Robin were laughing hysterically and making quite a scene. Luckily, the lunch crowd had mostly left leaving only a few people in the restaurant to witness this embarrassing display. As I sat down, Harvey regained control of himself and asked, "What did that bitch Diane say?"

Not understanding the hostility, I said, "Well, she said to enjoy the visit and that she'd see me when we were through." Harvey looked at me in a strange and angry way, but said nothing.

I felt very nervous and finally burst, "Is everything alright?"

Harvey snapped out of his stare, studied me for a moment, and then in the most gracious manner said, "Look Joe, there's a lot you don't understand yet. You were hired for one reason, and that was to eventually work with us at corporate. Don't worry about the details, just learn as fast as you can and expect a promotion within your first year. You're going to do great here, I just know it."

The way he said this last statement was so genuine and real that it made me feel great. But truthfully this guy was all over the board. One minute he was talking business, then the next he was angry as hell. Yet when he was speaking to me, it was if I was the most important person in the world. I was very confused but excited nevertheless because it appeared that I really was being considered for a promotion on my very first day. This was hard to believe.

Suddenly, Harvey was happy again. He ordered another round of drinks and began teasing Robin for being so quiet. By this time, with nothing in my stomach but a few beers, I had developed tunnel vision and forgotten that Robin was even at the table. When I looked at her I saw a surprised look on her face, like she had just discovered a long lost friend. It was probably the same surprised look written all over my face. We both began to laugh at each other and in seconds were making another embarrassing scene in the almost empty restaurant.

I never made it back to the office. I called Diane back from the same pay phone as before at 4:00 and told her I was still at the restaurant. She said not to worry about it and she'd see me in the morning.

I made it home around 6:00 and immediately had something to eat. Soon, I began to feel awful about what had just happened. It was so unprofessional to Diane, the one who had hired me. I felt as though I'd let her down. And she was my direct supervisor for the next six months to a year *if* the promotion Harvey had mentioned came through. If not, then she'd be my supervisor for longer...or shorter if I took many more afternoons off. The more I thought about it, the more I realized I shouldn't put much stock in the word of a man who started his Monday mornings with a drink in his hand. I decided to make amends by getting up early and pick up some breakfast for the office. I planned to be waiting for Diane when she arrived. After a long shower, I was in bed by 9:00 p.m. with the alarm set for 5:30 a.m.

I arrived at work at 7:15 a.m. the next morning with donuts for the whole office. Diane didn't arrive until an hour later. When she saw me she flashed a smile and said, "Well, how do you feel today?"

I had been very nervous about how she'd react to yesterday's antics, so when I saw the broad smile on her face, a deep breath escaped from my lips and I felt my shoulders drop from their tensed position. "Diane I am so sorry . . . "

Before I could say another word she cut me off with a wave of her hand. "I never really got a chance to warn you about Harvey but believe me, I know what yesterday's lunch must've been like. I've been there."

Instantly a huge weight was lifted from my chest and I decided to take a chance with my new boss, whom I suddenly felt much closer to. "Diane, would I be out of line if I asked you about Harvey? I mean, I'm not trying to pry but yesterday was kind of interesting."

"Not at all," she said. "Let me get some coffee and let's go into my office." We both got a cup and headed to her office. When I entered it Diane asked me to close the door, so I held the handle down until I was sure it would close quietly, then let go. "Okay," she said. "To start with, anything I tell you is confidential and doesn't leave this room. Agreed?"

"Agreed," I said.

"Two years ago Harvey was a consultant hired by United Health International. He was hired to close this home care agency as quickly and quietly as possible. The agency had come with the purchase of the hospital and was an unwanted and misunderstood asset, so Harvey was hired to make it go away. Once he got here though, he reported back to the V.P.'s at corporate saying that they were nuts to close down such a potentially profitable agency. They told him he had six months to put his money where his mouth was or both he and the agency were gone. So they made him the new administrator of this agency."

"Wow! Where were you at this time?"

"I was a billing clerk then. The agency didn't have a business manager, so Harvey upgraded my title and gave me a raise. He told me what needed to be done to organize the office while he began marketing the local physicians. And as I'm sure you found out yesterday. Harvey is a complete mess. However, when he wants to, he turns on his charisma and he has the ability to make people think the world revolves around them. The next thing we knew the referrals came pouring in and we were back in business. By the time six months were up, we were making good money and the guys at corporate were thrilled."

"That's incredible," I said. "Is he really that good?"

"Yes," she said. "Harvey worked his magic by befriending the local docs and enticing them to refer patients. He set up a rotation of golf in the afternoon with one doctor then drinks in the evening with another. He usually didn't come into the office until around 11:00 a.m. and he was always in a foul mood because he was still hung-over from the night before. At lunch he'd go have a few drinks and come back happy in the afternoon."

I shook my head as Diane continued. I was in utter disbelief at this mysterious boss of ours. If I hadn't seen it firsthand, I wouldn't believe it.

"After a year or so Harvey approached the guys at corporate and proposed the idea of starting home care operations as additional revenue streams for *all* of the hospitals owned by the corporation. They liked the pitch. They understood that it was a way to capture revenue from their patient's even after they'd left one of the company's hospitals."

Diane took a sip of coffee so I took the opportunity to pose a rather rhetorical question. "Is it safe to say Harvey might have a drinking problem?"

A rush of air came out of Diane's nose and mouth as she began to laugh. Her coffee spilled so she began to clean up the mess with a napkin as she regained control. "I'm sorry Joe, it's just that I've never heard anyone be that diplomatic about Harvey's illness. The answer to your question is yes; Harvey has a severe drinking problem. He drinks way too much, but

I can safely say that he's one of those people you really want to have a few drinks in him to take off the edge of his quirky personality."

I had known the answer to that question before I asked it and now felt silly for even asking it. Still, I decided to ask one more question. "Diane, Harvey sounds a bit unstable. Now you're telling me he is an alcoholic. Where does this leave us? I mean, he's the director of our division."

"Yes, he's an alcoholic and he'll be one until he faces it down and gets help, but that doesn't mean he's stupid. In fact, he has one of the best mathematical minds of anyone I know. His track record, at least with this company, is very impressive. He took this agency from losing money, to making over one hundred and fifty thousand dollars a month. He can be difficult to work for, but I think you'll find that most of the people around here are pretty loyal to him."

"Diane, if he put you through such hell, what makes you so loyal to him?"

"He gave me an opportunity that I never would've had otherwise. Harvey earns respect by putting complete faith in his employees. If he trusts you to do a job and you succeed, the next time he needs someone he'll call you. If he trusts you and you fail, you may as well look for a new job."

With those words, I grabbed my coffee and decided I'd better get to work.

3

My mom was dying to hear how my first day on the job went and since I wasn't in great shape on Monday, I dropped by the next evening to tell her all about it. Dad was mostly quiet while I talked about Diane and the office staff, but when I got to Harvey and all his idiosyncrasies Dad's mood took a turn for the worse. About halfway through my explanation of Harvey, Dad reared his head back and said, "He's your boss. In my day we didn't question the people we worked for. You don't even know him yet. Don't you think you should at least give him a chance?" This was said in an angry tone as if I was whining excessively and he'd simply had enough.

Mom's jaw dropped and she glared at him. "Vince, he was simply telling us about his first day. Don't be so crabby all of the time."

This seemed to anger him more so he sat up in his chair to address her statement. "This boy needs to toughen up. So his boss had a few drinks. So what? When I was young we respected people of authority no matter what they did. We knew our place and kept to it."

I could see he was about to get off the rails so I tried my little trick again. "Dad, who was your first boss?"

With that, he leaned back in his chair and his demeanor once again changed from anger to one of stress and frustration. He looked at me, sighed and said, "Lee Kosa," and then he gazed passed me, out the window with a pained look on his face. In a matter of seconds, he had gone from angry, to sad and very distant. I hadn't heard this name before and apparently, neither had my mother because she was the one who asked the next question.

"Honey, who's Lee Kosa?"

Dad continued gazing out of the window for a moment and then he began to speak. "Lee was my first squadron commander on the Ticonderoga when I finally made it to the South Pacific. He was a great man and I'll never forget him."

Then he launched in to his story. "After a long ferry ride aboard the U.S.S. Hornet, I joined the Ticonderoga in the Marshall Islands to begin combat flight operations. The air boss of VF-80 was a great big guy from New Mexico who was of Native American heritage and greeted his men with a hearty slap on the back every time he saw them. Even if you stepped away for five minutes to use the head, when you returned he'd be there waiting to slap you on the back and greet you as if you'd cured cancer while you were away. His name was Lee Kosa.

"We quickly became friends even though Lee was my senior officer. We had an informal relationship similar to two old school chums. Lee had an unassuming air about him, but he was fiercely loyal and had a reputation as a real ball buster when you crossed him. To Lee, as long as you did what you were supposed to do there'd be no issues. But when you got out of line he'd be the first to step in and aggressively change your attitude. The good men liked Lee because they knew where they stood with him. The troublemakers hated him with most asking for transfers away from his constant badgering to try and make them better.

"We got along great from the moment we met because I was clean-cut, easy to teach, and respectful. I desperately wanted to survive the war and figured the best way to do that was to listen closely to the advice of good men who had been around for a while. Lee fit the bill. He was smart, disciplined, and happy to help me. We spent hours talking about the correct way to approach a target, common defensive tactics used by the Japs, and even how to survive a prison camp if I were to be shot down and captured. Lee was a wealth of information. And he hammered into our heads the intricacies of the Hellcats. One particular detail he covered every day was locking the guns when we landed. Like all other heavily armed combat planes that landed on aircraft carriers, they were equipped with locking mechanisms on the guns, which were designed to stop the guns from accidentally discharging upon landing. These locks were manually engaged by turning the gun switches to the safe position, which turned off all electricity going to the guns and disarmed the trigger on the pilot's stick. Then the pilot had to turn the gun charging knob to safe which disabled the mechanical functions of the guns. These two actions ensured that the machine guns located in the wings wouldn't go off when the planes caught the arresting wire and came to their abrupt halt on the deck.

"My first combat mission was a strafing mission over the isle of Luzon. Since many of the South Pacific islands had already been heavily bombed by our boys and were, for the most part crippled, us fighter pilots were instructed to make low passes over them in an attempt to flush out the remaining Japs who oftentimes tunneled into the islands. Four planes were sent on the mission and I was one of them, assigned with a wingman that was an experienced pilot and had been in the South Pacific for months. As the catapult shot me off the carrier, I felt excited and fearful. We flew in formation until we reached our designation. The two other pilots said they were going to begin working the north end of the island so my wingman and I headed to the southern end.

"Once over the island we began a series of low level runs to try and find the enemy. By this point in the war, the Japs had been beat up pretty good and our intelligence had determined that all of their anti-aircraft guns had been destroyed. This meant that there was less of a risk of being taken out by one round since they'd most likely be using small arms.

"As I came in low and fast over the island, I saw small groups of Japanese soldiers running about the hillsides so I fired at them as I'd been instructed to do but the feeling of excitement was replaced with sickness as I thought of the lives I was taking. When I pulled out of my dive I heard a small thud on the side of my plane and realized that I'd been hit by small arms fire. In an instant my attitude adjusted and I realized the very real fact of war: if I didn't kill the enemy, he'd gladly kill me.

"I made a quick assessment and determined that the plane hadn't sustained any catastrophic damage and luckily neither had I. Since we were now officially engaged with the enemy, there was no longer a need to maintain radio silence, so my wingman raised me, 'Those Japs have to be holed up somewhere on that hill. Let's make another pass and see if we can locate the entrance to their tunnel. Then we can drop some fire on them.'

" 'Roger,' I replied.

"Each plane was equipped with a large canister of Napalm under its fuselage. Napalm's a nasty substance that resembles burning jelly and is extremely effective as an anti-personnel weapon. So we came in low and once again we could see the Japs running about but this time we noticed the men coming from a well-worn area. In the middle of the clearing we could just make out an opening and I even saw one man emerge from it just as we pulled up to make a third pass.

" 'I got it,' said my wingman.

" 'Me too,' I replied. Then we regrouped for another run.

"I settled in at a safe distance behind my wingman and we looped around and began our decent to the tunnel opening. As we reached five hundred feet, I could see fire from my wingman's machine gun obliterating the jungle around the tunnel, and then at just under four hundred feet I could see the Napalm canister fall from his plane. I avoided the blast and released my own canister, and then we pulled up and away from the island. As I was climbing, I could hear a muffled explosion beneath me. We took another pass but this time there was no opposition or fire. As we flew in low to survey the damage, I couldn't see any movement, but just as I turned away I noticed the clear outline of a human body burning in the clearing. It was my first sight of death, death caused by my own hands. I knew this was a fight against a tyrannical enemy but nevertheless the image was one that will stay with me forever.

After landing back on the carrier, I taxied to the staging area and cut the engine. When I pulled back the canopy, standing over me was Lee Kosa. He'd scaled the side of the plane to greet his newly initiated combat pilot. He slapped my back with his large hands and said, 'Congratulations! You aren't a virgin anymore!' And then he laughed his loud, infectious laugh, 'Haaa, Haaa, Haaa.' I couldn't help myself so I smiled back and, despite what I'd just done and seen, I laughed along with Lee.

After that first mission I fell into a routine of flying missions similar to the first one, then returning to the carrier for a day of rest and debriefing. While I was on the carrier I experienced a number of close calls. One time I was scrambled to the deck because a Japanese spotter plane had been seen in the area. My squadron was sent up to look for the plane, but heavy clouds in the area made visibility difficult. The plane was never found, but the impact of our failure was felt a day later when a small group of kamikazes struck the Ticonderoga. We were lucky as we lost no men and the ship sustained only minor damage, but we all realized the enemy still had plenty of fight left in them.

"After one uneventful mission I landed and headed below deck to answer the call of nature. A short while later all hell broke loose on the flight deck. I was two decks below and it sounded like the carrier had been attacked by heavy machine gun fire at very close range, yet the air raid siren hadn't gone off. As I ran to the flight deck I tried to imagine what could've possibly happened, but I had no idea.

"When I emerged onto the deck, I knew exactly what had happened: one of the pilots had failed to engage his gun locks when he landed and the result was tragic. I saw carnage like I'd never seen before. The fifty-caliber machine gun had obliterated the flight deck and many of the sailors who stood on it. Men were running everywhere and the scene was completely chaotic. I quickly scanned the deck looking for someone I could help when I saw a pile of rubble and noticed that a man's leg jutting out. I ran to the pile and began carefully removing debris. It was hard work but I eventually made it to the bottom of the pile and to my utter horror, it was Lee Kosa. He was badly hurt and barely conscious. I could see his right leg had been almost severed and he was losing blood fast. I yelled for a corpsman but over the roar of activity I wasn't sure if anyone had heard me. The corpsmen were doing their best but with the number of wounded they had to deal with I knew it could take some time before one made his way over to help. As I bent down next to Lee, I figured the majority of his blood loss was coming from the severed leg. I looked hard at the leg, fighting back a wave of nausea. I could see the femoral artery spilling blood in spurts with the rhythm of Lee's heart, so I clamped down on it hard. At this point all I could do was wait.

"Lee had lost a lot of blood but by me stopping further loss, his blood pressure rose enough for him to open his eyes. I said, 'Don't talk Lee, help is on the way.'

"Lee smiled at me and in a low whisper said, 'How many times have I told you boys that the gun locks are there for a reason?' Then he grimaced and continued, 'Don't let this damn war get you Vince. You're one of the good ones.'

"I said, 'Lee, you are going to be okay, now save your energy.'

"He closed his eyes and appeared to be sleeping when a moment later a corpsman ran up and said, 'What have you got?'

"I told him as he hurriedly bent down and started his assessment of Lee. I kept talking, telling him what I knew when suddenly, he cut me off, 'He's dead. Just let him be for now. We'll collect the body later.' Then he jumped to his feet and ran off in search of someone else to help. I looked at Lee in shock . . . he'd just been talking to me.

" 'What a waste of human life,' I said to no one.

"After a minute or so I went to stand up and it then I realized I was still holding onto Lee's artery. I let go and stood up but I couldn't stand the indignity of walking away from Lee's body and leaving it uncovered. So, I removed my shirt and laid it on top of Lee's head and upper body. Then I said a quick prayer, whispered goodbye to Lee, and jogged off to see what I could do to help out.

"That's who Lee Kosa was. He was a great man, he was my first boss and I respected him immensely."

I'd been engrossed in Dad's story and hadn't even looked at my mother as he was talking. When I did I saw that her eyes were red and watery. She looked at me and said, "I'm going to go freshen up." With that she got up and left the room.

I turned to Dad and said, "Lee sounds like he was a wonderful man."

"He was. He was twenty-nine when he was killed and not a day goes by that I don't think about him."

Suddenly, I not only had a different attitude for respecting my boss, but I was beginning to understand my father better. As I left my parent's house that day I thought I would give Harvey a chance. I knew Dad would.

It was time for me to head into the field and see what our agency did. Diane scheduled my day with a field nurse starting at 10:00 a.m. and I was feeling a little nervous because I honestly didn't know what to expect. I was picked up on time by the nurse, who didn't seem very interested in baptizing the new guy but she was pleasant nonetheless. It was a very cold day in December as we donned our coats and she began by telling me what our day entailed. Our first stop was at the home of two elderly women living together in a small trailer outside the town of Rockwall. The nurse entered first to make sure that the women were decent while I waited outside. After a few moments I was allowed into the trailer but upon entering I immediately wished I could leave. Both women were very pleasant and happy to have someone new to talk to, but the trailer was a complete mess.

Apparently the heater had gone out so the women warmed their little home by turning on several of the gas burners, leaving them on all day long. Their method was crude but it worked well resulting in heat that was oppressive. What made matters worse was that both women were chain smokers and the cigarette smoke was thick enough to cut with a knife. After thirty minutes or so I began to feel sick to my stomach. And when one of the ladies stood up to fetch another pack of cigarettes, I had an unobstructed view right through her well-worn cotton nightgown. If I'd been a doctor, I would've billed for an examination because unfortunately, I saw *everything*. That pushed me over the edge so I politely, but quickly excused myself from the trailer in search of fresh air and fresh thoughts. After a few minutes, the nurse I was riding with exited the trailer, took one look at me and laughed.

"Boy aren't you a sight!" she chuckled.

"Yeah, thanks for my introduction to the world of home care."

"Well, I'll bet you'll never forget your first patients."

She was right.

As time went on I learned a lot from my time at the little home care agency in Mesquite. Diane was part home care savant and part innocent country girl. As much as I liked her, I feared that as the agency grew, someone might replace her with more education and sophistication. She knew she lacked polish, and it seemed to make her insecure. This was obvious by the way she carried herself in large meetings at the hospital and with our referral sources. She tended to push me ahead of her in those meetings, preferring that I act as the mouthpiece for the agency. This was great for me, but not for her. I felt a good deal of loyalty to her and did what I could to prop her up, but as the administrator, she needed to be the one in charge and the one handling much of this on her own. And I was quickly learning that the large corporate environment was very cutthroat. I wondered, and worried, if Diane could survive.

One day, several months into my employment, Harvey called to explain that in years past he'd put together a golf tournament for the doctors that supported the agency. I thought this was a great idea and took it to the hospital CEO who liked the idea as well. Harvey told me that he liked his tournaments to have a guest speaker at the awards ceremony after the players finished their round of golf. He said that back when he first put the tournament together, he had landed a local DJ to speak and recommended I start with someone like that. I had a different thought. Since this was a golf tournament, I called Norm Hitzges, a local sports guru who had a radio show five days a week. He was well respected and I thought he'd be the perfect speaker even though I really didn't know if he would even consider speaking at our little tournament. I made a call to Norm and got right through to him. He agreed on the spot. Harvey, a sports nut, was so impressed I had landed Norm Hitzges that he promoted me to corporate on the spot.

I was suddenly thrust into the big leagues, something I had only dreamed of—and I had done it in just under seven months! I was excited and nervous but I was ready, I thought, to conquer my profession. So there was no way I could've known what I was in for. I always thought I wanted to go into health care.

What the hell did I know!

Two weeks after the golf tournament, I reported to the corporate office in Dallas and was officially transferred. I assumed we'd meet with the corporate team and develop some sort of plan, but they were nowhere to be seen. Gayle, our receptionist and administrative helper was there as was Robin and Harvey, of course, but no one else. An hour into my first day, Harvey said we were needed in Philadelphia the next day to solve some problems. We didn't do a lot on that first day and didn't make a plan or really discuss what the problem was that needed fixing. After lunch Harvey left early for the day and recommended that Robin and I do the same. Before he left, he told me to meet him at the airport at nine the next morning for our trip. And with that he was gone.

When the day was up, Robin and I left the office and went to a watering hole across the street. We both ordered a beer and toasted in celebration of our first day on the job together. Then I headed home early to start packing, not wanting to overdo it the night before my first business trip with Harvey.

I had no idea what to expect so I packed a lot of business attire. I imagined sitting in important meetings with the hospital executives, discussing our newly intertwined strategic objectives and tossing around the latest business lingo *synergy* and *rightsizing*. I was prepared for anything and determined to make a good impression on whomever we met in Pennsylvania.

The next morning our plane took off at 10:00 a.m. with Harvey in first class and me sitting in coach, near the first class section. I assumed he was in first class because he'd accumulated a lot of travel miles. About an hour into the flight I noticed Harvey waving at me from behind the little curtain that separated the two cabins. I unbuckled my seatbelt, walked over to him, and immediately noticed he'd been drinking. With the flushed cheeks, the glossy eyes, the certain slur in his speech that I'd seen before, there was no doubt. Not that this was a huge revelation based on my previous experience, but it was only 11:00 a.m. and Harvey had told me that our plan after landing was to meet with our Philadelphia hospital's CEO. Granted I didn't know much about how these meetings went, but I assumed that a meeting with the CEO of a large Philadelphia hospital would require a certain degree of sobriety. Then again, I gave Harvey the benefit of the doubt since I was still young and new to this industry.

Our plane was fairly empty so Harvey asked me to sit in the vacant seat next to him. The second I did, a flight attendant appeared.

"Sir, do you have a first class ticket? Why are you here?"

Before I could stammer out a reply, Harvey spoke up. "Look, I'm a platinum member and we need to discuss some important business. And by the way, could you get us a couple of vodka martinis?"

This was before 9/11 and the flight attendant didn't seem to care a great deal about any rules we were breaking, so she headed off to grab our drinks. At this point we were one hour into our three-hour flight and I could see where this was headed. When she came back with our drinks, I tried to sip it slowly. I didn't want to be too obvious on my distaste with drinking before a big meeting and there was no way I was going to be wasted by the time this plane landed. After all, I'd been to college. Meeting the CEO of a hospital drunk was on the top of my 'DO NOT DO' list.

When we arrived in Philadelphia, Harvey decided for some random reason that a rental car wouldn't be necessary and that we should requisition a van from the hospital's motor pool. Unfortunately, the hospital didn't keep spare vehicles at the airport. So this meant that two maintenance workers would have to leave the hospital in two vans so that they could drop one off for us. This was going to take a while and it clearly was not the best use of our time or theirs, but Harvey was the boss. After a forty-five minute wait, Harvey began to get upset because the van still hadn't arrived.

By the time the van arrived, Harvey's rage gauge was about to redline. We were going to be late for our meeting at the hospital, the same hospital the van had come from, and we still had to get there. We began driving and made it about halfway before the van simply turned off at a stoplight and refused to start again. I honestly thought that the van had recognized Harvey's presence and shut itself off, not wanting to cooperate with the strange little man. Whatever the case, we were now stuck in the middle of Philadelphia still miles from our destination.

It didn't take a genius to figure out we'd be late to our appointment with the hospital's CEO. On top of everything else, it was 95° with approximately 99% humidity and my boss was as drunk as a skunk. I wasn't drunk, but the one martini I had choked down to placate Harvey, combined with the oppressive heat was making me feel like I could throw up at any moment.

I was about to suggest that we call a cab when Harvey suddenly began running/waddling frantically up the street. My pores were already secreting bucket loads of sweat, and I was trying desperately to suppress the vomit that kept creeping up my esophagus so I made the immediate decision not to run after him. I looked ahead of Harvey, trying to figure out what sent him into his frenzy, and saw that he was running to another van that had our hospital's logo on it stopped at a traffic light. It was close, but Harvey made it to the van before the light turned green. He scared the poor driver of the van half to death. Then, once the man realized he wasn't being carjacked, he did what most sane people would do in his situation— he drove away.

By the time Harvey got back to our broken down van, he was a huge mess in every sense of the word. I mean he was sweaty, nasty sweaty. Of course he was really mad too—mostly at me for not running with him, but also at the driver of the van for not pulling over. And worst of all, the run had somewhat sobered him up. I knew we were in trouble and I remembered Dad's advice about respecting your boss so I did two things. First, I saw a cab and made my own run to catch him. Luckily I only had to go about thirty yards. The cabbie had someone with him but he said he'd call us a ride. Second, I went into a convenience store and bought Harvey a tall boy. This made Harvey happy since he was once again consuming alcohol and also that he was no longer alone in his sweaty attire. While we waited, I said a silent prayer the cab would actually show up. Luckily, about ten minutes later, it did show up.

By the time we arrived at the hospital we were forty minutes late for our appointment. It ended up being forty-five minutes after I suggested a quick stop into the men's room might be a good idea. It helped a little but we were really disheveled and needed a full shower and change of clothes. I couldn't help but notice that Harvey smelled like a he'd rolled around in a pile of sulfur and showered with alcohol, but I doubted I was in much better shape.

When we arrived at the CEO's office, Harvey announced very officially who we were and said we'd experienced a slight setback on the way from the airport. The secretary looked up and almost fell out of her chair. I'm sure she didn't expect a couple of executives from her company's corporate office to look like two homeless guys who had just wandered in from the street.

The receptionist told us to have a seat because, since we were *extremely* late, the CEO had moved on to his next scheduled meeting. I wondered if the person in that meeting had actually splurged and spent thirty dollars for a rental car.

While we waited, Harvey pulled out a stick of gum and chewed it vigorously. When the door finally opened, the CEO emerged and he was exactly the type of person I had feared he would be: tall, put together, and meticulously dressed. The guy looked like he'd just showered five minutes ago and it was almost 3:30 p.m. He even smelled good. All this was excruciatingly painful, because it even further highlighted how bad we must have looked.

Harvey jumped up and introduced me to Dr. Simmons. After the introductions we went into his office. I couldn't help but to notice that besides being an M.D. the guy also had his Columbia MBA hanging prominently on the wall. Obviously this guy was intelligent. I guess CEO's tend to be like that.

I knew right off he'd see through the two of us. Still, when we began discussing business, Harvey, for all of his various problems, was very adept at conversing at an official level while intoxicated. Though it was impressive, I don't recommend it. Dr. Simmons didn't seem to notice Harvey's altered state, nor did he seem to notice that we looked like a couple of street hooligans. He simply told us what he'd like to see from us, which included various projections for our home health agency, which was now a part of his hospital. He also wanted to know specifics on national and regional trends for home care utilization in hospitals, which were similar in size to the hospital he ran. As the new guy, I sat there, nodded thoughtfully and took a few notes. I assumed that as the newbie I should just listen and speak when spoken to.

After twenty minutes or so, the CEO thanked us for our time and said his secretary would call us at the agency with a specific time to reconvene. Then he politely dismissed us so he could get back to running his massive hospital.

After the meeting, we went down to the maintenance department to tell them where they could find their broken-down van and to request another one. When the guy who was helping us explained there was only one van left and he wasn't sure if he could loan it to us, Harvey took the information surprisingly well. As soon as the guy walked off to ask his supervisor for permission, Harvey reached across the desk, grabbed the keys, and ran out of the room. Stunned, I gave chase and tried to talk sense into him. But, the next thing I knew we were peeling out of the parking garage as fast as Harvey could drive.

As we exited the hospital I assumed we would head to our home care agency, find a place to work, and begin pulling together all of the information we'd been asked to compile. Yet Harvey and I obviously weren't on the same wavelength. When we were on the main road, he turned to me and said, "Have you ever been to the dog track?"

"No," I said. "Why?"

Harvey smiled. "You're going to *love* this."

It was about 4:00 when we pulled into the dog-racing park where we walked into the facility, ordered two beers, and Harvey placed his first bet. The funny thing was that everyone seemed to know Harvey. *Go figure.*

As the afternoon dragged on, I noticed that occasionally Harvey would head over to the pay phone and make a call. This seemed a little weird to me, despite Harvey being the strangest person I had ever met, so finally I asked who he was calling. I expected to get my head bitten off, but Harvey didn't seem to mind the question at all. He responded that he was calling the agency's marketing girl and that he was trying to get us a place to stay for the night. This, I have to say out of all the events that had occurred that day, really threw me for a loop. So I asked a few follow-up questions, "Who is the marketing girl?" "What do you mean find us a place to stay?" "Aren't we staying at a hotel?"

Harvey glared at me, signaling I had crossed one of his imaginary lines. Then he smiled as if he decided to let bygones be bygones and said, "Tara's hot! She lives in a condo that's close to Atlantic City and it's nicer than any hotel. And, her husband is out of town. We're staying with her."

I carefully processed each one of these nuggets of information and a series of words came to mind: married—adultery—husband—mad—gun—homicide—morgue. I decided to stop asking questions. I mean, how can you argue with idiotic reasoning like that? It was wrong on just about every level, but once again, who was I to question this guy. He *was* my boss.

We spent the rest of the afternoon gambling at the dog track before it was time to go find the marketing girl. We got lost twice on the way to her condo but eventually we found it. Harvey wasn't kidding about Tara, she was very pretty and extremely nice. Tara took one look at us and started laughing. We must've looked like a couple of overused, dirty hotel towels. She was also really nice about the fact that we were completely invading her space. I hopped into the shower first and when it was Harvey's turn, I got to know Tara.

She met Harvey via her father who was one of Harvey's cronies in the medical supply business. Harvey did her dad a favor by getting his daughter a job as a marketer in the Philadelphia agency. I couldn't help but wonder if Harvey would've been so willing to help this nice young lady if she were as ugly as mud fence. Throughout the conversation, her husband wasn't mentioned and on top of that she was very flirtatious. I could tell it was her personality, but despite that I sensed she really was available. Then she came right out and told me that she had a very open relationship with her husband. I didn't dig too deep into what that meant; at least she finally mentioned that she *had* a husband. Needless to say, this was an interesting twist in a never-ending soap opera that was my job.

When Harvey emerged from the shower, he looked much the same as he had before. He had decided that the best way for the three of us to spend the evening was at the casinos in Atlantic City. At this point I was somewhat immune to his random suggestions and just said, "Sure." He explained that he knew all the good casinos and it would be a lot of fun. Tara was thrilled with the idea, so off we went.

While Tara and I sat at a table, Harvey wandered around like a kid in a candy store gambling on anything and everything. Unfortunately he didn't have very good luck so his results weren't good. Harvey proclaimed, "It's like, whatever bet I make always loses," then he slumped down into his chair and ordered another drink. Tara and I simply watched and carried on a normal conversation actually getting along fairly well.

At some point in the evening I realized that I hadn't had a lick of food since we had arrived. So Tara and I ordered some food, which we didn't eat until eleven that night. We both began to wilt soon afterwards. Tara had actually worked all day and I had done . . . well, all that I had done, so we were both pretty tired. Tara broke the news to Harvey that we'd like to leave at around midnight. He was pretty upset, but then he grew more concerned about the slot machine he was pumping dollar coins into, saying, "This should be the best machine in the casino but it won't pay out! What the f . . .!" Tara and I nodded then slipped away to her car and headed for home, or actually Tara's home. And her husband's too.

We had been back at Tara's for about forty-five minutes when an angry Harvey called. He had lost all of his money, and he couldn't remember how to get back to Tara's condo. Tara got on the phone with the cab driver and they eventually made it to her place. I decided this day needed to end, so I pretended to be asleep on the couch to avoid the fallout when he arrived.

It turned out I didn't have to act for long because I soon nodded off and missed whatever fireworks there were.

As if day one of this 'business trip' had not been weird enough, day two started off even weirder. First, my bipolar boss who went to bed annoyed woke up in a great mood. I assumed Tara had something to do with that. He said he needed to make some calls and run some errands. Then he asked if he could use Tara's Lexus, having grown tired of driving a hospital van. She graciously allowed him to drive it. Next, he suggested the two of us take the day off and hangout by the pool. Tara was downright gleeful with this suggestion and I was left scratching my head . . . again.

I borrowed some shorts from her absent husband and imagined how the police report would read: Victim, Caucasian male, lying face down in Suspect's house next to Suspect's wife and wearing Suspect's shorts. But, I made the best of it and the two of us headed down to the pool while Harvey headed off to do whatever he needed to do. Tara plugged in some music and explained that Harvey was probably going to see his bookie. We sat by the pool for about two hours before Harvey showed back up around 12:30 p.m. and said the hospital CEO's office had called the agency and wanted to schedule the follow-up visit with us at 2:00 p.m. so I needed to get cleaned up. Finally, it appeared we would be doing something other than screwing around.

I felt better about going to see Dr. Simmons the second day because I was clean, freshly shaven, and my clothes didn't look like they had been slept in. Harvey, even though he was clean and freshly shaven, looked just as he did the day before. Regardless, we were going back into the lion's den and I felt pretty good about things for the first time since we left Dallas. We even arrived a few minutes early for the meeting, adding to the good impression we were about to make.

When the secretary said we could go into the office, we collected our things and headed in. Dr. Simmons greeted us with, "Good to see you again. I'm anxious to review the data I requested from you yesterday. Do you have it together?"

A large smile formed on Harvey's face. "Of course." Then he turned towards me and said, "Joe, show us what you found out."

My heart stopped. My mind rushed a thousand miles per second and a red hot flash shot up my body as I began to sweat. I glanced at Harvey, and saw him looking back at me with a devilish grin on his face.

With both of them looking at me I knew I had to say something, so I said, "Well, I have some of it together but we had a problem with the printer back at the office and well, I couldn't print out the information. I should've saved it on a floppy and brought it over but I, well, *honestly* I thought we were going to submit this information tomorrow so I'm very sorry Dr. Simmons. I take full responsibility for the confusion."

There was a moment of silence. Then Harvey, with a disgusted look on his face, turned toward the doctor and said, "Well, I'm very sorry for this Doctor. I assure you that this is not the way my team usually operates."

Then the most amazing thing happened. The Dr./CEO/Columbia grad stopped Harvey cold and said, "Hold on, he didn't try to pass the buck. He accepted responsibility for his mistake and that's something I admire in a young person. Besides, I wasn't clear about wanting those reports today. I didn't know you two were going to be in town tomorrow, but that would be fine. I can wait. How about we say same time tomorrow?" I couldn't believe my good fortune. Lying, when done properly, can actually be beneficial. Who knew?

Harvey gave the doctor a you-just-let-this-idiot-off-the-hook look and said, "Of course, we will be here tomorrow and this time, I'll check the reports myself before we leave the agency."

Dr. Simmons, who I think was done with us at that point, simply stood up and said, "That'd be fine." With that, I slinked out of his office and almost ran past his secretary.

Once outside, I looked at Harvey and said, "What was that!?" Harvey glared at me as if to say don't push it. But I pushed it anyway. "I'm serious, that was complete bullshit! You're the one who wanted to go to the dog track yesterday afternoon. I . . . " I never finished the next thought because Harvey lit into me like I was a Marine grunt on the first day of boot camp.

"Don't you ever speak to me that way again! I make the rules on this team! It's not your job to question them and it sure as hell ain't your job to question me!"

Harvey had a way of speaking when he was really mad that made you feel you were really stupid. But during his little tirade, he then did something that got my attention. After he'd dressed me down for his addictive behavior, he defended himself in a pitiful sort of way by saying, "Besides, that stuffed shirt jackass doesn't know what he wants. We'll give him the reports when *we* want to." This took me back a little because it was very childish. Right then, I felt I'd glimpsed inside of Harvey for a brief moment and what I saw was a very immature and sorry little man. He was acting as if the teacher was at fault for us failing a test we hadn't studied for. It was weird and confusing and it made me feel like I was fifteen and in trouble, not twenty-five and in the business world.

I looked at Harvey and said, "Okay, how about we go to the agency, pull together the information he needs, and then go have a drink." It just kind of fell out of my mouth and before I could take it back, Harvey looked at me and smiled.

"Okay Joe, let's go."

When we were done running the reports and they were safely tucked away in Harvey's briefcase, with an extra copy in my briefcase just for good measure, we headed out. This time we ended up with Tara and her brother, Steve, for the evening.

Steve was a handsome fellow who still worked for his father's medical equipment business. He was nice but he acted like a used car salesman much of the time. As a result, we ended up at a cheesy tourist bar with some bimbo serving us multi-colored shots of unknown liquor that was guaranteed to make us all sick.

When the night was over, Steve suggested that we crash at his buddy's apartment that was conveniently located right around the corner. I thought this was one of the worst ideas I'd ever heard, but Harvey thought it was brilliant, and that's all that mattered. So Harvey, Tara, Steve, and I ended up spending the night in a partially furnished one-bedroom apartment that was a complete dump. I ended up sleeping on a disgusting love seat that was half as long as I am tall and awoke feeling horrible and looking even worse. As I glanced around at the disaster scene, I wondered if anyone else went on business trips like this one.

Tara drove us back to her place so we could clean up and then we headed to the hospital for round three with Dr. Simmons. At twenty-five, I could rebound pretty quickly after a night out on the town but after two nights out and sleeping on small, hard couches, I had bags under my eyes and knew that I looked as bad as I felt.

When we sat down with the good doctor to go over the numbers he'd requested, Harvey started messing with his briefcase/satchel thing and babbling about all the good information he had for Dr. Simmons. After a long painful two minutes, he emptied the entire contents on the floor looking for the reports. There, amidst the small, airline-sized liquor bottles, cigarettes, and bottles of Tums, Harvey finally found some of the reports. He started to present them to Dr. Simmons, but they were badly wrinkled and since he hadn't found all of them, they were incomplete. I said, "Hold on Harvey, I believe I have another copy here." I quickly pulled out my clean copies and handed them to the doctor.

As I stepped past him to hand the reports to Dr. Simmons, I caught a glimpse of Harvey and he was glaring at me. I realized immediately that I had accidently upstaged him and he was not pleased. We made it through the meeting discussing the reports and actually talking some business, which pleased the doctor. Once we left the hospital, the fireworks started.

Harvey let me have it with both barrels for making him look bad in front of the doctor. I stood up for myself, but it didn't matter what I said. He was in orbit with rage. We went to the agency and Harvey immediately holed up in one of the offices with Tara. After an hour or so I saw the door open and they walked out of the office. Tara looked at me and smiled. As they walked in my direction, I heard Harvey say, "Come on. We're going to have a drink."

I was happy he was in a better mood but wondered what in the heck was going to happen next. After all, the last thing I wanted to do was have a drink. However, this time Tara was in charge so we ended up at a five-star hotel sitting by the pool sipping Sea Breezes. At least this was better than multi-colored liquor shots served by the bimbo from the night before.

At one point Harvey got up to use the restroom and I turned to Tara and said, "What did you do? He was so mad I thought he was going to stroke out. And the reason he was mad is because I saved him from looking like a fool. What the hell is happening here?"

Tara smiled and said, "Harvey's a child and he can't process the basic facts of life. He was mad because he thought you made him look bad. I simply explained that he needs you since organization is easy for you and hard for him. He shouldn't fight you but he should use you in a way that benefits him." I could see where she was going but I must've had a weird look on my face because she said, "What's wrong?"

I said, "I'm a little hung up on the term, 'use you'."

Tara smiled again, and placed her hand on my arm. She leaned in close and said, "You obviously missed the part where I told him he needed you. And you know what, I think he does. You're organized, reasonable and, well . . . everything he's not, so you may as well play it to your advantage."

I thought about this advice and it dawned on me she was right. I was so preoccupied with what a jackass this guy was and how uncomfortable he made me feel that it hadn't even occurred to me he might need someone reasonably normal to offset him. Maybe he actually knew how screwed up he was and took his frustration out on guys like me. I felt more comfortable in my own skin with this new perspective. With Tara in charge, we still stayed out too late but at least we did it at really nice places. After drinks at the hotel, she drove us to a top-notch steakhouse. After dinner we headed back to her house where I slept on her couch again. Thankfully there was still no sign of her husband.

In the morning, Harvey announced that our work was done and it was time to go home. With my head pounding and my back a mess from sleeping on couches for three nights, we headed to the airport and flew home. When I got back to my apartment I had a message from Robin on my voicemail. I called her back and when she answered the phone all I could say was "Wow!" and she began laughing. That made me start laughing and we kept at it for several minutes.

After we both calmed down a bit Robin said, "Well, it's official, you're now a healthcare executive." And with that we lost it again for several more minutes. This was to become a common occurrence for the two of us since Robin and I had the same sense of humor, we made each other laugh—a lot.

I thought a great deal about my new career and decided that as weird as it had been so far, I was going to stick it out and see what happened.

4

After my experience on the Philadelphia trip, I was really contemplating the advice my dad had given me about bosses and respect. I decided it would be best to ask him out to lunch and maybe approach the topic with more sincerity. I knew that dementia affected people in different ways and was glad that Dad seemed to fully recall his past, even though he struggled with the present. He was now seventy-one and his dementia had become worse but it didn't affect our talks, which I had really begun to enjoy, and I was pleased to have found this window to his past. Our time together highlighted how little I knew about him, but also how much he still had to offer me. For such a long time I'd been unable to effectively communicate with him and now I felt I was seeing him for the first time in a way I never thought I would, and it was all because of this crazy job. Even when there wasn't a direct lesson to be learned, I loved hearing about his experiences. His stories held a real importance, regardless of whether or not he was my dad.

When we sat down to lunch, he said, "How's work?"

I said, "It's fine so far. I just got back from Philadelphia and had several tough days." It was an offhanded comment and I didn't mean it in a serious manner, but Dad looked ruffled and mumbled under his breath, "*Tough days, I doubt that.*" I rushed to make up for my sour start, "Hey Dad, did you have any other tough days like the one with Lee Kosa?

The serious look on his face subsided and he took a sip of his drink. His eyes got that glazed over look, signaling he was recalling another memory from back in the day. He said, "Yes, I did have a lot of tough days but one does stick out." He put the glass down so that he could use his hands to speak. "After I'd been in the South Pacific for about four months, I had a day that I'll never forget. It all started very early in the morning.

"During my time on the Ticonderoga, I saw many men come and go. Some of them were lost in battle and some, who had done their time, just shipped out and went home. Eventually, I became the flight leader. This had its benefits of course, but it also had drawbacks. One morning at 0500 I was roused out of bed to fly a mission. A nighttime radio operator had heard what appeared to be a Japanese supply ship report it was delivering it's payload to one of the nearby Jap held islands, so my fellow pilots and I were being sent out to destroy the ship before the delivery could be completed.

"As I ran to the deck and climbed into my plane, the catapults were warming up to launch me off of the deck. Back then, the catapults were run by steam and anything run by steam is not much use unless it had enough steam built up to work the internal mechanisms. As a result, warming up the catapults was absolutely necessary before attempting to launch a plane.

"On this day, because of the urgent nature of the situation, the deck-hands did not give the catapults the appropriate amount of time to warm up and the result was a cold launch which sent me off the end of the Ticonderoga and into the Pacific a few hundred yards out in front of the carrier but that was about it. As I opened the canopy and deployed my six-foot rubber raft, I glanced back and realized that the Ticonderoga was bearing down on me. My plane sinking fast, I knew that it could take me under so I had to get away from the plane. I quickly scrambled onto my raft and tried to figure out what to do next.

"Aircraft carriers back then were not as big as a modern aircraft carriers but it was still a 900 foot long, 27 ton ship. From the vantage point of a six-foot long rubber raft, it looked like a moving mountain coming directly at me.

"My first thought was to try and paddle out of its way, but I only had seconds to try and create distance between me and the hull of the ship. Unfortunately, despite my efforts, I wasn't very successful. I just didn't have enough time to create the distance necessary to get me out of harm's way. When the ship was about forty yards away, I pretty much figured I was about to be sucked under the huge ship and chopped to pieces by its massive propellers. Then, I had an idea, a desperate idea but it was my only chance.

"As the hull was cutting through the water, I realized it was creating a large bow wave pushing out from the front of the ship. My rubber raft was hard to paddle because the bottom was flat and not streamlined like a boat. This particular feature was bad for paddling but might be good for surfing. I was just off the center of the hull so I prepared to lean forward as the ship displaced water and hoped it would help me jet away from the boat. When the bow wave hit me I rode it about ten yards from the huge ship, but knew it still wasn't enough to survive so I decided to jump into the dark water and swim as fast and hard as I could while towing the raft. I really felt like I was making some progress but could tell I was still being sucked back to the propellers. I thought about letting go of the raft, which was dragging me, but that would've meant certain death by drowning or even worse, sharks.

"Standard procedure back then was for the ship to cut engines immediately. The ship couldn't stop for the sake of one man but if the screws could slow down just a bit it might make survivability more possible. So I swam for my life away from the ship and didn't look back. If I got sucked in, so be it. But it wasn't going to be for lack of effort.

"I could feel the end was near and figured I needed to climb back on the raft for a better chance of survival. As I did, I could see the stern looked like a boiling cauldron of death. Just as it swept close to me, I began spinning in one of the whirlpools created by the ship as it cut through the water. I held on tight assuming that one of them would spin me down towards the propellers but it didn't. Cutting the engines just barely saved me.

"By the time I caught my breath, the Ticonderoga was out of sight. All I heard was the sound of water slapping against my raft. That's when the hopelessness of the situation slowly dawned on me. I knew the ship would continue its current heading into the wind so the rest of the squadron could be launched and proceed on their mission. This was well before helicopters were around so they weren't coming back for me. But I also knew my position would be given to any other friendly ships in the area, *if* they were in the area. Now I was truly alone on a six-foot rubber raft in the middle of the Pacific Ocean. The raft had a provisions pocket, which contained a small amount of drinking water and a few chunks of chocolate. But it didn't provide any way to shield me from the sun that was starting to come up. On top of all of this I was starting to see fins circle my raft. Things were looking grim and I figured it was going to be rough day.

"I soon learned the sharks routine: they'd start circling the raft in a broad circle then slowly tighten the circle until they were brushing the raft. I figured they'd eventually tip it over so they could get at me. It was obvious they had experience at this. I looked at my standard issue .38 Smith & Wesson service revolver still strapped to my leg and the extra ammunition in the pocket of my flight suit and decided to put it to work. My plan was simple: when a big shark nudged the raft, I'd shoot him in the head a few times. The wounded shark's blood excited the other sharks and the feeding frenzy began. Then I broke out the paddles to put some distance between the blood bath and me. This process took about thirty minutes or so then they refocused their attention on me. I let it play out for as long as I deemed safe then plugged another one with only two shots hoping to conserve ammo. It still worked and a new thirty-minute routine was in place.

"After several hours and four dead sharks, I started getting hungry. I was thirsty too but despite wanting to gulp down the water, I forced myself to only drink small amounts because I had no idea how long I'd be in my raft. I had to conserve my water for as long as I possibly could.

"I was running out of ammo just as the long, hot day turned to dusk, and I was beginning to have thoughts about how long I may have to survive in the open ocean on this tiny raft. I was studying the sharks and was pleased to see they were in a wide circle, which meant I had a few moments to think about my situation. Suddenly, I heard something behind me. It was a bubbling, gurgling noise. I had become used to silence so the noise gave me quite a start. I was lacking water so my brain was having a hard time comprehending what was happening. Then it hit me: a submarine was surfacing. I'd seen subs during my time in the Navy but I didn't know much about them and had never been this close to one as it surfaced. One thing I knew for certain, this was not a coincidental surfacing. This sub was surfacing because of me.

"Now the question was whether this was an American sub or a Jap sub. In my current situation there wasn't a lot I could do either way except wait. As the sub materialized before my eyes, I convinced myself that it was a Jap sub, and that I was about to die. I got my pistol fully loaded and ready to fire at whoever was manning the gun. I knew I would lose this shootout but thought I may as well take one with me.

"As the ship settled in the water, it was about seventy yards away giving me a chance to study the mast where the sailors would emerge. It took two long minutes before I saw any activity then finally a body emerged. I gripped the pistol and waited a moment to get a clean shot off when I heard a man's voice call out across the water, "Ensign Lynch, Ensign Lynch we are the U.S.S. Devilray. Are you hurt?" I dropped the gun and collapsed back into the raft, a stupid grin spread across my face. I was in disbelief of my good fortune. Then I raised up, waived to the sailor and yelled out, 'Never been better. What took you so long?'

"After boarding the sub and debriefing with the CO, I was shown around, fed, and allowed to clean up. They told me when and where I could sleep because there weren't enough bunks for all of the men so hot bunking—the act of sharing beds between men on different shifts—was the norm. I was quickly bored stiff since I had no assigned role on the sub so I did my best to stay out of the way and took the opportunity to catch up on some letter writing to my parents and friends back home. I ended up being stuck on the sub for almost a week, during which time I smacked my head more than a dozen times on the low hatchways. Most of the men who signed up for sub duty were relatively short because of the cramped quarters. I, on the other hand, stood all of six-foot-four, causing me to have to stoop when entering certain areas of the ship or when stepping through one of the hatches. It was frustrating, but I wasn't complaining; it definitely beat floating around in a raft before being eaten by sharks.

"I developed a lot of respect for those sub boys and promised all of them that the drinks were on me if we ever met up again on dry land. The supply ship was a bit more comfortable due to its larger size but the men were a surly bunch who I didn't much care for. After a few days on this vessel I was shuttled back to the Ticonderoga where I almost fell to my knees and kissed the deck, I never thought I'd be so happy to be back on that ship. And the boys welcomed me back with open arms and a bottle of whiskey one of the guys had been saving for special occasion. It was great. Then, reality set in. We were at war and had to fight. I learned from this experience how much I loved flying and it was now time to get back in the air and do my job."

After this story Dad paused a moment. He was looking at his glass that had gathered quite a bit of condensation during his story. He placed his finger on the outside of the glass and wiped away some of the water.

Then, to no one in particular, he said, "God I miss flying." At that moment he looked tired. In fact he was beginning to look tired a lot these days. When our food came he picked up the fork and said rather nonchalantly, "That was my rough day at work. Now tell me about yours."

When I went into the office the next morning after the Philadelphia trip, I had no idea how Harvey would act toward me. I was relieved when he initially seemed at ease. He even offered to get me some coffee. The more time I spent with him that morning the more I realized he was acting like I was his good buddy. This was a pleasant surprise. It reminded me of those times in college when I'd been thrust into some crazy fraternity rush situation. Where I was asked to entertain some kid I'd never met before in hopes that he would join our fraternity and we had ended up hanging out together all night. In the morning, even though I still didn't truly know the guy, there was this feeling of camaraderie between us. It was a mutual respect that we had achieved through acting like idiots together. I wasn't sure how I felt about this comparison because I assumed that those days had ended once I left college. I now felt that I'd entered Harvey's gauntlet of crazy, psychotic debauchery and exited the other side alive and still willing to work. To him, I was now worthy!

I didn't really know the other members of the team except Robin, but they were there that morning. There was Dale the cerebral, a very quiet older guy. When I say older, I mean he was in his mid-thirties and had some experience that Robin and I did not have in health care. He was, like Robin and me, a generalist in that he'd go anywhere and do anything Harvey decided needed doing.

Then there was Kathy, a very outspoken nurse who was also in her mid-thirties and also had a lot more general and practical healthcare experience than us. She was our compliance specialist. Like all aspects of healthcare, home care has a ridiculous amount of regulatory issues that need to be addressed or else the state and federal authorities will rain hell down on you until you're forced to close your doors.

Gayle was our receptionist/secretary. It was her job to keep us all on the same page as we spread out across the country. Gayle was efficient and pleasant. She was relaxing in a very real way. She was in her late forties and had been around the block a time or two. She had silver hair and wore little rectangular glasses on the tip of her nose. She had the good-natured appeal of a grandmother watching out for her grandkids.

Then of course there was Robin, Harvey, and me. Harvey called the meeting to order by telling "us assholes" to shut up. He then told everyone that he and I had a very productive trip to Philadelphia. He also mentioned that I had done a good job representing our team in a professional and classy manner. I would've laughed out loud if I hadn't been so relieved that Harvey had lied through his teeth. I had feared he'd tell these professional's, whom I hardly knew, the truth: that we'd bounced around the east coast like a couple of buffoons. The only one who had a smirk on her face was Robin.

Harvey began by stating our big picture goals. We were, for lack of a better term, rogue agents of the corporation traveling from city to city in an effort to add home care agencies to the corporation's existing hospitals. Once agencies were established, we were the ones overseeing their daily operations. So when a state surveyor walked into one of our agencies anywhere in the country we'd receive a call and one or two of us would drop everything and fly out there to help them through the survey.

Harvey began laying out a plan of attack in very general terms. He did this by speaking about each of the projects we would be involved in over the course of the year. First, there was Philadelphia. He said our goal was to get the Philadelphia agency fully integrated. The agency already had its license and was fully functional, but Dr. Simmons was very uptight and we needed to provide some good PR in that market to get a full buy-in from hospital administration. Next was Lexington, Kentucky. Harvey had just transferred one of our nurses from the local Mesquite agency (where I began my illustrious career) to this agency to get it going. It wasn't licensed but would be soon and they'd need our help getting it off the ground. Third was Tyler, Texas. This project was just getting going so we would need to help it along. Fourth was San Lorenzo, California. This had been an existing agency with the hospital that UHI Corporation had just acquired. They were fully functional but needed our help with integrating into the corporate culture. Next up was Orange and Escondito, both in California. They were starting up and needed one of us to serve as project manager. Also on the horizon, but not yet ready for any real due diligence, were Austin and Fort Myers. Finally, we had our little agency in Mesquite and Kathy's home agency of Fort Worth, Texas. These two needed little or no attention from us since they were fully established and had experienced associates working in them.

After his recap, Harvey declared that he and Robin would be going to San Lorenzo, Dale would go to Lexington, Kathy would go to Orange, and I was to stay here at home. With no further explanation of what anyone would do once they arrived at their destination, the meeting adjourned with a flurry of activity as everyone set out to make their plans for the week.

I was a little relieved to be staying home because my trip to Philadelphia had created some problems for me on the home front. My fiancé had gone ballistic about all that had gone on with Harvey on the trip, and she thought

I needed to resign immediately. I wasn't impressed by Harvey's actions, but I viewed this as a real opportunity if I could just cut through his idiosyncrasies. I knew that opportunities didn't grow on trees, and I wasn't about to walk away from this one just because my boss was nuts. Parts of the trip had been fun, and I did enjoy the business we were in. Basically, I viewed my job the way an old west cowboy viewed a beautiful wild stallion—if I could hold on in the beginning, I'd have a really sweet ride.

In the office, I spent the next several days laying out a plan for helping to promote our agencies in all of our different markets. At home though, things with my fiancé continued to go south. There was a lot that had gone on between Lisa and me over the years and I was really beginning to question if this relationship was a good fit for me. She drew a hard line on anything I did that she didn't like and at this point of my life, I felt as if I needed a little bit of latitude to take a chance and venture into the unknown. Sure I'd make some mistakes, but that didn't make me a bad guy.

The truth is I shouldn't have proposed in the first place. Being young and stupid only goes so far as an excuse. I was prepared to accept the blame for making a poor decision, but I was beginning to realize that if I didn't take action, I might end up making a bigger mistake by actually going through with the wedding.

Then, the next day, my buddies called to remind me of the float trip they had planned for us down the Guadalupe River. We had never done this before, but had heard it was a blast. What we had been told was you get a bunch of people together and float in inner tubes down a river letting the current lazily pull you along. When they asked me if I was still in, I said "Of course."

This pushed Lisa over the edge and was the proverbial straw that broke the camel's back. While the trip hadn't been in the front of my mind recently, it was something my buddies and I had been planning for quite some time. Her severe reaction was based on the fact that we were not getting along and she thought I should stay home and be with her. I had a slightly different point of view: I wanted to get as far away from her as I could.

We argued back and forth for days, before I finally said the four most dreaded words in a relationship, "We need to talk." I came clean and told her I was having serious doubts about our relationship and I wanted to speak with the priest who was supposed to marry us in a few months. The priest was an old friend of the family and someone who knew me well. He had been the one doing our pre-marriage counseling so he seemed like a good person for me to consult with. She hated this idea because I think she knew the priest would tell me to run for the hills. She could tell that I was adamant so she finally just said, "Well then, call me immediately when you're done."

I went to see the priest and told him everything that had happened. Once I was done talking, he said, "Joe, I've known you all your life, and I can tell that you're obviously not ready to marry this girl. One should not enter into a marriage with doubts and it appears to me you have a good many of them." I fully agreed with him and was happy to hear his honest assessment of my situation. However, the next step of the process was going to be tough.

It was Friday afternoon when I walked out of the priest's office. As I opened my car door, my 1992 brick phone was already ringing. It was Lisa and she wanted to know everything that was said. I told her I was on my way to her house and would be there in five minutes. That wasn't the answer she was looking for.

When I arrived at her apartment, she had the worst look on her face and knew exactly what was coming. I explained that I'd made a horrible mistake and that I just couldn't marry her. Her reaction was pretty strong and besides getting angry, the first thing she did was call her parents and tell them what had happened. They said they'd come and get her and bring her home with them. The only problem with this plan was that I knew I couldn't leave Lisa alone. It crushed me to see how much pain I'd caused her and to have to sit there watching her sob uncontrollably was one of the lowest points of my life. And unfortunately, things didn't get better.

When I finally heard a knock at the door, I opened it to find her father giving me the steeliest glare I've ever seen. He simply said, "I think we can handle it from here." I left the apartment and never looked back.

When I got home, it was around 6:30 p.m. and my buddies had left me a few messages asking when I would arrive in Austin for our trip. I called them back and told them what had happened. I apologized and told them I didn't think I'd make the trip. One of my buddies said, "Why? What the hell are you going to do there?"

It was such a simple statement, but it resonated with me. I realized he was right, what was I going to do here? Mope around all weekend? He followed up by saying, "Man if anyone needs to float down a river and relax, it's you."

I appreciated his caring tone. This was a guy who knew me well and knew I needed to get away. So, I threw some gear in a bag and I headed to the airport. The truth was, it was exactly what I needed to do. I'll always remember the good time we had that weekend.

The next week Harvey dispatched me to Lexington. I welcomed the trip with open arms because it allowed me to keep my mind on something other than the breakup.

My parents were out of town when the breakup occurred, but they supported me fully on my decision not to get married. Especially when I mentioned I didn't feel ready. And let's face it, what parent wouldn't? They arrived back in town while I was in Lexington, but I went over to see them as soon as my plane touched down. Mom hugged me and said, "It's easy to love someone Joe, but if you're going to go through all the challenges life throws at a married couple, you'd better love your spouse completely or the two of you will never make it."

It seemed like good advice, and I appreciated the unwavering support she was giving me. While Mom and I were talking, Dad sat quietly and nodded the whole time seeming to agree with the sage advice my mother was doling out. Then, unexpectedly, he burst into the conversation and said, "What have you gotten yourself into now?" His statement confused my mother and me. It took me a few seconds, but then it clicked he was angry because he was confused. And he was confused because of his dementia. Mom started to speak to him in an annoyed tone, but then she too seemed to reach some sense of what was going on.

She stopped herself and said, "Joe, why don't you talk alone with your father for a while and fill him in on what's going on with you?" She knew he did better with one-on-one conversations when he was feeling confused or out of the loop, so she excused herself and let us talk.

I explained again what I'd done, and this time he seemed to completely understand saying simply and innocently, "How does this make you feel?"

It was the first time someone had asked me that question since I had made the decision to break off the engagement. It was something I hadn't given a great deal of thought because I was afraid of how I'd react if I did. For the first time since I last saw Lisa, the weight of my decision hit me head on. I had gone from the rafting trip to Lexington, constantly keeping busy, and now that I was in my parent's house with nothing to do, I could feel the emotion welling up inside. I didn't want it to come out so I leaned forward and placed my face in my hands. Dad knew what was happening and he instinctively stood up and placed his large right hand on my back. He didn't say anything because he didn't need to say anything.

After a few moments I managed to control myself and looked up at him with bloodshot eyes. "I'm sorry dad."

He waived his hand and said, "I've known sadness too son. You don't have to apologize to me."

My voice wasn't back to normal yet but I managed to say, "When?"

"Lots of times. By the time I was your age, I'd buried a lot of my friends. Sometimes you just have to get things off your chest."

"Yeah, I know. It already feels better."

"I'm glad to hear that," He paused and then added, "You know, my relationship with my father wasn't always the best. I had a lot of things on my chest and one night during the war, I was missing him so I wrote a letter."

I lifted my head, wondering where this was going. "You did? What did you say?"

He seemed to be waiting for me to say just that. "You know, he kept it and I got it back when he died. Let me show you." He got up and went to get it. He was gone for a minute, and then returned with an old piece of paper in his hands. "Dad was running patrol off the Northwest so I wrote to him there, just after I got back to the ship from shore leave. Here, read it for yourself."

"Sure," I said taking the letter. It was dated December 1, 1944.

Dear Dad:

As I sit down in the squadron ready room to write you tonight, I can't help but wonder how you are and what you're doing right at this moment. I've just returned from a short stroll on the flight deck and it would've made me extremely happy to have you along. The night is a perfectly beautiful one. The moon is shining brightly and the stars are all out. The planes silhouetted against the horizon made a beautiful sight, as did the nearby ships, which looked like powerful phantoms just visible in the distance. It's a funny feeling to stand up on that deck with the full realization that the only purpose of this amassed might is to kill as many people as possible and yet to realize at the same time that it presents a beautiful, rather majestic sight. I feel a certain thrill and pride in being a part of all it stands for.

Undoubtedly you can't figure out what in the devil has gotten into me tonight. No, I haven't done any drinking since that first day ashore. Perhaps it was the stroll on deck. Have you ever had the feeling you wished with all your heart that you were a talented poet, artist or composer so you might put into one of those mediums the emotions you felt deserved to be recorded and preserved? That was the rather helpless sensation I encountered tonight as I stood there by myself and began to realize what a full and wonderful life mine has been, and will be, I hope. I thought of all the breaks providence has been fit to give me up to this time.

First of all, I thought of the family the Gods or God, whichever the case may be, saw fit to make mine and I thanked those above with all my heart for that gift. It was the grandest, most wonderful one they could've given me, and for everything else which is fine and which has given me happiness and the chance to live to the hilt my twenty-two years. Then I thought of how lucky I was to be blessed with such good health, with a body that responds unerringly to my will and a mind that's adequate, if not astounding. As I look over the rail at all the ships around this one, I began to realize very fully what I believe every man in this area knows, at least in his subconscious, the reason why it all exists, the reason why so many of the best men out here are killed, and the reason why others who find themselves in a tough spot against a fanatic enemy usually come out on top. It's that same deep heritage of country and family which I'm so thankful for and which all the others feel to varying degrees, whether they admit it or not. I know myself, now that I think about it (it was something I very much took for granted) that there must be nothing in this world which even threatens the heritage you and Mom have made possible for me, and I'd personally feel it a great privilege to spend half my lifetime out here, if it were necessary to ensure such a heritage. I've learned, not recently either, that thing's worthwhile in life must be fought for, whether it be mental, spiritual or physical fighting.

Please don't think that I am writing ads entitled "Why we fight" or that I'm envisioning myself as a noble patriot. As a matter of fact I've done a good deal less than I consider my fair share in this war. For some reason I just started thinking and dreaming tonight and the above is the incomplete result. Perhaps thirty years from now the world will have a more complete picture, and I hope like hell it does you and Mom credit. For you two are the ones who will deserve it, if any is due.

Today I was standing near the quarterdeck talking with an old friend when a little fellow with a face that looked extremely familiar walked up and called me by my name. It was Bill Weir, your Pensacola friend. He's in VT-81 out here and of course he wanted to know all about you and just what you're doing now. He wanted me to send very cordial greetings to you.

Keep up the grand job you're doing with the Northwest Frontier Dad. Who knows? I might get lost in that area someday soon myself. So be prepared if you hear "Flash, this is Big Swede Maltress Angelo .5. Visibility 2. How 'bout a fix? Over." There's no one I'd rather turn it over to either Dad.

My dearest love to Mums and Rogie, tell them both that I shall write to them both very shortly a more explicit and thorough letter than I'm afraid this one is. Take care of yourself, and if you have a moment, just drop me a short line. I'd love the word on everything.

Lots of love to you Dad.

As always, Vince

R. Vincent Lynch, Ensign, A1, USNR

When I finished reading the letter I looked up at Dad and said with watery eyes, "That's an amazing letter, Dad." Then I decided to go a little bit farther. "You know, I'm sorry for not getting to know you better when I was younger. I guess I was an immature teenager followed by a self-absorbed college kid who had no idea what his dad had been through."

Dad turned from the golf tournament he was watching and looked disturbed and somewhat confused.

"Sorry Dad, I didn't mean to startle you."

"Oh, I must've been caught up in the tournament."

Knowing the moment had vanished, I nodded and said, "Who's winning anyway?"

He paused and tried to get his mind working. It was obvious he didn't know who was winning and frankly I didn't care one way or another when he finally said, "Jack . . . Jack Nicklaus is winning. Anyway, what's on your mind?"

Jack Nicklaus hadn't been active in professional golf for years, and I felt bad for putting him on the spot even though that was the last thing I had been trying to do.

"I enjoyed your letter very much Dad, where should I put it?"

Dad pondered the question for a minute then said "You keep it, I have no use for it anymore."

I looked down at the yellowed piece of paper and suddenly felt as if I were holding the Magna Carta. I knew it was a big deal for Dad to give me something like this so I walked over and I kissed him on the cheek.

"Thanks Dad, I'll take good care of it."

Dad smiled at me and then he went back to watching the golf tournament. I stood next to his chair for a moment and then glanced over at the television. As I did, the announcer mentioned that Fred Couples had the tournament well in hand. I looked at Dad to see if his expression changed, it hadn't. As I left the room, I looked back once more and noticed he had the exact same look on his face that he did before I had startled him. It was an intense yet distant stare. I wondered what was going on in his head. I wondered if maybe he wasn't seeing Jack Nicklaus after all.

5

The very next week Harvey wanted to go to Lexington. He also wanted me to go with him, even though I'd just been there. He said he was only going to go for a night, but wanted me to stay for the entire week. Because of this, he said we would stay at the Embassy Suites. We'd only have to get one room—he'd stay him in the bedroom and me in the foldout sleeper sofa the first night. Then when he left, I'd move into the bedroom.

Once we reached the city, Harvey's first order of business was to 'strategize' over drinks and dinner with the local administrator, Eva. Eva had moved from Dallas to run the Lexington agency and seemed to really enjoy the job Harvey had given her.

We headed out of the Lexington office around 4:30 p.m. and found a bar. Over vodka on ice (Harvey) and a couple of beers (Eva and me), Harvey began to tell us about his grand vision for our little home care division. Most of what he had to say was merely rambling: increase profits; tighten expenses, expand agencies, etc. Eva and I started to get a little bored, but we could tell after three or four straight vodka's over ice, Harvey was starting to get pretty tight. Harvey was the type of drinker that had to have a lot to drink before he started to slur his words and fall down. But until that happened, he just got real loud and animated. There was a point in his drinking progression when I actually enjoyed talking with him and felt he could teach me something. That was at the point when the alcohol had loosened him up but had not yet turned him into a psychotic idiot. That was when he was at his kindest, most insightful and easiest to communicate with. Unfortunately, it was usually a brief window of time before he tipped into the Godzilla state where everyone ran from him. It was a few vodkas after that point that we headed off to dinner and that's when I really stopped enjoying the conversation.

At the restaurant, Harvey ordered some wine with dinner. I enjoy some fine wine every now and then, so I was happy to go along. Besides, I could tell where the night was going and I figured I might as well have a glass of wine before the fireworks went off. Predictably, the wine put him over the edge. He stopped making sense, then got loud and began swearing. The customers nearest to us began flagging down their waiters, whispering in their ears while pointing at us. Sure enough, moments later a smiling waiter approached our table, looked right at me and said, "Might you ask your friend to speak more quietly and to refrain from using obscenities?"

I was sitting eight inches to the left of Harvey when this poor unsuspecting waiter said all of this, so obviously he heard every word. And I knew he didn't like being spoken about without being spoken to. I gripped the table, knowing well enough what was coming.

"Are you talking about me?" Harvey slurred. With this question I threw out my best 'Yes, we are shocked' look.

The young waiter looked a little rattled. He paused a moment then said, "Sir we've had some complaints. I'm merely asking you to lower your voice and not use profanity." For a moment I thought it might work, but then he tossed in, "And perhaps you should abstain from any more alcoholic beverages." That's when I leaned away from Harvey and looked for cover.

The look on Harvey's face was so full of rage I thought he was about to punch the waiter in the face. Instead he said, "I will drink as much as I please . . . but not here, you ungrateful jackass!" And with that he stood up and left the restaurant with Eva running behind him.

I gave the man a credit card and asked him to run it quickly while I endured the nasty stares from the customers. When he returned with the card I apologized to him and said, "Hey, sorry about that. He's my boss and can certainly get carried away on occasion." He wasn't impressed.

The waiter had had enough of us by that point. He looked at me and said, "If I were you, I'd consider finding a new boss."

I smiled, gave him a good tip and said, "I was sort of thinking the same thing." He took the bill and turned away without saying another word.

When I got outside, I couldn't see Harvey or Eva anywhere. Then I spotted a bar. Going on a hunch I looked inside the door and sure enough, there they were, sitting in a corner booth that only had two chairs. They were laughing and seemed to be having a great time. Harvey saw me and said, "Joe! How in the heck are you?" Then he politely suggested that they should move to a table so I could sit down.

Eva winked at me as if to say, "New bar, new attitude. Roll with it."

Nothing untoward happened the rest of the evening and Harvey never mentioned the altercation with the waiter. It was as forgotten as was his mood at the time. When we arrived back at the hotel, Harvey opened a bottle of Vodka that he'd apparently brought with him for just this occasion. Seeing my look, he slurred out that he needed a nightcap—he was just under his daily recommended allowance of alcohol. I went to bed shaking my head. The next morning as we left the room, I couldn't help noticing that the bedroom Harvey had slept in looked like a bomb had gone off. Knowing I'd be sleeping in that room the next few nights, I prayed the maids were good at their jobs.

The next day we met with the agency staff and Harvey explained how we had big plans though like the night before, the details were nonexistent. Then, we stopped for lunch where he piled in several more drinks before taking a cab to the airport.

When I got back to the room the next evening, I was relieved to see that it looked clean and tidy. I was exhausted, so I was more than happy to call it a day. Stripping down to my boxers, I collapsed on top of the bed, turned on the TV and switched to the news. As I lay there, trying to enjoy the solitude, I kept smelling something that was intensely unpleasant. I couldn't figure out what it was, but it was so bad it was starting to give me a headache. Feeling a bit desperate, I started looking around the bed, wondering what in the world could produce such a rank cheese smell. I couldn't find anything under or around the bed, so I peeled back the bedspread and found one of Harvey's nasty, discolored socks. It'd been only a couple of inches from my head when I'd been lying on the bed. I didn't want to touch it, so I used the garbage bag from the bathroom and picked it up in the same manner that dog owners pick up droppings. I really thought I might be sick, so I decided that I had to get it out of the room.

In my haste to dispose of the sock—anywhere other than in my room—I locked myself out, wearing nothing but boxers and a tee shirt. A nice lady who was just entering her room for the night said she would call the front desk for me, but for some rude reason she refused to allow me into her room while I waited. Luckily, a man from the hotel arrived quickly. I guess they didn't want random people walking around the hotel in their underwear. He asked me what had happened and I told him about the sock, but left out the part about my crazy boss leaving it behind. He asked if the sock was mine and I said that it was not. He was so mortified, he offered to comp my room for a night, an offer I accepted with a "Just don't ever let this happen again!" attitude. But after I'd had a chance to process what had just happened, I began to feel like kind of an ass for accepting a freebie over Harvey's sock. I mean, I hadn't lied, it really wasn't my sock, but I'd conveniently left out that it *was* the sock of someone I was with. Also, I knew that there wasn't a maid on the planet who could adequately clean up after a man like Harvey.

This is about when I truly started to question if my career with Harvey was the best thing for me. On one hand, I did appreciate the opportunity. On the other hand, Harvey was an unstable nut and not a good influence. For some reason I thought of my father and wondered if I could talk to him about it, what he'd have to say. Would I get the "respect your boss" speech again or something new? I made a note to see him when I got home.

Mom had told me she was going shopping Saturday morning and that would be a great time to catch Dad. So I arrived at 10:00 a.m. just as Mom was leaving. "Hey Dad, how are you doing?"

"Good to see you, Joe, what've you been up to?"

I sat down and spilled my guts about everything. I told him I was having a hard time working in such a crazy environment, but I remembered his advice about respecting my boss and having rough days. Then I put it right to him, "Dad, do you think I should hang in there?"

He pondered the situation for a moment but said nothing. A few moments later I began to sense that he was at a loss for words. This happened sometimes when his brain became clouded. I redirected him in my customary way by saying, "Dad I'm in a tough spot at work. I enjoyed hearing about your day in the ocean and your submarine rescue. What other tough days did you have in the Navy?" Dad rubbed his chin and I could see that his brain was functioning again. Then he said, "It was around March of 1945 and we were still taking it to the Japs on a daily basis. I remember because we had recently transitioned from the Hellcat to the new F4U Corsair—man that was a great plane. I was flying a good many missions and with each one I noticed that the Japs seemed to be thinning in numbers and more desperate. As an officer, I was privy to some of the intelligence reports regarding the general condition of the enemy and the status of the war. These reports confirmed what I was seeing: the Japs were battered and bruised with dwindling supplies and too few men left to give us a one-to-one fight. That's why Kamikazes had become a part of their fighting strategy; it was their best chance to inflict damage on our fleet, despite the fact that it meant depleting their own ranks even further.

"One day my squadron was sent on a mission to protect some B-29's on their approach into Tokyo. While we were gone, all hell broke loose back on the Ticonderoga. The ship was hit by several Kamikaze's causing a great deal of damage. When we got back, we couldn't land on our ship and had to land next door, on the Lexington. After landing, we were told of the major damage and loss of life on the Ticonderoga. We were given bunks for the night and told that we'd be taken back to our ship in the morning.

"Early the next morning, we were taxied to the ship for the Naval custom of burying the dead at sea. We were totally unprepared for the sight before us. The ship was in ruins and stacks of bodies lay on the deck covered in flags, waiting for the official military ceremony which would mark the end of their service, and of course, their lives. These were our buddies, men we'd worked with day in and day out—men who'd had our backs. So the first thing we had to do was find out who had made it.

"It turns out that three of the men who worked on my plane had died in the attack. When I found out, it took all the strength that I had not to weep openly. As I headed to my cabin below decks, I felt an emptiness that only a select group of warriors will ever know. It's the emptiness that comes from a sudden loss of young life during a time of war.

"When I got to my cabin, I found the nicest khaki uniform I had and took special care to make sure that every aspect of my appearance was as buttoned up as it could be. Then I went back up to the flight deck with every other sailor from the Ticonderoga, living and dead, for the burial ceremony.

"On the flight deck, all the flags on the bridge were at half-mast. The men were quiet; so quiet the only sound I heard was the shuffling of feet as the men made their way to their designated spots. Once in position, the ceremony started. The commanding officer took his position next to the first body. All the bodies had been sewn into canvas cloth with weights placed around their feet to ensure they would sink to the bottom of the ocean. Eight sailors stood above the body being buried, holding a taut American flag. The CO called out 'All hands bury the dead,' which was the signal to begin. The men on the deck of the Ticonderoga stood at parade rest as the formal process of saying goodbye to their comrades began.

"The CO began by reading scripture and leading the men in the Lord's Prayer. He finished the religious portion of the ceremony by saying a personal prayer for the man lying before him, calling him by his first name, before asking God to grant the brave sailor peace and entry into the kingdom of heaven. When he was done, a firing party was ordered to 'Present Arms.' Seven sailors fired their guns in unison, three times each, to give the deceased sailor a twenty-one gun salute while the platform with the body was tilted over the side of the ship and it slid into the ocean. As soon as the last volley was fired, the bugler played taps and the flag was folded and placed in storage for the man's family. Then the ceremony began all over again for the next sailor.

"In all, there were twenty-three men buried over the course of two days. It was a long, hot process, but not a single man complained. These men were our friends and they deserved every moment of respect they could be given by their crewmates. The surviving men aboard the Ticonderoga knew that, but by the grace of God, this process could be held in their honor at any time.

"So, remembering that day I learned a lot about life. Life's short, real short. Don't waste your life doing something you hate. Find something and *someone* you truly love."

For another hour, we carried on as if he were twenty-years younger. We talked about sports, my friends, his friends, and the future of the country. It was a great time for me and I was sure for him, too. When I left, I gave him a hug and said, "Thanks Dad."

He said, "Anytime son." He smiled at me and it was then that I realized I'd never felt as close to him as I did right then.

By this time we were in a routine. Harvey told us where to go and what to do and that's what we did. The guys in Atlanta were really behind it all, getting word to Harvey of where they wanted the next agency. Surprisingly, we were actually able to accomplish a lot. We were also making friends with important the VP's from corporate because we were creating new agencies that made money for the hospitals—*their* hospitals. I learned a lot along the way, primarily because I had to figure things out as I went. For me, that's always the best way to learn.

Harvey occasionally joined me, but these excursions were becoming rarer. Harvey had decided that he didn't really like to go to places like Lexington. The fact that this was work and we were supposed to go where we were needed didn't matter to him. Places like Lexington put him in a bad mood, mostly because he thought they were such 'boring towns.' I couldn't help thinking the lack of nightlife in these towns was what bothered him since there weren't enough places for a business traveler to go screw around.

Robin and I had already been friends, but the time we were spending working together was bringing us closer than we'd ever been before. We were thrust into so many strange situations with Harvey that we came to rely on each other to maintain some degree of sanity and normalcy. We fed off of each other, laughed all the time, and when work needed to be done, we worked hard as a team. Of course, we were both dizzy from all the travel and very exhausted, but we were still having a lot of fun. We talked often about where all of this was heading, which was unclear at best, but not having any answers made it easier to just enjoy the ride as much as possible.

Our airline of choice was Delta, mainly because Harvey liked Delta better than American Airlines. We were in the air so much that, more often than not, we were able to use our frequent flyer miles to upgrade to first class. That made life a little more tolerable. Still, our company got reamed on the price of the tickets, mostly because Harvey rarely gave us any notice and we had to pay last minute prices for everything.

It was a cold and rainy Monday when Harvey and I happened to be in the Dallas office together. It was pretty clear it was going to be a slow week. I had my head down making notes from a call when Harvey walked into my office and in a very confident voice said, "Joe, San Lorenzo has some things going on and I think we need to go see what's up."

"Okay," I sighed. "When are we going?"

"Why don't we both head home and pack. I'll meet you at the airport at around three."

I sighed again. There wouldn't be much time—my watch said 1:00 p.m.—so I immediately reached for my briefcase and headed home to pack. Even though I was tired of traveling, the truth is I really love the west coast and was thrilled to be getting out of Dallas on a nasty, rainy day. Also, I'd never been to San Lorenzo before, so that was another plus.

The San Lorenzo agency had come with a hospital acquisition and was run by a bunch of people who had been with the agency for years. From what others on our team had relayed, getting them re-acclimated to our way of doing things had been proving quite a challenge.

At home, I threw some things together, slapped my bag shut and arrived at the airport a little before three. We knew from experience that flights would be heading out to Oakland on a regular basis, so we didn't even check into flights before leaving the office. When we got there I found a flight leaving at 4:15 p.m. so I purchased my ticket then headed to the Delta lounge to wait for Harvey. I never worried about buying the wrong ticket. Full fare tickets are like cash and fully refundable, which came in handy when traveling with Harvey. When he was a little late (which was often), we just applied it to the next flight.

I sat in the lounge waiting and by 3:40 p.m., I was beginning to wonder what was going on. Suddenly, Harvey rounded the corner and said, "Change of plans. We're going to Vegas." This was an interesting twist . . . I'd never been there either.

"How are we going to do that?" I said.

"Easy. We fly into Vegas tonight, do some gambling then fly on to San Lorenzo tomorrow."

"Okay, I'm in." Of course I was in. I worked for this guy.

Harvey handed me his ticket and told me to duplicate his schedule for myself. I left to go change my ticket while Harvey sat down to have a drink or three. The lady at the counter informed me the flight to Vegas didn't leave for another couple of hours, and with an ominous warning, said, "So you'll have plenty of time to relax in the lounge with your travel companion. Enjoy your trip sir."

I smirked and headed back to the lounge where I found Harvey with two dark brown drinks in front of him. Based on my college experience and now life in the pros, I knew these drinks packed a wallop. Either he was planning to get plastered or he'd ordered one for me, in which case we both were in trouble.

He slid a drink over to me as I sat down and said, "You ever been to Vegas?"

I said that I hadn't, to which he said, "You just can't go there without a scotch buzz. It's in the rules."

I'm not sure Harvey had ever gone to *any* city without a buzz. Seeing that we wouldn't be working or professionally interacting with anyone either tonight or the following morning, I said, "What the hell," and took a sip. It tasted like jet fuel.

After a very rough flight through the storm that had been pounding much of the country we finally arrived in Vegas. It was only 8:30 p.m. local time but 10:30 p.m. for us. I'd been up late both nights the last weekend (one of my buddies had gotten married) and the time of night coupled with the eventful flight had me totally exhausted.

Still, there was life to be lived and the moment we got outside the airport doors Harvey flagged down a cab and said, "Caesars Palace."

I said, "Do we have reservations at Caesars?"

"No, I've been there a few times and I think I can get them to comp us a room."

When we arrived at the casino, I was thinking that the first order of business should be to secure us a room but Harvey thought otherwise. He wanted to go directly to the blackjack tables and worry about the room later. This meant that we had to check our luggage in with the concierge, which luckily wasn't a big deal in Vegas: they also wanted us to get to the blackjack tables as fast as humanly possible.

We sat down at a $20 table where Harvey whipped out a couple of C-notes and was handed a stack of chips. I had come on this trip with about $80, because stupid me, I was thinking we were going to San Lorenzo, not Las Vegas. With only $80, I thought the $20 tables seemed a little aggressive, but hey, what did I know? This was my first time here.

Over several minutes, we went up and then down, winning as much as we were losing. Sadly, Vegas won out and I was flat broke. Harvey turned to me and said, "Hey, that happens here. Don't worry about it. Here's another $20 chip. Our luck is getting ready to change."

Incredibly he was right. We started winning . . . *everything*. I could split kings and win. I could stand on five and win. I could order a drink and win. We were winning so much I could feel the cameras above zooming in on us. After an unbelievable run, I made a major Vegas faux pas and spilled my drink on the table. And I didn't just spill it, I launched it with my forearm and it went everywhere. The dealer was noticeably upset and the other players at the table angrily pushed away from the table and left.

At that point I was up over $900 and Harvey was up to around $3,000. We didn't want to leave this magical table so we waited out the cleaning crew but unfortunately, when the game started back up, the magic was gone, having been sucked up by the cleaning crew's vacuum cleaner. I lost $200 almost immediately and decided being up by $700 over my initial $80 and Harvey's gifted $20 was good enough for me. I told Harvey I hadn't eaten anything since breakfast and was going to get something to eat and wait for him (since we didn't have a room) in the restaurant by the front desk.

I was there about ten minutes before Harvey showed up and asked to borrow my money. Not some of my money, he wanted all of it. He'd had around $2,700 when I had left him so this was a little bit of a shock to me. I said "Harvey, the table's gone cold so why don't we just call it a night?" It was around two in the morning by this time (four our time) so it seemed the next logical thing to do.

Harvey, who was in a very altered state by this point twisted his face into a that's-not-what-I-want-to-hear-right-now look and said, "Just give me the money. You wouldn't have anything if I hadn't loaned you that $20 chip. Besides, I'll pay you back." I simply didn't have the energy to fight with him, so I gave him $600 dollars, which left me with $100, and off he went.

He was back by the time I finished my sandwich and dead broke. I was actually relieved he lost, because now we could go see about a room. When we arrived at the front desk, Harvey began to haggle with the lady helping him, but his method was a bit heavy handed and she wasn't reacting well. The push to get a free room was not going our way and Harvey started to get agitated. It was important to get the room comp'd, because he didn't want to put it on our expense report since this Vegas diversion would most likely be viewed unfavorably by our bosses back at the corporate headquarters. Personally, I was so exhausted I didn't care if I had to pay for the room myself, and seeing him cause a scene sent me into a semi-panic. If Harvey went south on this poor lady the way I knew he was capable of doing, then we'd most likely get kicked out of Caesars. The thought of walking around the Vegas in search of a new hotel was not that appealing to me; I was close to falling asleep right there in the lobby. I walked up to Harvey and volunteered to pay for the room myself, but Harvey gave me a very serious stay-out-of-this look and I gave up, slumping back to my chair and praying for an end to this madness. A few minutes later, Harvey walked up with some keys and a victorious look on his face. Somehow he'd managed to get us a room.

Our room was pretty nice, but then it could have been a pit of pig shit and I wouldn't have noticed. As soon as my head hit the pillow I was asleep and had absolutely no desire to ever wake up.

When I woke up Harvey's bed was empty and I assumed he'd gone down for breakfast. Worrying about whether I'd slept too late and was delaying our departure to San Lorenzo, I jumped up and raced into the shower. As I was getting ready, I thought, despite the usual shenanigans associated with traveling with Harvey, I had had a good time on our little side trip to Vegas. I doubted I would ever see the $600 dollars again, but I still had more now than when I'd left Dallas. After I was ready, I headed downstairs to seek out Harvey. The front desk hadn't seen him and we hadn't been checked out. I looked in the restaurants and he was nowhere to be found. At a small stand I bought a bagel and some orange juice and started to walk around trying to find him.

Eventually I found Harvey sitting at the same blackjack table we had been at the night before, and with a drink in front of him. There was only one other man at the table and they both looked like hell. They were making small talk with the dealer and chain smoking, probably taking a few more years off the dealer's life. I approached Harvey and said, "Good morning. What's our schedule for today?"

Harvey looked up at me blearily and said, "Have a seat." It was now about ten in the morning and I was in no mood to gamble. It was a depressing scene in the casino. The cleaning crews were lazily wandering around pushing vacuum cleaners and cleaning out ash trays, while a few die hard gamblers slumped at their tables, leaning on elbows, and gambling away their paychecks, 401k's, and for all I could tell, their children's college fund.

I sat on the edge of a chair close to Harvey, but did not belly up to the table. Harvey noticed this immediately and said, "Aren't you going to play?"

I'd been prepared for this, so I tried to deflect it by saying, "I thought I'd get us ready to go and make a few calls. I just wanted to check your timing first."

In response, Harvey just looked at me blearily (as opposed to exploding). I couldn't help noticing how drawn out and gaunt he looked. "I don't know, Joe, we'll just have to see how it goes." This wasn't an encouraging answer and I couldn't help thinking he was acting like he really had no control over the situation. I got up and told him I'd check in with him later.

Later turned into much later than I'd expected. In fact, we blew the whole day in Vegas. Harvey gambled and I fumed, stuck with no option but to wait until he'd decided he'd had enough. I hated to watch a man trapped by his own demons. I also felt guilty that we were supposed to be in San Lorenzo working. It was a tough spot to be in but surely better than the one he was in.

When I started out on this adventure, I reasoned that the company was paying the same amount of money to fly me to Vegas then to Oakland as it would've to fly me directly there. And we'd have burned up a whole day traveling anyway, so I felt like I was still technically being productive. In fact, I was justifying this trip in every imaginable way to avoid feeling like I was slacking off. But now, seeing another day wasting away while this demon-for-a-boss was chained to the blackjack table, it was official: I was slacking off.

Eventually though, the demon inside him released its grip from the tables and we finally left for the airport around 4:00 p.m. I could tell Harvey was pretty intoxicated especially when he told the cab driver to take us to the Bare Fort. To my amazement the cabbie just gave us a knowing nod and began to drive off in a different direction. I leaned up and said, "You are taking us to the airport, right?"

He looked at me with a strange look and in a thick Middle Eastern accent said, "Oh, *airport*. I thought you go to nudie club. The Bare Fort is very nice. Very, very nice. It's all nude, you know."

"That's great," I said. "We'll try it out next time."

When he changed directions, I could see Harvey's eyes were closing. It seemed better to let sleeping dogs lie so I didn't wake him until we reached our destination.

When we arrived at the airport, Harvey awoke and we headed inside. At the ticket counter, I discovered that all the flights to Oakland were booked so we were going to have to fly into San Francisco. I didn't think it was any big deal, after all, San Francisco is just across the bay from San Lorenzo, but for some reason it threw Harvey for a loop. I figured it was because it was a longer drive, but I didn't press it. When we landed, I made a point of handling the rental car—Harvey had had several vodkas on the plane and was really not in any condition to drive. I think he knew he shouldn't be driving, but because he was drunk, he argued and made a big deal over me having control of the keys. I held firm and kept the keys.

I asked the clerk for directions to San Lorenzo and while I was getting those, Harvey walked around looking for someplace to buy a beer for the road. The guy told me the most direct route was south to the San Mateo Bridge and across the San Francisco Bay. I took a small map and off we went.

I started driving and we were making good time, but Harvey was unusually silent. I thought he might have been passing out, but when we approached the beginning of the San Mateo Bridge he began babbling loudly. Clearly, he was upset, but I really couldn't understand why. He kept slurring, "Bridge, dammit Joe, bridge, long, earthquake."

I was trying to concentrate on driving, but his ramblings were extremely distracting. I finally said, "What the hell's wrong with you?" Suddenly, he reached his foot across and stomped on my foot, mashing the accelerator to the floor. As my body was thrown back into the seat, I saw we were just entering the bridge *and* there was a lot of traffic around so I did what anyone would do: I panicked! Twisting my foot loose, I was able to remove it from below his but he still kept the accelerator pinned to the floor. With my right foot I tried desperately to remove his foot while my left foot rode the brake giving my brain an opportunity to calculate when I should mash down on the brake or perhaps crash the car in a controlled way to keep us from going over the bridge and plunging to our deaths. My brain reminded me I still had a few weapons left to use, one of which was my voice. I turned and screamed at him at the top of my lungs to stop, hoping to reach something deep inside him. It didn't work. Now the speedometer was passing sixty mph, and the point of no return was just about gone. I made two evasive moves just missing three cars and still, he had the accelerator floored. When I saw the speedometer cross seventy, I knew I was dead.

Then an idea hit me. I remembered what my brothers used to do to me when I was an annoying little kid. They called it frogging. It's when you stick out your middle knuckle and punch someone really hard in the thigh muscle. If done right, it causes a lot of pain and stuns your leg for several minutes. I didn't have a lot of time to weigh the pros and cons of striking my boss, so without any hesitation I reared back and I punched his thigh as hard as I could, driving the knuckle deep into any muscle I could find.

"*Aarrggghh!*" he shouted.

It worked. He retracted his leg to his side of the car and began rubbing it, making more babbling noises. Now that I was back in control of the car, I moved to the right lane slowing us just under the speed limit. My heart was still racing and I needed to regain my composure. I would've gladly pulled over had I been anywhere but on a bridge, but without any other recourse resigned myself to breathing deeply to steady myself. It wasn't until I'd gotten a hold of myself some that I remembered Harvey. Glancing over, I saw his head leaning against the window and hands gripping the spot where I'd just hit him. It occurred to me that I might have really hurt him, since I'd hit him with all I had. He probably was hurt, but at least we weren't dead. And he didn't say anything more about it as we made our way across the bridge into San Lorenzo where I found a hotel near the agency and left him at the hotel bar while I decompressed for the rest of the night.

The next morning Harvey was extremely hung over and walking with a limp so I said, "Are you hurt?"

"Yes, did I run into something yesterday? My leg really hurts and I have a bruise the size of a softball on my thigh."

I said innocently, "Hmmm, not that I remember."

"Huh, it feels like someone hit me." He paused trying to get his soaked hard drive to work. "You didn't hit me for any reason did you?"

To this I gave my best, innocently shocked look and said, "No! I would never strike my boss! How dumb do you think I am?"

He relaxed and the subject was dropped for the remainder of our wasted and worthless trip to San Lorenzo.

6

I arrived back in Dallas late on Friday afternoon, so I skipped the final two hours of work and went to my apartment, thoroughly sulking about my boss, my job, and my career. I couldn't believe the working world was like this—company's like The American Coupon Company with the Boob and now UHI with a guy like Harvey. It just seemed like there were no normal jobs out there.

I called my mom to check in and see what was up. "Your dad's doing well. Would you like to come to dinner?" Although it could change, this was a code Mom and I had been using to tell me Dad was fairly coherent at this moment. Over the past year or so, Mom had been urging me to get all the face time I could with my father.

"Sure Mom. Put a plate out for me and I'll be over shortly."

When I got there, I tried to maintain a happy façade, but it didn't work very well. Dad asked, "What's wrong Joe?"

I wasn't sure if I really wanted to get into it, but when I saw that he looked like he really wanted to hear about it, I relented. "I'm thinking of leaving my job and I guess I may need some help making the decision."

He looked at me as if I were crazy and said "Is this about your boss again?"

"Yeah Dad, my boss Harvey Waller. He drinks so much I heard some employees calling him Harvey Wallbanger. I didn't even know that was a drink until someone else told me."

"What?! For crying out loud, don't these people respect authority?" I could see he was getting agitated, which could lead to all sorts of problems, so I decided to go to Plan B.

"Dad, how did you get out of the South Pacific? Did you just quit? Or did the war end?"

It worked. Dad got that distant look on his face like before and then began, "Well, you don't decide to leave a particular duty in the military; they decide for you. One day I was in the officers' mess on the ship—the war was still going on—when I was called to the commanding officers' quarters. The CO told me I'd put in enough time to earn the right to transition back to the states. I wasn't going to be out of the Navy, but I was going to get off the carrier and be stationed somewhere out of the danger zone. I didn't know where, but just like that, my fighting days were over."

"I took a transport plane to Luzon, then hitched a ride on a B-29 for the flight back to the Treasure Island Naval Station in San Francisco. After saying goodbye to the other men I had been traveling with, I made my way to the front gate and hailed a cab. I didn't know any of the local hotels, so I asked the cabbie to take me to one of the economical ones nearby. When the cab arrived, I pulled out my money and was surprised when the cabbie refused to take my money.

'I don't take money from servicemen,' he said, looking directly into my eyes. 'Thanks for your service, son. You boys sure have done a bang-up job.' I was touched by his generosity, particularly since it was my first experience with the patriotism felt by the American public.

"After a couple of days of R&R in San Francisco, I received orders to head back to the Naval Station in Newport, Road Island. My mission was to run patrols up and down the Eastern Seaboard in a brand new F4U Gull Wing Corsair with my old friend from flight training, Cliff Thompson, as my wingman. I just knew this was going to be fun.

"Cliff was a big Texan who had been stationed aboard the Essex and had just finished a good run in the South Pacific himself. He was as relaxed as any man I'd ever met, and he spoke with a drawl that seemed to stretch each word into several syllables. I hadn't seen him in quite a while, but we instantly picked up where we'd left off, as old friends do. When on land, most pilots still call their fellow pilots by their call signs, but not Cliff. He liked to call me 'Yankee', primarily because when we'd met at flight training in Corpus Christi, I was the first Yankee he'd ever met.

"Since the war was almost over, this was a cake walk of a mission. All we had to do was fly our planes from Newport down the Long Island Sound to New York City and back several times a week. VE day had occurred two months earlier so we knew the likelihood of spotting any rogue German ships or subs wasn't high. It was summertime, the weather was perfect, I was flying in a new plane with an old friend as my wingman and no one was shooting at us. Life was good."

"Lucky for me, my whole family lived in and around Greenwich, Connecticut which was only a short drive from the base down I-95. I checked in on my mother and siblings every chance I got. With Dad still running patrols off the Oregon coast, they enjoyed having me drop in for visits as often as possible."

"I still remember clear as day when I learned that the war had ended. It was the night of August 14, 1945 at 1:30 a.m. and Cliff and I were flying one of our weekly nighttime runs down the Long Island coastline. All of a sudden, Billy, the tower operator back at Newport, was trying to get our attention over the headset. He was a winey young sailor who had yet to sprout any facial hair and was constantly teased because of his youthful appearance. This time he was as excited and animated as I'd ever heard him. And he was reaching out to us since he knew we were the only ones up at this hour. 'Hey boys, I've got some news for you!' Billy said over the radio."

"Cliff responded first, 'What is it Billy? Did you finally get laid?'"

" 'No, no that's not it, I mean, *hey*, I've gotten lucky lots of times,' he said stuttering and stammering. 'Why are you guys always busting my chops? I may look young, but the ladies love me, and very often, if you know what I mean.'"

"We started laughing and I said 'Billy! Your sex life is fascinating, but why don't you get to the point and tell us what's up?'"

" 'Oh yeah, I just heard over the wire that the big bombs did the trick. The Japs have surrendered! The war's over, boys!'"

"In the darkness I couldn't see Cliff, but I sure could hear him as he gave his best West Texas 'Woooooo Hooooooooo' scream. It caused my ears to ring, not that I minded. It was something we'd all been waiting for."

"As the news began to sink in, I had an idea so I clicked on my radio, 'Hey Cliff, my Uncle has a house on the Connecticut coast in Belle Haven. What do you say we celebrate by giving him a buzz?'

"Cliff didn't have to think long before giving me the thumbs up, saying, 'Hell yeah! Lead the way Yankee!'

"I banked off and Cliff fell in next to me. In fifteen minutes we were over Belle Haven and I called out, 'Commence buzzing run on my mark.'

" 'Roger,' said Cliff, laughing.

"Our two planes came in low and fast at about 200 feet off the water. It was a clear night with a full moon, so visibility was very good. We were excellent pilots and could've come in lower, but considering this impromptu mission was strictly for fun, I decided to play it safe and not risk crashing into the mast of a poorly placed sailboat. As we approached the outcropping of land marking Belle Haven, we leaned on our throttles causing the two eighteen-cylinder, 2,000 horsepower Pratt and Whitney engines to scream even louder, cutting right through the quiet early morning darkness."

"We came in over the land hot and then pulled the nose of the planes upward as both planes spun straight up into the night sky. We followed this little stunt up with some barrel rolls and spins. Of course, no one could see this show, but that didn't matter to us. We were so happy, we didn't have a care in the world. However, the good people of Belle Haven could hear the show going on above their heads and since they didn't yet know the war had ended, they weren't too happy about it. In fact the local police station logged countless calls from frightened, frantic citizens who were sure they were under attack. This in turn prompted countless calls to the closest Naval Base, which happened to be in Newport. And all of these calls ended up with Billy, who just laughed and laughed.

"Now that the war was over, I wondered how long it would take before I could get out of the Navy and begin a normal civilian life. My answer came soon enough. Within days, our CO summoned all of the officers of the Newport Naval Base to the general assembly hall. This was a relatively small base, so there were only thirty-five officers present. The CO started in by congratulating us for winning the war. This statement brought raucous applause. We felt tremendous pride for what we'd done, both in Europe and in the Pacific. The CO went on to explain that though there was no longer a war to fight, the United States military could not just summarily discharge all reserve soldiers all at once. The process would take time and we would have to be patient. Just as the draft had happened in stages, the process for discharging soldiers out of the military would be handled through a selection process, much depending on a man's rank and current responsibilities. The phrase 'Be patient' was repeated fairly frequently.

"For a week or so Cliff and I were content to hang around the base and drink in celebration of the part we'd played in defeating the Japs. Then, it caught up with us as we realized we were both pickled, bored and missed flying. We hadn't been assigned any more patrol missions, because the brass thought there was no need to endlessly patrol during peacetime. We understood, but thought that there must be something we could do for our country that didn't entail sitting around the base wasting time.

"It turned out our superior officers had had the same thought. They decided to select a few men in different parts of the country to form small groups and train in the art of formation flying. Of course, we already knew the basics of flying in formation, but not in the way the Navy had in mind. In wartime we'd been taught to fly in a way that would maximize the efficiency of the planes and ensure destruction of the enemy, while at the same time giving ourselves the best chance for survival. Now, we were to be taught how to fly flamboyantly, all for the purpose of glamorizing the Navy. Apparently the Navy wanted to show off their assets and keep people interested in the military, even though there was no war to fight.

"Both Cliff and I were selected. I confess, we were absolutely thrilled to be flying again. It took just a few weeks to complete our training, and then we were sent across the country to air shows where our group was the feature attraction. The people loved it. A country that had been mired in war for years was now turning out to bask in the glow of victory, all while watching the men who fought on their behalf perform death defying tricks in our planes. The shows packed 'em in. Eventually our group of barnstorming pilots became the Navy's elite flying team known as The Blue Angels."

Dad had a big smile on his face as he saw my jaw hit the floor.

"No way! You were one of the first Blue Angels? Are you kidding me?!"

"Well, I was the opening act, the Angels were formally established in the Spring of "46". The question is, what's all that have to do with your situation?"

"I don't know. Take up flying?"

Dad chuckled, assuming I was kidding. "No. I was willing to reinvent myself and learn something new so I could stay productive. I can't tell you to leave your company or stay, but having a willingness to learn new things can sure open doors for a person."

I leaned back and thought about what he'd just said. Not only was it stunningly good advice, the fact that my Dad was capable of such advice was yet another new awakening for me. And I was still having trouble processing the Blue Angels bit. Then I heard my mother.

"Boys, dinner's on. Come on in."

Dad stood up and headed into the dining room as I sat for a moment longer pondering what I had just been told.

What an amazing life! And after all these years I was just now learning about it.

In the winter of 1993, I was assigned to open an agency for a hospital in Austin. One day while I was working there, I received a call from Harvey. He asked me to get on a plane ASAP and fly to Plantation, Florida. Austin was the first full start-up I'd done completely on my own and I was really enjoying feeling productive. And I was learning a lot. The project was ahead of schedule and under budget. I was proud of this and I wanted to keep working it. On the other hand, I'm a team player, and if I were needed in Florida, then that's where I was going. Besides, a break from Austin to take a spin out to Florida sounded nice. But there was a problem with all this and it started with Harvey's telephone call to me.

I picked up the receiver. "Hello Harvey, how's it going?"

"Those damn dykes in Florida are driving me crazy."

"Huh," I said, "What dykes in Florida?"

"Robin and I are trying to get a project off the ground at Florida Community Hospital and it's run by two dykes. Has Robin not told you about any of this?"

"No Harvey, we haven't spoken in a while. Do the two . . . uh, ladies have titles other than dykes?"

Harvey chuckled, "Yes, one's the CEO and one is the COO. But I swear they've got to be sleeping together. They never do anything apart."

I was confused. "So where do I fit in with the dykes in Florida problem?"

"Robin hates them and says she'll never go back. She swears they want her to join them in a threesome."

I was stunned. "Knowing Robin, if she's truly worried about it, then it's a problem."

Harvey cut to the chase. "Listen, I know you. You aren't threatening the way Robin can be. When she feels uncomfortable, she gets that damned chip on her shoulder and then nothing gets done diplomatically. So, I want you to go to Plantation and meet with the dykes and smooth this whole thing over."

"How do I go about doing that? Are they mad at us for a particular reason or just because Robin won't have a threesome with them?"

"Joe, the threesome issue is a real problem, even though they haven't actually proposed it to Robin."

"So," I said, "Let me ask this another way. What's the problem I'm trying to smooth over?"

"You know, just be yourself. They'll like you because you're a guy and they're not into guys."

That's when I realized two things: first, Harvey didn't know exactly what the problem was, so he'd created this dyke/threesome issue to cover up his lack of knowledge; second, Harvey didn't like having to deal with ladies who possessed a lot of authority so he was passing this little gem off to me. Knowing all this made my decision-making much easier.

"When should I go?" I said.

"Fly out tomorrow."

"Okay, I'll take care of it."

"And let me know how it goes."

"Okay, I will."

Click . . . dial-tone.

I immediately picked up the phone and called Robin. "Robin, it's me. Harvey just called and he wants me to fly out to Florida Community and smooth over some situation with the dykes, apparently because you refused to have a threesome. What the hell have you done and what the hell am I supposed to do to fix it?"

Robin began laughing hysterically.

"Yeah, very funny," I said. "But seriously, what am I going to do there?"

Robin, still laughing, said, "He called you and wants you to . . ." as she erupted into laughter again.

Robin eventually went on to tell me the whole story, which, for the most part, was no story at all. Florida is what's called a certificate-of-need state, which meant each home care agency needed a special certificate to be able to do business. At that time, there was a moratorium on new certificates of need for home care agencies. For us that meant we had to buy an existing certificate of need.

According to Robin we had found one and negotiated the purchase, but the actual closing wasn't going to happen for another couple of weeks. In the meantime, Harvey had hijacked Robin and flown with her to Plantation to 'work,' then had driven her down to Miami to sample the dog tracks there. While all of that was going on, the 'dykes' from the hospital had called corporate to see when Harvey was coming to town so they could discuss some of the logistics involved with their new acquisition and had been told that Harvey was there now, which of course he wasn't.

This obviously baffled the 'dykes,' because they hadn't heard from or seen Harvey in weeks. Word apparently got back to Harvey and Robin and it really put a crimp on their trip. Harvey had made up some BS story about doing market research, which the 'dykes' probably read right through and the end result was that Harvey now hated these two women, because he feared they may be onto him. And now I was going to Florida to run interference and possibly take a bullet for the boss.

I left on a redeye the next morning, arrived at the hospital, and went straight to administration. I didn't have an appointment, but that was part of my plan. I wanted the ladies to see that I had arrived early and to know they could see me whenever they had time. They weren't available so I left a detailed message with their receptionist and headed over to the makeshift office to get settled in.

After running through my checklist of required start-up items the agency would need to begin operations, I started making a list of what would be needed prior to the closing date. Next to nothing had been done, so I began placing some orders and speaking to the hospital supply department about what could be obtained in-house. I knew the agency wouldn't require a full complement of staff, so I began making some notes on the personnel that I thought we would need in place to get the agency going.

At around 12:30 p.m., I received a call from one of the ladies, Patti. She was the CEO of the hospital and she was clearly excited I was in town and actually available. She wanted to start right away and I was over there in ten minutes. The very first thing I noticed when I got to Patti's office were pictures all over the place showing Patti with her husband, Patti with her kids, and Patti with her new granddaughter. So much for Patti being a flaming lesbian, as if that mattered to begin with. The COO, Barbara, was also there and they were very both nice, appreciating the fact that I was clearly there to help them.

Many of the hospital CEOs weren't particularly thrilled at our arrival. They (understandably) felt they knew best what their hospital needed. They certainly didn't want some punk from corporate forcing a home care agency down their throats. These ladies, however, were excited to have a home care company affiliated with their hospital. They wanted to get the process going and be involved every step of the way. For me, this was a dream scenario. Harvey's aversion to them led me to wonder whether he actually liked the CEOs who wanted nothing to do with us. That way he had an excuse to fly under the radar and not have people questioning his whereabouts.

The work was easy. I gave them what they needed to do to get their hospital ready for the new agency and showed them what I'd already done. I left them with a punch list of things they could do to help and told them that I'd be around for the next day and a half, before needing to get back to Austin for interviews I'd set up. This whole process took about thirty minutes and made them my new best friends.

A day and a half later, I tried to track down Harvey to give him an update while waiting for my flight. I started with Gayle, who told me he was in San Lorenzo. I asked her to tell him I'd called, then I tried to call the office in San Lorenzo. They didn't know where he was and hadn't seen him in weeks. With the trail gone cold, I left a message with them before boarding my flight and let the matter go.

Once back in Austin, I began the process of interviewing for the position of administrator for that agency. This was the person who would lead the agency once my part of the start-up was complete. The agency wasn't officially open yet and the phone didn't ring a lot, so my receptionist doubled as my secretary. She had appointments set up all day Thursday and Friday and I was hoping to find someone who fit the bill during that time.

After interviewing all day, Harvey called and asked to speak with me.

"Hi Harvey, where have you been?"

Harvey was very annoyed at that question. "What are you, my mother?! The question is, where the hell are you?"

I was confused. He'd called me at the office in Austin. Surely he knew where he called! "Uhh, well, I'm working in Austin."

"No! I mean why aren't you at the airport picking me up?"

"In Austin? Are you here?" At this point I was totally taken aback.

"Yes, how could you not know that?"

"Well, because no one told me you were coming in."

"Dammit, I'm here! Come get me!"

"I can, but, I mean, I have interviews scheduled all afternoon. Can you take a cab?"

"DAMMIT, GET DOWN HERE NOW!!! I DON'T WANT TO WAIT AT THE AIRPORT ANY LONGER!!"

I knew that if I didn't pick Harvey up, then I may as well start looking for another job. So, I asked my nursing director to manage the rest of the scheduled interviews for the day and headed to the airport. When I got to the airport Harvey was somehow in a good mood.

"It's good to see you," I said. "What brings you to town?"

"Well, I just wanted to see how everything was going, so I flew in."

"Great, do you have a room or are you going to stay in the corporate apartment with me?"

"I don't know, let's just go grab a drink."

I looked at my watch and saw it was 3:30 p.m. We were heading to a bar instead of interviewing candidates for the administrator position, yet another waste of time. Once we arrived and Harvey had some alcohol flowing down his esophagus, he thanked me for handling the situation in Florida, but never really asked about any of the details or about what had happened. He did ask a few vague questions about what was going on in Austin, but nothing too involved. He abhorred operational details. After about an hour and a half, during which I nursed a beer or two while he sucked down four vodkas over ice, Harvey said, "Well, I better get on back to the airport and fly home."

Behind his back I shook my head. This was all incredibly ridiculous and it made me rather sad. Sad for him, because he had a lot of responsibility as well as a wife at home, but rather than work or go home, he obviously just wanted to waste time. And he was doing it by buying an expensive airline ticket and flying, unannounced, to another city to have a few drinks, drinks he could've had back in Dallas. In the process, he was derailing my efforts to actually get some things done.

As previously stated, I'd been doing a lot of thinking about Harvey and my career, but this episode put my brain into overdrive. I was growing professionally and Harvey seemed to be regressing further as we became busier and busier. I knew this couldn't go on forever and I began to wonder when the end would come. I thought it could be a simple audit of Harvey's expense report or it could come in some other more dramatic way such as a DWI arrest or automobile crash. I hoped it wouldn't be the latter, but based on his behavior, I couldn't help fear the worst.

Each a month Harvey had to make a full report to corporate so beforehand, he held a meeting in Dallas with all of us to prepare. I always came in the night before the meeting, and often used the time at home to go see Dad. On one such occasion Mom was having a dinner to celebrate my brother Bruce's birthday so my other brother who lived in Dallas was coming, too. I was excited to see everyone and even more excited to be around some normal people. At the dinner table, we all were having separate conversations when Dad raised his voice higher than normal and said, "Joe, how's work?"

I was less than enthusiastic about telling everyone the truth about my job so I just glazed over the whole Plantation and Austin incidents and gave a thin overview of my situation. For some odd reason Dad wasn't satisfied and took on his grumpy demeanor.

"Is that it?" he said.

I could sense my brothers and my mother getting uncomfortable with his change in behavior, but I was used to it. I felt like I knew something they didn't, because I understood Dad well enough now to know how to redirect him.

I smiled at him and confidently said, "Hey Dad, why don't you tell us about what happened to you when the Navy made you one of the first Blue Angels."

My brothers all looked at me as if I had a screw loose, but I knew what I was doing. Then Dad did something unpredictable: he stood up from the table and barked out, "No one wants to hear about that crap."

I realized I had made a fatal mistake. He knew I enjoyed hearing about his past, but he assumed no one else did. By asking this question in a group setting, I'd boxed him in and made him extremely agitated. I looked at my brothers and said, "Sorry for that, I'll explain later." Then I got up from the table and walked after Dad. I found him in his study looking out the window. He looked at me but didn't say anything. So I said, "I'm sorry dad but I really would like to hear more about your past."

He looked at me and said, "Do you really like hearing about that stuff?"

"Yes, I really do."

"Why?" he said in a way that bordered on innocence. I knew right then he was in a vulnerable state. Sometimes his brain worked and sometimes it didn't. I had no choice but to accept it and adapt, just like him.

I moved closer to him and said, "Because you're my father and you're telling me things about yourself I didn't know. I also really enjoy hearing about a dangerous time in our nation's history, and you lived it. I just think it's really cool. Besides, I never know what you'll tell me next."

Sensing my sincerity, he smiled and gave a slight chuckle. Then he pulled out a cigarette, lit it and said, "Alright. Where did I leave off?"

"You and Cliff were taking part in the air shows."

He looked away for a moment then said, "Right, right. Okay, let's see, I'd been flying in those shows for a while and it was fun, but the precision flying was taxing and I needed a break. So, after one show in Philadelphia, I left the squadron to head home for some rest.

"I was excited, because my father had finally arrived from the west coast and we hadn't seen each other in over a year. Plus, I'd managed to get a date for the night with a beautiful woman I'd been eyeing for quite some time. I took off early on a picturesque fall day and headed north to Greenwich. I was relaxed and happy to be going home. I received clearance to fly right over New York City and I gotta tell you, that's an amazing sight!

I loved New York and made a mental note to head into the city as soon as I could for some good food and maybe even a show. Then it happened.

"I heard something that made my heart flutter: the engine in my Corsair skipped. Now I knew a cold engine skipping or coughing when it was started was one thing, but an engine missing an hour into a flight was something entirely different. I waited a moment, and it happened again. I told the tower at North Beach Airport that I might have a problem. Because I was in such a densely populated area I knew couldn't risk ditching the plane right there. I told the tower of my concern and received permission to increase my altitude while I still had the chance. Simultaneously, I asked for a change in direction so that I could take a direct route to the water. I was thinking if I had to ditch, at least I wouldn't hurt anyone.

"I received permission and headed to a higher altitude as fast as I dared. Once situated at the higher altitude, the plane seemed to steady. I reported back to the tower as soon as I reached the water's edge and told them the plane seemed to have normalized and I thought I might make it. My confidence rose even higher as I headed out over the Long Island Sound.

"After fifteen minutes of smooth flying, I began to allow myself to think that I might be in the clear. Then it happened again. This time the plane began to sputter and cough and smoke. I was a pretty good pilot, but I wasn't much of a mechanic. Still, even I knew what was coming next. I radioed in that I was going down. Because of my flying skills, this little set-back was really more of an annoyance than a serious problem. After all I'd been through, I wasn't real worried about landing safely in the calm waters off Long Island Sound. I was, however, very worried about my shoes. I only owned one pair and they were on my feet. If I jumped into the water with them on, then what would I wear for my date that night?

"I surveyed the beaches below and saw one that appeared to be a tad bit less crowded than the others, so I aimed my dying plane toward the open water in front of the beach. I knew I needed a spot far enough out to avoid any swimmers. I was still deciding whether I really had to ditch or not. My engine was making pitiful coughing noises but hadn't stopped yet. Just as

I was considering everything, it gave a jolt and made a sickening metal on metal noise before stopping cold. I was now gliding and out of options. So I settled into a suitable glide path and landed the plane in the water of Long Island Sound just off the Mamaroneck Beach Club.

"The landing gave me a jolt, but was otherwise uneventful, at least, as far as crash landings go. As soon as I was able to unbuckle myself, I began to remove my shoes. My plan was to jump into the raft and paddle to shore, but the time it took to untie my shoes in the cramped cockpit caused me to miss the opportunity to deploy the small six-foot raft that had been my lifesaver in the Pacific. And the plane was sinking faster than I'd expected. Seeing that the shore was only a few hundred yards away, I slipped off the plane's wing and began my short swim to the beach, carrying my precious shoes over my head.

"As I made it to shallow water, I looked toward the shore and noticed a strange sight. In the surf, walking toward me was a man in a suit with his shoes off and his pant legs rolled up past his knees. When he got a little closer, the man called out to me and said, 'Welcome to Mamaroneck Beach Club!' as if I were some celebrity arriving for my reservation. I was surprised that the man wasn't angry, and even more surprised to receive a small hero's welcome from the people sunbathing on the beach. They clapped as if I'd just done something really special, not crashed my plane into the water. I gave a half wave as I walked out of the water and thanked them under my breath, although for the life of me I couldn't figure out what I was thanking them for.

"Once I was fully out of the water, a pretty girl approached me with a towel and a glass of iced tea. The club's manager said, 'We have stronger if you'd like. How about a gin and tonic?' I was tempted, but declined the cocktail since I still had to figure out how to get home.

"After I borrowed some dry clothes from the club manager—the guy in the suit who had waded out to greet me—I called in to my CO and told him what had happened. Afterwards I hopped a commuter train for my trip up the coast. When the cab pulled up to the house, I got out wearing my ill-fitting clothes, paid the Cabbie and walked up the sidewalk. There standing in front of me was Dad, in his full dress uniform. We looked at each other for a moment before I said, 'Welcome home, Commander.'

"Dad smiled and said, 'Thank you Lieutenant. I hear you made an unscheduled stop, and apparently picked up a new uniform in the process.'

"I laughed and said, 'Yours seems to be all there. What's the occasion?'

" ' I was going to come pick you up at the airport and wanted to look my best. Come on inside, let's have a drink and catch up.'

"The next day I received a call from the club manager to tell me that the Coast Guard had dredged for my plane, but hadn't found a thing. In fact, they never found that plane. They blamed it on the currents. I always wondered how a plane could have disappeared that quickly into the ocean.

"I enjoyed my time at home and especially enjoyed catching up with Dad. The time away had been good for our relationship and what I'd done in the South Pacific proved to Dad that I was indeed 'tough enough.' From then on Dad treated me with respect.

"As for Dad, he'd totally enjoyed his second stint in the military. For the generation of fighters who'd known so much success in WWI, WWII gave them a reason to feel important all over again. They'd suffered for years due to the Great Depression and now they felt they were contributors once again. In fact, Dad was so proud of his service that during that long weekend, he wore his Navy uniform more often than not. I never questioned him about this, but it was obvious he was extremely proud to play a part in America's great victory and clearly, he wanted others to know of his involvement as well."

Dad was still chuckling about his father wearing his dress uniform while running household errands around Greenwich that weekend when my brother Bruce walked in. Bruce stared at us and said, "What's so funny?"

Dad looked at me and winked, then turned to Bruce and said, "It's a long story."

7

A few weeks after my initial visit to Plantation, I received a call from Patti, the CEO of the hospital I'd visited to solve the nonexistent 'dyke' problem. She was very cordial and asked if I could come back out to Florida and assist them with a couple of issues. They'd taken their home care project seriously and completed a good deal of work while I was away. Fortunately, buying a pre-established certificate meant that the process was not that complicated-especially since they'd been working off my punch list. Now it was time to check back in, give some input on a few more details, and help them select the right person to run the agency. I called Gayle and asked her where Harvey was. She said she thought he was in California this week, and for sure he would be in California next week. Of course, when I asked where in California, she said she hadn't been given that information.

By this time we had agencies in Escondito, Orange, and San Lorenzo. Because I knew Harvey wanted to know where each person was at every minute, I told Gayle I would be in Plantation instead of Austin for the first two days of the following week. Since I'd been tasked with handling the situation there, I knew Harvey would be okay with me changing my schedule.

I left for Plantation on Monday and arrived mid-day, going straight to the administration offices. Patti and Barbara had jumped right in and from what I could tell, were doing a great job. The administrator candidate was coming in after lunch, so I headed out to get a bite and returned just in time to meet the candidate as she walked through the door. We were able to chat for a while before the interview and I have to say, she seemed excellent. She had a lot of high-level experience and seemed very grounded in every way. A short while later, Patti and Barbara were ready and we headed back to Patti's office. Right at that moment the receptionist called me back and said "Mr. Lynch, you have a call from Bill Swinson. He says that it's very important he speak with you and it can't wait." Patti looked at me and was very impressed Bill, a VP at corporate, was calling me regarding important business. Of course, I didn't feel important—I felt dread.

Bill Swinson was a big shot at UHI who oversaw all the home care operations as well as a whole division of UHI. He was one of our biggest supporters and also second in command of the entire company. I'd never spoken to him alone. Every meeting or discussion I'd ever had with him occurred with Harvey right by my side. Bill had never, ever called me directly and the fact that he had tracked me down in Plantation didn't seem like a good thing. I told Patti to begin without me and the receptionist escorted me into a small conference room so I could have some privacy.

Picking up the receiver, I said, "Hello Bill, how are you?"

"I'm okay, Joe. How's it going in Florida?"

"Pretty good. Patti is doing a great job with their new agency. We were just getting ready to interview a new administrator candidate."

"Great. Listen, I'll get right to the point. There's been an incident in California and I'm going to need you to get back to Dallas as soon as your interview is over."

"Okay, but can I ask what kind of an incident?"

"Well, initial indications are that Harvey became inebriated and attacked Robin physically in a hotel lobby. He then had to be restrained by Dale so he wouldn't hit her again."

My heart started racing as I began sweating.

"Uh, is Robin okay?" I stammered.

"She'll be alright," Bill said, "and she has every right to press charges against Harvey personally and against UHI for putting her in this situation. She's been checked out by one of our physicians at West Coast Community and she's okay physically, but I think she's still pretty emotionally shaken."

"Where is she now?"

"She flew home this morning. I've given her a few days off and asked her to come to Atlanta as soon as she feels up to it. We'll need to debrief with Human Resources. I'll be in that meeting as well."

"What's next?" I asked.

"That's what we need to determine and why I need all of you to be in Dallas tomorrow morning for a conference call."

I was still stunned. "Okay, thanks for the call."

"Thanks, Joe. We'll talk in the morning."

I tried to wipe off the sweat and straighten my tie before I lightly knocking on Patti's door. She motioned me in and asked if everything was okay; I must have looked like I'd seen a ghost. I said everything was fine and we proceeded with the interview. After the candidate left, I recommended that Patti make her an offer. As I got ready to go, Patti told me she was very appreciative of my efforts and would throw in a good word for me to Bill the next time he was in town. I thanked her but as I left, I wondered if I'd still be employed with UHI the next time she ran into Bill, because when the axeman swingeth, more than one head can be lopped off.

When I arrived at the airport, I called Robin knowing she probably wasn't there yet. When the machine came on, I left a message telling her I would be home soon and we could talk whenever she liked. Then I caught my flight and for the first time in a long time, I had a drink on the plane.

The next morning we all assembled at the office for the conference call, except for Robin. I hadn't heard back from her yet. Prior to the call, Dale had given us a blow-by-blow account of the assault. I wasn't surprised to learn it was the same old story. Dale had already been working in California and had decided to stay to visit some friends over the weekend. On Sunday, Harvey and Robin had met up at the airport mid-day so that they could fly to Orange and then head to Escondito later in the week. They started drinking the minute they got to the airport and by the time they arrived in Orange, they were both hammered. Dale ran into the two of them as they were all checking into the hotel. At that point, they all agreed to go to dinner together when Robin said something Harvey didn't like. It wasn't anything over the top, but in his altered state it set Harvey off. Robin has a strong personality and when she realized he was mad, she popped off again about him being a big baby. This sent him over the edge.

According to Dale, she was walking in front of him when Harvey reached up, jerked her backward by the hair, and then hit her hard in the face. When Harvey moved to hit her again, Dale quickly pinned Harvey to the ground. Harvey remained extremely belligerent throughout and had to be subdued until Robin could get away. The hotel concierge called the police, but Robin refused to press charges. Once the police left, Harvey was booted out of the hotel and disappeared.

All of us were still picking our jaws up off the floor and were just beginning to ask Dale questions when Bill called and the conference call began. He wasted no time. Harvey was being relieved of his duties. He could still serve as a consultant to help transition our division to new leadership, but other than that, he was being stripped of any responsibility or authority. Harvey was, at that moment, on his way to Atlanta and it wasn't clear what would become of him, but a full investigation into his actions was already underway. We were told to go back to the projects we were working on and wrap them up as efficiently as possible. Bill wanted weekly reports. Any trips to places other than our primary project location needed prior approval. I was still setting up the home care offices in Austin so I had authorization to go there and back, but not anywhere else. When the call was over, I felt like the end was near.

As soon as I had a minute, I put in another call to Robin and got her voicemail again. I left her a long message pleading with her to call me and teased her with information from the call we just had. It worked. About an hour later she called me back. She immediately began crying, but desperately wanted to know what had happened on the call. Once I'd repeated everything Bill had said, Robin apologized for messing everything up. I told her she wasn't to blame for the actions of a crazy, drunk lunatic and encouraged her to get some rest. I asked her if I could come see her later and she agreed.

I dropped by immediately after work. When she opened the door, I was appalled to see a large red welt on her face as well as a black eye. She stepped out of the door, hugged me and began sobbing. My heart broke as I held her and felt her warm tears soaking my shirt. There was no laughter on that day.

The next week I received a call early one morning from my mother. She informed me that Dad's condition was deteriorating. She'd taken him to the doctor many times over the years, but on the last trip he was so confused that he'd been admitted to the hospital to be certain that he hadn't had a stroke.

Mom knew that there was nothing I could do; she just wanted me to know what was going on. Since I was in the Dallas office working for a few days, I headed to the hospital after work to pay Dad a visit. I arrived at his room around 7:00 p.m.—Mom had already gone home. He looked sad as I entered the room, but then smiled broadly when he saw me.

"Hey Joe, glad to see you!"

"Hey Dad, how are you feeling?"

"Oh, this is so silly. I shouldn't be here. I'm fine." I realized in an instant that Dad was giving me a sales job on how well he was doing in the hopes I'd call Mom and convince her, too. Even so, I was so relieved he was in a good mood, this tactic didn't bother me.

We talked about the tests he'd been through and made guesses when he'd be released. He asked me about my job but I kept it brief, not wanting to rile him up with the whole Robin/Harvey incident. As strongly as Dad felt about having respect for one's boss, he felt stronger about men hitting women. That story would have enraged him, and I didn't feel that he needed that now.

Then, out of nowhere and catching me completely off guard, he said, "Hey, where did we leave off on the story?"

I was shocked. "Do you mean the story of *you?*"

He chuckled and said, "Yes, that's a good way to put it, yes, the story of *me.*"

"Well, if I recall correctly, you'd just crashed your plane into the Long Island Sound."

Dad laughed hard and deep. It made me happy to my core to see him laugh that way. In fact, I hadn't seen him that jovial in more years than I could remember.

"Oh yes," he said once he'd regained his composure. "Well, a few days after that crash I received a call that changed my life. I was back at the base and when Uncle Mac called. Uncle Mac was married to Dad's sister and was an executive at the Vought Corporation. He asked me when I'd be able to leave the service. Of course, I had no idea, but said I assumed it'd be within the next year or so. Uncle Mac told me Vought needed good men who could fly and the company might be interested in employing me as soon as I was free. The Vought Corporation was an aircraft manufacturing company that had produced some of the most important airplanes of the last twenty-five years, including the F4U Corsair, which I was then flying. I thought this was an intriguing proposition, especially since I knew I needed to find meaningful employment after I finished my degree at Yale. Being considered for a job that would involve flying, honestly, seemed too good to be true. I told Uncle Mac that I needed another semester or two to finish college, but if they still wanted me after that, I'd definitely be interested.

"A week later I was told I'd be honorably discharged from the Navy at the end of November. This was perfect—now I could jump back into Yale for the spring term and wrap up college by December. Then I had a dilemma: money.

"I hadn't needed much money during my years in the service, and had been sending most of it home to help pay the bills. Now, I had two semesters worth of credits to complete, but only enough money for one. Thinking about the job at the Vought Corporation, I decided to cram all of the remaining credits into one semester. This would get me a degree faster and not risk having my flying skills become too rusty. It was a brutal spring, but I made it through, earned my degree and then went to work for Vought.

"I started as both a test pilot and part-time executive working with the sales and marketing department. They had me working out of the company's Stratford, Connecticut facility, but since the government was the primary purchaser of our planes, I ended up spending a good deal of time in Washington, D.C.

In those days I flew everything Vought produced, all of which was very exciting. I also found the business aspect of my job was equally as challenging. I earned a lot of friends on my job, both among the seat-of-the-pants test pilots and among the businessmen and politicians. Then one day, I met the ultimate friend.

I was late to an early morning meeting and was walking quickly down the streets of Washington D.C when I turned a corner and ran directly into a man by accident, almost knocking him to the ground. He was as stunned as I and when I had made sure he hadn't fallen and we both straightened ourselves out, I said, "Gee, I'm so sorry. I wasn't looking . . . " Then I stopped in midsentence and stepped backwards. "Mr. President . . . " I was about to apologize when he held up his hands.

" 'It was an accident son,' he said looking at my uniform, 'Say, are you a pilot?'

"I looked around and saw he was by himself. At this time the secret service didn't follow around each President like they do today. Also, the White House was undergoing a large renovation, which caused President Truman to live across the street at Blair House. Truman made it his habit to walk the short distance to the White House every morning and it was during one of these walks I inadvertently ran into him.

"He asked me about my service and wanted to hear about my perspective on the front lines. I could see he liked hearing the stories. I would walk with him as far as I thought proper then turn around and go about my business. But each morning, I made it a point to get up early and catch him during his walk.

"This went on for awhile until two things cut it short: first, Vought moved its operations to Dallas. They needed to expand their footprint and that coupled with the Navy's concern for having multiple aircraft production facilities in close proximity to each other meant moving elsewhere. Then there was an assassination attempt on Truman's life, which ended his casual walks and boosted the Secret Service's protection. Still, I treasured those walks with the President of the United States of America and was glad to give him my perspective.

"By this time I'd married that girl I crashed my plane to go see on that Labor Day weekend. We'd started a family, your half-brothers and sister, and were now moving to Dallas for my job with Vought. The move presented a wonderful opportunity for my career, but it put a heavy strain on our marriage. The high-pressure job combined with lots of travel and unfamiliar surroundings, all factored in strongly to my divorce. I could handle the relationship dissolving, but when she took your brothers and sister with her back to the East Coast, that really hurt. I compensated by throwing myself into my work and eventually ended up running one third of the Vought Corporation, while visiting the kids or bringing them to Dallas every chance I got. In time, I met your mother and we were married in the fall of 1958.

"I remember one time shortly after we were married, Nancy and I were on a trip together in Houston. I was going there for business and wanted her to accompany me to a social gathering which included a number of my Houston associates. When we got to the party, I had to tend to business so Nancy wandered off to find the bar. As she turned around with her drink, she was met by a group of men who seemed very anxious to meet her. Introductions were made all around, but none of the names meant anything to her. They said they were good friends of mine and they'd been anxious to meet my new wife. They knew me from our Navy days and now, our friendship had overlapped with each other in the aircraft business. During a lull in the conversation, Nancy asked the question, 'What do you guys do now?'

"The one doing most of the talking was named Alan. He perked up and said, 'We're astronauts.'

"Nancy wrinkled her nose and said, 'What's an astronaut?'

" 'Well,' Alan said, 'an astronaut is a person who pilots a spacecraft.'

"Nancy told me she'd enjoyed their boyish charm and delightful sense of humor, and even went so far as to assume this last statement was a joke as well. She began laughing and said, 'Seriously, what do you guys do for a living?'

"Allen wasn't put off. He said, 'Let me give you a global perspective. Several years ago the U.S. Government decided to form a division which would be responsible for the exploration of the space. Eventually they realized the crafts they were trying to build would need to be piloted by men who understood the inner workings of an aircraft. That led them to the Navy and the Marine Corps, which led them to us. We're the men who'll fly their spacecraft and we're called astronauts.'

"Nancy now understood they weren't joking. 'I see, and when will this happen?'

" 'It's happening now,' said John Glenn.

" 'You mean you guys have flown in space?'

" 'No, not yet, but we're building the vessels now and training for the day when we'll get there. We hope to be ready in the next few years.'

"Of course, Nancy had never heard of such a thing and was amazed by the whole idea. They continued talking throughout the night and years later, she was glued to the television along with the rest of America when Allen Sheppard, John Glenn, and the rest of the men of the Mercury 7 program launched into space and then orbited the earth.

"By the late sixties, I'd seen Vought head off in a new direction and by then we had you and your two brothers, so I decided to take my career in a new direction as well. I was anxious to try my hand at starting my own business, so I paired with an old friend and began a holding company, which owned companies in industries from mobile home manufacturing to real estate investing. The business started slowly, but within a few years it really took off and once again I was running a large organization with a lot of responsibility.

"In February of 1968, I received an unexpected call from your uncle Bill in Greenwich—Dad had died. He was attending a cocktail party with Mom at the home of one of their friends in Greenwich and he was sitting on the couch when he suffered a massive stroke. It was traumatic to Mom and a shock to us kids. It hit me especially hard, because we'd become very close in the years after the war. Now at the age of seventy-five, he was gone."

He took a break from talking and gazed at all the monitors and tubes spread along his bedside and he suddenly looked sad again. For my part, I couldn't believe what I was hearing. The movie *The Right Stuff* hadn't been out long and it had quickly become one of my favorite movies of all-time. I looked at him and asked, "You knew Alan Sheppard, John Glenn, Scott Carpenter and those guys?"

He smiled and said, "Sure, I knew Alan better than the others, but yes, they were my friends."

I was kicking myself for never asking about all this earlier in life. But at least I was now.

Over the next few weeks, I worked exclusively in Austin and hardly spoke to anyone else from the team, other than Robin, of course. I never heard from Harvey, but I spoke with Robin almost daily. She was getting better and slowly she seemed to be letting go of what had happened in California. She said she'd spoken with Harvey and he'd apologized profusely. Harvey was also now temporarily back in charge of our division because, apparently, the guys at corporate had no other logical option. But the word was he was being watched like a hawk. No one knew what would happen with him and I assumed his time with UHI would be over soon.

When my time in Austin drew to a close, I called Bill Swinson and asked him what I should do next. He asked me what I wanted to do and I told him that the constant traveling was getting to me and that I would like to start an agency and then stay there to run it for a while. He asked me where I wanted to go and I said, "I'm a team player, I'll go wherever I'm needed."

He said, "Good enough, I'll see who needs an agency the most."

A couple of days later I got word my agency was going to be in Midland, Texas. I wasn't thrilled with the location, but I remembered what I'd said to Bill and I wasn't going to back out just because the location wasn't to my liking. I did make one request, though. I asked if I could get a review and a possible transfer after one year, if all went well in West Texas. They agreed, so it looked like I was moving to Midland.

A week later, I needed to fly to Midland to meet with the hospital CEO and tell him corporate wanted start a home care agency and they wanted me to run it. Gayle called to tell me that Harvey was working out of our Dallas office for a few days and had set up the meeting for me with the CEO for the next afternoon. I had no idea what Harvey's current capacity with the company was and frankly, I didn't give a damn, especially after what he'd done to Robin. It did, however, dawn on me while driving to the airport that Harvey may have just told Gayle to tell me to go to Midland without actually calling the CEO. I imagined showing up at the CEO's office and being told that the CEO had no idea who I was so, I decided I should call Harvey from the airport and verify the appointment. I placed the call and asked Gayle if I could confirm the appointment with Harvey. She hesitated and said "He's not really in a great mood these days. Are you sure you want to do that?"

Frustrated that Harvey could actually still be controlling anything with his moods, I said, "Yes, I'd like to speak with him."

When he picked up the phone, I said, "Does the CEO in Midland know I'm coming?"

He exploded, "Goddammit Joe . . . YES . . . he knows you are coming!"

I was in no mood for his erratic behavior so I simply hung up. That was the last time I spoke with him.

After that, it didn't take long for our little team to disband. Robin used the blow up in California as a negotiating ploy to work out a sweetheart deal with UHI. They were so worried about her suing them, they probably would've agreed to anything. She stayed on with the company for a few more months, but like the rest of us she was burnt out on travel and Harvey and eventually walked away. She couldn't handle home care anymore, so she parlayed her experience into another opportunity in the staffing industry.

Dale stayed on for a similar amount of time and then left UHI to go work for another home care company. Kathy made it about six months and then started her own home care company. Sadly, she passed away ten years later from breast cancer. Harvey managed to stay on with UHI in a consulting capacity for several more years, after which he disappeared into the woodwork and was not heard from again by any of us. As for me, I had just started to date a girl I really liked in Dallas, and now was moving to Midland.

In the time we were all together, we'd started, acquired, and eventually ended up managing over fifteen million dollars of home care revenue for UHI. Harvey had put the wheels in motion to make it happen and for that, I give him full credit. I'll also give him a nod for hiring me in the first place. He gave me a chance when I needed one and for that I'll always be grateful. It's too bad his behavior was our downfall, as I have no doubt our team could've stayed together and kept growing the division if the man who created us hadn't also derailed us.

After I'd been away from Harvey for a few weeks, I began to feel the tension in my body start to melt away. I hadn't even realized how much pressure working for a man like that had put on me. In the end we all ended up happier to be out from under the little tyrant named Harvey.

8

After moving to Midland, I quickly settled into my new position as administrator of the hospital's home care agency. I was able to land with my feet running and quickly made friends with a couple of the doctors who then sent us a lot of patients. I also hired a staff that interacted well together. The thing I noticed most about running an agency was my closeness to the actual patients and staff. I liked the degree of interaction. I was used to being the guy from corporate who did what needed to be done to get an agency going, then left. Now I was the day-to-day manager and it had an entirely different feel. Daily operations were my focus, so while I still worked for a huge company, my life centered on our little west Texas hospital community. I liked the job itself a lot, but living in Midland was much more of a transition. It really was a nice community and full of nice people, but it just wasn't for me. Plus, I missed my regular conversations with Dad. Sure, we spoke on the phone quite a bit, but it wasn't the same. Lucky for me, Southwest Airlines ran about eight flights a day from Midland to Dallas, so I was able to make it back home frequently.

Throughout my time in Midland, I came home regularly to see Dad. Each time he was slipping farther away, and the moments he was coherent were getting fewer and farther between. Then, six months into my new position, a new head of home care was brought in at UHI, which is what officially relegated Harvey to a part-time consultant. I wondered if this new person would have some bearing on my transfer out of Midland after my first year, but I didn't really worry about it. I merely kept working and things continued to go well.

After my year was almost up, I put a call into Bill Swinson and asked him if he remembered our arrangement. He said he did but that all such requests would have to now go through the new director. Bill was nice about it, but I felt a little uneasy about my chances of winning over someone I really didn't know. I'd met the new guy once at a company-wide conference, but that was it. I tried to politely ask Bill if he'd put a good word in for me and he laughed and said he would. I waited a few days for that good word to be 'put in,' then called the director of home care operations. He told me that I was doing a great job in Midland and that there would be no transfer.

By this time I was receiving a good many calls from recruiters looking for folks who knew the ins and outs of home care management. I didn't know how they were finding me, but when one of them called shortly after I was told that I'd have to live in Midland for the rest of my life, I talked to him. He said he represented an agency in Dallas that was looking for an administrator and asked if I knew anyone who may be interested. I told him I'd be interested and complimented him on his timing (though I assumed I was number eighty-six on his list of one hundred folks he had to call that day).

The agency owner he connected me with was very interested in meeting me and flew out to Midland the next day for an interview. He was a great guy and we really clicked. So good, in fact, that in no time, I was writing out my letter of resignation that would end my tenure with UHI.

As I put Midland in my rearview mirror, I thought back to all the crap I put up with from Harvey and how bad it had worn on me. One full year away from the lunatic made me realize how screwed up my life had been with him as my boss. And truly, my time in Midland had been good for me. It had cleared my mind and made me appreciate the profession I'd chosen. I now realized that it was all about the patients and providing the best care I could. I was also happy to be moving to a small company environment, complete with all the challenges it provided. I knew there was something out there for me and hopefully, I'd find it back in Dallas.

When I first arrived in Dallas, I immediately went by my parent's house to see how Dad was doing. He had just been in the hospital again, this time for several days having numerous tests run. The results weren't great. As we already knew, he was in serious decline, but nothing was acutely wrong with him. So they sent him home and gave Mom a list of things for him to do which consisted of such startling revelations as drinking less, smoking less, getting more exercise, and resting. Mom suggested I rally my brothers and take Dad golfing. She thought it would be good for him to get out and spend some time with us. Since it was a Friday, I made a couple of calls and set up a game for us the following morning. The club we played at was very close to Love Field airport in Dallas where an air show was being held that weekend.

The next morning I picked up Dad and headed to the course. As we drove past the airport I noticed my father craning his head out of the window trying to see the vintage airplanes that were flying over. When we were past the airport he looked at me and said, "You know, I can still identify those old planes just by hearing the sound of their engines."

I smiled, not really believing him, and said. "I'm sure you can, Dad."

When we arrived at the golf club I put my shoes on and told Dad I'd meet him out on the putting green. My two brothers were already outside practicing. We talked for a bit, before Dad finally emerged from the locker room. He waved at us, smiled, and then began ambling towards us with his slow and steady gate. While he was heading toward us, I began to hear the distinctive sound of an old piston engine airplane. With the air show going on we'd heard a lot of planes that morning, but this one really got Dad's attention and it caused him to stop cold in his tracks, then he tilted his head and began looking for the source.

Just then a WWII Japanese Zero became visible from behind a group of trees as it made its decent into Love Field. Dad studied the plane for less than a second then raised his arm, extended his middle finger and shot the bird in the direction of the plane. My brothers and I laughed out loud at the sight of our elderly father standing among a number of weekend golfers giving an airplane the finger, but one of the onlookers didn't find it funny. A smallish man of about fifty approached Dad. We were twenty feet away but could hear the man.

"I don't find your actions funny or appropriate. This is a nice club, not a barracks."

I started to walk towards the two, but my brother Bruce put a hand on my shoulder to stop me. "He can take care of himself."

Dad looked at the man and in a slow drawl that sounded as much like John Wayne as my father, said, "If you had ever fought in a war, you might have a different attitude."

The man looked somewhat defiant, but then gave a smug chuckle. "That war was a long time ago."

With this my father raised himself up to his full height, pushed all of his 230 pounds into his chest and took a step closer to the man. Upon seeing my large father move in closer, the man turned slightly, took a step back and suddenly looked very uncomfortable. Dad pointed at the man with his finger approximately one inch from the man's nose and in a booming voice, said, "Not to me!" Then he turned and continued walking over to where the three of us stood. The little man slinked away.

As we greeted our father, three older men also in their seventies walked over laughing. One of them said, "Good for you. That little shit will never know what it's like to be shot at by one of those damn Zero's. I sure as hell do. They gave us hell at Guadalcanal."

They spoke for several minutes reliving their youth and then invited Dad to join their foursome. Dad smiled and said, "Thanks men but I promised my boys I'd play with them today." With that he proudly turned and introduced the three of us.

A few moments later we said goodbye to Dad's new friends and began walking to the first tee. As we walked, I heard the sound of another piston engine overhead. I turned to my father and said, "Hey Dad, what's that one?"

Without missing a beat or looking in the direction of the plane he said, "That's a P-51 Mustang. Great plane. Saved our ass in Europe." Then he began digging in his golf bag for a ball as I looked up and saw the signature silver skin and protruding belly of a P-51 Mustang emerge from the trees on its way into Love Field.

When I brought Dad home later in the afternoon, he immediately retreated upstairs to take a nap. I sat down with Mom at the kitchen table and told her all about what had happened at the golf course. Mom laughed at Dad's antics and was very happy he was able to spend the afternoon with us. Then we talked about my work and my life for a while, before moving on to a subject I really wanted to know more about but didn't feel comfortable asking Dad. "Mom, would you tell me about when Dad left his development company?"

"Why do you ask?" she said.

She knew I'd been speaking to Dad about his past, but hadn't followed the progression of our talks and she didn't know her explanation would fill in the next chapter of the story Dad had been telling me. I answered honestly that it would be helpful for my career—especially at this critical time—to hear how he progressed from one job to the next.

"That makes sense," she said. "Well, as I'm sure you already know the development company was a huge success, but your father didn't like the direction his partners were taking it. They had several disagreements over the course of several months and Vince decided the time was right for a change of scenery. Your father has never liked controversy and the result was he began drinking more than he should. I hated to see him that way, so I recommended he go ahead and leave.

"In the summer of 1975 he headed out on his own. From there he dabbled in the oil business for a few years, managing a few properties my father had left me. The properties provided a little investment income for us but more importantly, they intrigued Vince and made him extremely interested in the oil business. He'd also taken a liking to Texas and being in the oil business appealed to him now that he considered himself a Texan. So he slowly built up the properties and by the mid-eighties, he had a robust company. Because of his success, he was asked to serve on the board of a savings and loan.

"In about 1985, savings and loans companies began failing, mostly because of crazy real estate loans. At the same, the price of oil had dropped from $35 a barrel to under $10. This took the wind out of the sails of

Vince's company. Bruce had joined the business in the early eighties and told me about a meeting between Vince and Larry Newman, our accountant. Larry began the meeting with 'Vince, you've done well in the oil business, but we both know that a commodity like oil has its ups and downs. Right now, we're headed into a down cycle, but that doesn't mean you have to suffer. I've done the math and I think that if you liquidate 75% of your properties, you can pay off all your debts and walk away with a sizable amount of money for retirement. You can even keep a small office, play some golf and go back to managing the remaining properties on a part-time basis. Honestly Vince, it's a win-win scenario. Would you like me to proceed with the sale of the properties?'

"Vince wasn't happy with that plan at all. He was proud, too proud for his own good. He looked at Larry and said, 'Larry, that's the dumbest thing I've ever heard. I'm not a quitter and I don't agree with your assessment. Do *not* move forward with that plan; do move forward with finding a new place of employment.'

"Both Larry and Bruce were shocked. As a result, Vince left the room and Larry left the company. And just as Larry predicted, the company headed down. A few months later Bruce was forced to leave the company, too. He was young and he needed stable employment. At the same time he hated to leave his father in such a bad situation. As the condition worsened over the next several years, Vince turned more and more to alcohol to help him cope with the pressure of managing a dying business. Stress coupled with getting older, alcohol, and a lifetime of cigarettes began to affect his cognitive abilities. That was about the time he began showing the first signs of dementia. And that's where we find ourselves now."

It was sobering to hear the cold hard facts like that. Mom didn't hold anything back. Mom's telling of Dad's story wasn't as elaborate or exciting as Dad's—she was more of a 'get to the point' storyteller—but this didn't make it an easier to hear. Then again, this part of Dad's life wasn't very glamorous and I doubt she felt a sense of nostalgia about it. Despite all of this, she did a good job filling in yet another piece of the puzzle that was my father's life.

9

After leaving my parents' house, my next priority once I got back to Dallas was to reconnect with Ann, the girl I'd been so interested in before I left. She was beautiful, with blonde hair and brown eyes. She was smart, funny, and lucky for me she was still interested! Our relationship had been put on hold when I moved to West Texas, but once I was back in town it quickly turned serious. We were married in the summer of 1997 and soon after she became pregnant with our first child.

At work, I found my new boss Jim to be even-keeled, smart and sober—a great guy to work for. His company was called CTS Care and had been around a while, but hadn't been aggressively managed. It was secondary to his other ventures and he simply hadn't invested a lot of hours into managing and growing it.

At the time I came on, CTS consisted of a small agency in Dallas and one in Hillsboro, Texas. The Hillsboro office actually had more patients than the Dallas office. That seemed strange, as there are far more people in Dallas, not to mention we took Medicare patients. The reason? Competition. It turned out that the Hillsboro office had virtually no competition. That, combined with a population of older Americans who used home care as a primary source of health care, brought the agency close to bursting at the seams.

Small towns were pretty new to me. I could tell things were different, but I didn't yet have a handle on it. So I decided I needed to spend some time in Hillsboro to get the feel of how things worked. It was a different world all together. And these people were country. Real country!

I sat down with the nursing director of Hillsboro and began asking her questions about how things were done. As she spoke, she kept talking about the clout she had, phrases like, "I have the power," and "The power's in my hands."

After a few of these references, I finally said, "Excuse me, but what do you mean when you say, 'the power'?"

She looked at me as if I wasn't all there and said, "The power to schedule people to work." Still not fully understanding, I began subtly asking more questions. It was then I learned the scheme she had going. CTS's field staff were paid for each visit they made to their patients, not by the hour. Since employment opportunities were scarce in little Hillsboro, Texas, she was referring to the power to put money in people's pockets. As it turns out, she certainly *was* wielding a lot of power in dictating who got to work and pay their bills and who didn't. And I soon learned she wasn't wielding it in any kind of a logical manner. If she was mad at someone or just didn't like them, she'd cut them off, despite how good they were with their patients. Absolute power tends to corrupt a person. Because of this, I immediately knew this woman was going to have to go, but I needed to build a case first.

My first day in Hillsboro started with a bang. After interviewing the nursing director, a call came into the agency from a very distraught woman. She was the daughter of one of our patients. The call was routed to the nursing director who quickly realized that the woman was very upset, so she passed the call on to me.

It took a few moments, but I finally understood the situation. It seems her mother, who evidently really liked the nurse taking care of her, had decided to give the nurse her car. Obviously, *wanting* to give someone a car is a very nice gesture and it would've made a great story for this nurse, if that had been as far as it went. But it didn't. In this case, the nurse accepted the car and actually called her husband to come pick it up. What really makes this story special is the type of car the patient gave the nurse: a mint condition 1967 Mustang convertible. The daughter of the patient had been looking forward to getting that car for years, and now it was in the hands of a home care nurse the family had just met. I apologized to the daughter and told her I would make the situation right.

I called the field nurse and told her I would be getting a ride to her house so that I could pick up the car and in midsentence, she hung up on me. At this point I knew I was in for a long afternoon.

When I showed up at the nurse's home and saw the Mustang parked out front, I politely told her she couldn't keep the car. That was when her large husband met me at the door and informed me the car was theirs to keep and I'd better move on. I told him that accepting a gift of this magnitude could land them both in a good deal of hot water, particularly if the family chose to pursue them for taking advantage of a helpless old lady who had been clinically diagnosed with dementia. I explained that the daughter was hopping mad and that I wouldn't be surprised if the police were to show up any minute. I also pointed out that since they were not in possession of the car's title (a minor detail completely overlooked by either of these geniuses), it would be pretty easy to make a case against them. After some back and forth conversation about how he couldn't afford to be in trouble with the law again, the man opened the front door and threw the keys at me, hitting me hard in the chest. It stung, but not as hard as if I hadn't been able to return the car.

After this excitement, I decided that I'd had enough of Hillsboro for the day, so I called the nursing director and told her I was taking the car back to the daughter and would return the next day. She acted like this really was going to put her out, but I pressed on and told her I wanted to go into the field with one of her nurses the next day. Would she please make the necessary arrangements? She said she would and we hung up.

The next day I showed up early, ready for my day of seeing patients in Hillsboro. I was paired with a nurse who was very quiet and in fact, I had a hard time getting her to string two sentences together. The first couple of stops were uneventful, but our third stop was at the home of what had to be one of our more pitiful cases. The patient lived with her son and his wife and was kept in a small side room of their house. The room was tiny and had no ventilation. This was bad news for the little old lady (and for us, too!), because her bedside commode hadn't been cleaned in some time. I didn't need to actually check it to make this determination—the horrendous, nasty smell permeated the room, my nostrils and eventually all of my clothing.

The room had a door that sealed it off from the rest of the house and was very difficult to open. I only know this because the nurse asked me to open it at one point to let in some air and it took all my strength to accomplish the task. I quickly started to sweat because of both the effort and the extreme heat. The seventy-five-year-old patient was seated in a chair next to the bed. At first I just said hello to the woman and observed the care that she was receiving. The nurse introduced me as an observer, which seemed to satisfy her but she kept looking over at me and smiling like she was really happy I was there. But there was something else, like she wanted to say something directly to me. The situation was very strange and uncomfortable. Frankly, I wanted to learn more about what was going on from the nurse; she hadn't given me any information before entering the home. Now I really wanted to know the backstory.

As the nurse was trying to complete her Q & A, the patient kept trying to ask me questions. The nurse told her she could speak with me in just a moment, but that she would just need a minute more of her time. When the nurse was done, the lady began a full inquiry of who I was. Her questions were not with the attitude of someone angry or even curious. They seemed to come from a sense of desperation and I got a strong sense she was scared and needed some help.

About the time I came to this conclusion, the door burst open and a large woman of probably thirty-five years old entered wearing a flannel nightshirt. She was very upset! She wanted to know if I was a person with any authority at my company. I told her I was the Administrator. When the patient heard this she began screaming and asking me to help her. The younger lady in the flannel nightshirt began screaming at the older lady to shut up. It was a mess and I was right in the middle of it.

The screaming went on for a minute or so and before they both calmed down enough for me to say, "Exactly what is the issue here?"

The younger lady immediately began to berate me for what my company had done to her. I really didn't want to stoke her fire in any way, but since I didn't have a clue what she was talking about, I said, "I am sorry ma'am, but what did we do to you?" She looked at me as if I were Satan himself and began telling me my nurse had been coming out on a regular basis and filling her mother-in-law with lies about how she should be treated.

With this, the older lady began crying and reaching out to me—literally reaching out and grabbing my arm. By this point she was sobbing and could hardly get her words out. It was one of the saddest things I'd ever seen. This made the daughter-in-law even more belligerent. She turned to the older woman and said, "What the hell do you think you're doing?" Then she addressed me and said, "That bitch don't need no sympathy from you."

I looked at this overweight woman who was still in her nightshirt at 11:00 a.m. and said, "She wants to speak with me. I can't see the harm in that, unless there's something you don't want me to hear?"

The daughter-in-law looked at me with sheer hatred in her eyes and said, "That bitch is lucky to have me taking care of her and I don't need no disrespect from her—*or you!*"

I turned my attention to the patient and said, "What's the problem ma'am? Is my company not helping you or is the problem with your family?"

The daughter-in-law started to answer this question with protests but I snapped my head in her direction and said, "If you say another word, I'll call the police right now." She shut up and let the older woman speak

"Please take me with you. Please take me with you. *Please, please* take me with you." Her pleading was heartbreaking. I repeated my question.

"Tell me what the problem is, ma'am. I really want to help, but I need to know what is going on."

She looked at me for a while and then pointed towards her daughter-in-law. "She is so mean to me. Please take me away from her."

With this I turned to my nurse who I had not looked at during this whole exchange. She was openly crying. I told her, "Please go call APS (Adult Protective Services) and you should probably call the police as well."

The daughter-in-law went ballistic. As my nurse ran out of the house to make the call, the daughter-in-law lunged at me as if she were going to hit me. I held my ground, even though I was honestly scared to death—this woman was huge! She didn't hit me, but she certainly acted like she was going to. But now she was standing so close to me I could smell her. She was certainly giving that bedside commode a run for its money. Then she spat out, "I'm going to go call my husband and he's going to kick your ass!"

This didn't sound like very good news for me, especially since I had caught a set of car keys with my ribs the day before. I watched her run out of the side door and noticed it had a lock on it. I had to struggle to get the door closed, but I was highly motivated and managed to lock it. A short while later the daughter-in-law began beating on the door, yelling obscenities. About that same time, I heard some commotion outside the other door so I opened it, thinking that the police had arrived. They had, exactly as the fat woman's husband did. I was really glad he hadn't arrived before the police! He was a big, old, country boy and he would've beat me like an old country mule. Fortunately he wasn't very bright, because he decided to engage the police in a little one-on-one fisticuffs, which of course didn't turn out well for him. I was going to tell the officers I had a trained nurse with me, but decided against it. They had medical staff at the jail and they'd take a look at him so long as he was still alive.

When the police came into the room and asked me what was up with the older lady, I let them know I was fairly certain she was in an abusive situation. The police, the same police who had just kicked the country out of this woman's son, were as gentle as if they were handling a newborn baby. It was awesome to watch. As they helped her into a wheelchair, she looked over at me and said, "Thank you."

I knelt down next to her and said, "I didn't do a thing. You spoke up when you needed help and that took a lot of courage." She grabbed my hand and smiled, as her eyes welled up with tears. Then I watched them roll her out to a car and take her away to a hopefully much better place.

I later learned that the son and daughter-in-law had sued a local hospital for something or another and had been awarded $100,000 in the settlement. To them, this meant that they were *rich* and suddenly resented taking care of the man's mother. They wanted to live the highlife they thought they deserved. Instead of doing something smart with the money, they spent it on trucks and frivolous stuff. Now, they were running low and taking their frustrations out on the poor woman, the same woman they were supposed to be caring for. I never did learn what happened with the lady, but I assume that she was put in a home.

I have little patience for people who abuse children or the elderly, and was privately glad the son got his face rearranged. Forget the fact she was elderly—that was his mother! How could someone do that to their own mother?

Afterwards, I bent my nurse's ear pretty good about not preparing me better for the situation. I learned we'd called Adult Protective Services before on these people and this is most assuredly where the tension had started between the family and us. I don't like being surprised, although my nurse couldn't have known what would happen in their home that day. But if she'd just told me some of the story, I could've at least known where to go with my questioning when the screaming started.

While dealing with Hillsboro, we began to grow the Dallas operation. The Dallas agency had a good reputation, but it had never been marketed effectively. Now that we began to spread the word, it began to grow much more quickly. One thing that was a relief is that it was never really a problem to manage the Dallas operation. Things there ran smoothly. Hillsboro, on the other hand, was very different story. There was a lot of infighting and drama, all of which centered around the nursing director.

She was a bully and abused the staff. This meant the staff hated her. Eventually, she made her final mistake and it was time for me to fire her. I've never relished firing anyone but in this case, I knew it was for the best. Still, you never know how people are going to react. As angry and unpredictable as this woman was, I thought the situation could get ugly. In the end though, she did what most bullies do when confronted: she went away with hardly a whimper.

During my first year with CTS, the agency grew substantially. This growth put the agency on the radar screen of larger companies looking to expand. So when Jim received a sweet offer to sell the company, he decided to cash out. I wasn't aware of this—as the employees rarely are in these situations—and learned the hard way. I was at an appointment one day, and when I returned to the office, guess who was sitting in the reception area waiting to meet with Jim? My old buddy Harvey. I almost fell down when I saw him. When he saw me, he jumped up and began pacing around in his Charlie Chaplin manner. Of course, neither Harvey nor Jim figured that anyone would know who he was or why he was seeing Jim. When Jim realized how well I knew Harvey, he decided to loop me in on the sale. Before long I was working for a division of United Health International again. How unbelievable is that?!

I met my new UHI boss and she was nice enough, but I'd read this book before and knew how it ended. So I decided that, despite being newly married and having a baby on the way, it was time to go in a new direction. But which one?

The old woman in Hillsboro had really stayed with me. She made me think about what my career *should* be about. And it finally occurred to me the talks with my father had meant something more than just a son figuring out how to communicate with his aging, sick father. Those sessions lined up with what I was doing in my professional life, because the people I was professionally responsible for looked a lot like my Dad.

I don't know why it took me so long to figure all of this out. Maybe I was just too caught up in all of the junk constantly swirling around me to focus on what my professional life should be about. But there has to be a purpose to what you spend your days doing, otherwise all of your effort only serves the purpose of paying bills and little else. I guess I didn't understand that until I saw firsthand what a bad case of elderly neglect looked like. Even today I find it humbling that I needed to actually see an abusive situation before I truly understood the immense responsibility which is placed on anyone involved in the care of an elderly person. The fact that the ones who most needed the services we offered were frail of body and sometimes of mind, now resonated in me and I wanted to cut to the chase and help more of them in any way I could.

This called for a meeting with Dad, so I called him and asked if we could go to lunch. He said okay and we set a time the next day at his favorite restaurant. I needed some advice and hoped he had enough left in him to give.

During the previous weeks, Dad had been sounding and looking better. He still had an office nearby that Mom would drive him to. He would shuffle to his desk and sit in his comfortable chair and do what? I had no idea. But it was a way for Mom to get out of the house without worrying about him. And there was a restaurant, Pierre's—his favorite—right next door. He'd often wander over to eat, then go back to his office for a nap. At the end of the day, Mom would pick him up and Dad was happy because he felt productive. It was a win-win situation.

I showed up on time and eagerly awaited sitting down with him, and asking him what I should do. But I wasn't sure if I should tell him my problem first or get him started on some more stories before telling him what was on my mind. I truly enjoyed hearing a firsthand account of the decisions he'd made in his life and had come to love these encounters. I think he liked them, too.

As I sat there thinking about his life and what I would ask him to tell me, I suddenly felt very selfish. It dawned on me I was gaining a lot from his stories, but I wasn't telling him how his stories were helping me learn and grow as a man. It was only right he should know that he was helping me become not only a better person, but also a better husband and father. He should also know that I loved and respected him a great deal and I hadn't ever told him that. While I sat there, this suddenly weighed on me a great deal.

I waited thirty minutes before I finally found a phone and placed a call to his office. No one answered. I then called the house and no one answered there either. I thought of walking to his office, but decided against it. If he'd forgotten, there was no chance we were going to have a meaningful conversation anyway. So, when an hour was up, I told the waiter that my father must have forgotten so I would just need a check for the iced tea I had ordered. The waiter looked sadder than I felt. He knew Dad well. Dad always liked to go places where people knew his name. I think it was from his younger days on the east coast where it was a sign of status—when you took a date to a restaurant and everyone knew your name.

The waiter, in his thick French accent said "Oh nooo, what happened to Monsieur Vince? Is everything alright?"

I smiled and said, "I'm sure he's fine. He just gets a little forgetful sometimes. He'll probably be back in tomorrow for a visit."

The waiter seemed to be somewhat placated by my answer, but then looked at me and said, "Monsieur, your father . . . well, he order zee same meal every time he come to the restaurant. When you told us that you were having lunch with him we prepared zee dish in advance. Please Monsieur, allow us to serve it to you free of charge."

I said, "Oh no, I couldn't do that. Isn't there someone else that could eat it?"

The waiter chuckled and then he persisted, "Please Monsieur, we love your father and he is such a good customer. Besides Monsieur, no one else would like this particular meal. It is ready to serve so please . . . we insist."

It was one o'clock and I hadn't eaten a thing all day except a banana at seven in the morning, so I finally said, "Sure, thank you very much."

With much pomp and circumstance the waiter brought out a plate while another waiter snapped a clean linen napkin open and placed it delicately on my lap. Then yet another waiter lit the candle on the table. When I looked at the plate, I saw lunch consisted of one chicken breast. On the side of the plate were two anchovies, one sliced hardboiled egg, and a small bowl of béarnaise sauce and with it all, they served me a cold glass of chardonnay. It was not exactly my idea of a perfect lunch, but I had to laugh because it was everything my dad loved. I could just see him cutting a small piece of the chicken breast and scooping it up with an even smaller piece of the anchovy and then dipping the bite into the béarnaise sauce before putting the whole mess into his mouth. The hardboiled egg would be eaten on its own with a light sprinkling of salt and pepper. Then he would wash everything down with a gulp of wine. What a unique way to get to know my dad better!

When I was done, I thanked the waiter for his generosity and left him a tip that was more than I would have spent on my usual lunch at Subway. At the same time I left feeling sad I'd have to wait to tell Dad what was on my mind. I brooded on this until I got back to work, where the minute I hit the door and was hit with new problems, I forgot I'd even had lunch.

When I arrived home that evening, I saw my favorite sight in the whole world: my lovely wife Ann cooking dinner and my one-and-a-half-year-old daughter sat in her high chair picking at her food. They smiled at me and instantly, the day melted away.

After I kissed my two girls, Ann said, "Hey, by the way, is everything okay with Peter and Libby?" Peter was one of my brothers and Libby was his wife.

"I haven't heard anything either way, why?"

"Well," she said. "It's probably nothing but they've called here a few times and there was only one message left, but it seemed unintentional because Libby didn't speak into the phone. But in the background I could hear her talking to Peter before she hung up. I thought she was crying."

A cold chill ran down my spine. Was it possible there was another reason why Dad didn't make it to lunch? Suddenly, my pleasant homecoming turned ominous. I was just about to dial the phone when it eerily rang in my palm. I set the phone down and refused to answer. Instead, Ann gave me a funny look then picked it up.

"Hey, how are you?" she said in her usually friendly voice as her facial expression changed from happy to slightly annoyed, "Okay, sure, he's right here." She cupped the receiver and said in a hushed voice, "It's Peter. I guess he only can talk to you because he didn't have much of anything to say to me."

Dread overcame me as I slowly took the phone. "Hello."

"Joe, Mom let Dad sleep in and when she got home later in the day she found him slumped over in his bed."

Still hoping this had a happy ending, I said, "Well, did she get him un-slumped?"

That's when he got to the point. "Dad is dead."

10

I had the phone to my ear, but wasn't taking in a word of what was being said. I wasn't ready for this. No son or daughter is ever really ready for the death of a parent. I could feel my throat constrict and the tears begin to fall. Peter said, "We need to go over there. I'm headed your way to pick you up, okay?"

"Sure," is all I could say as I hung up the phone, sat on the couch, and placed my head in my hands gasping for breath. My wife knew it was bad, but with me lacking the ability to talk, she would have to wait.

Finally, when I lifted my head to tell her the news, my daughter, who had been studying me carefully, immediately began to scream. She had only seen me acting goofy in an attempt to make her laugh. Now, I sat a few feet away crying and it really threw her little one-year-old mind for a loop.

The scene at Dad's house wasn't much better. We were all crying and hugging each other, wishing a grumpy old man would come down the stairs and ask what in the hell was wrong with all of us. But it wasn't going to happen.

The next few days were a blur—planning a funeral, writing an obituary, and receiving family and friends. Then, before I knew it, I was sitting in the church listening to my brothers eloquently eulogize our father. I was impressed by their ability to speak so beautifully on the heels of such a loss. I knew I couldn't speak at the service; I was getting choked up watching the setting sun. A funeral would be too much. As they spoke, my mind drifted to a young version of my father standing on the deck of the Ticonderoga with all of his surviving shipmates as they honored the men who had died in that kamikaze attack. He must have been heartbroken watching as man after man, friend after friend, was buried at sea. Yet my father was one of the lucky ones. He escaped the war and was able to work, play and raise a family. I wondered if right now he was up in the air again with his buddies, flying for the sheer fun of it. This thought actually brought a smile to my face.

Then reality crept back in as I thought of all the conversations I hadn't yet had with him. I had found a lot of the scattered pieces of my father's past, but in all the time we'd spent together, I hadn't told him how special he was to me, how I felt about him. I hadn't said what I needed to say and that more than anything else filled me with regret.

Something else was bugging me. While I was out learning about the working world by dealing with people like Harvey and all of the other random people I encountered, my father had died alone; I hadn't been there when he needed me most. I had all this health care knowledge, but now none of it would help Dad. How could this happen? How did I overlook that? More importantly, what was I going to do about it?

Then there was my job; I was at a crossroads and knew I didn't want to stay with UHI. It was a good time to make a new start for myself, one where I really could make a difference in people's lives. And as I thought about it, I could almost hear Dad saying, "Go ahead Joe, take a chance. I'll be with you." So, sitting there in the church that day while the funeral was going on and selfishly thinking about me, I decided to start my own company. It seemed like the best way to take the knowledge I'd accumulated and really make a difference in the lives of the people I admired the most.

After the service all of our family were allowed to leave the church first. As Ann and I exited the sanctuary the first people we encountered were Tom and Loraine Terry. The Terry's were old family friends and Tom Terry had provided a lot of support to me as I transitioned into the working world. I didn't realize it at the time but in retrospect I am certain that their presence was God's way of passing the torch. The Terry's, and more specifically Tom, were going to be an important part of my life in the months and years to come, I just didn't know it yet. Eventually many others showed up to pay their respects. I didn't think a lot of seeing many of the people there that day, but as it turns out, I would end up taking care of a good many of them before a service like the one we'd just attended would be held in their honor.

"Joe. . . *Joe*, are you there?"

I was standing by myself when Mom snapped me out of it. "Sorry, I was just thinking about Dad."

"Sure, I know it's hard. And it's going to be for a long time. But I need you to come by the house later if you can, and come by yourself. It won't take too long."

This was an odd request coming from a grandmother who loved visits from her grandkids. "Sure Mom, I'll be by later. How about after dinner?"

"That would be good," she said and turned to talk to some friends across the way.

That evening Ann just let me wander around in a daze and didn't ask questions when I said I was going to see Mom after dinner. I kissed Ann and my daughter and left the house wondering what Mom wanted to discuss.

I found her sitting by the fire and I thought she looked tired. "How are you doing?" I asked.

She looked at me with haggard eyes and said, "I'm fine, but it's been a long day and I'm tired. How are you?"

"Fine, I guess." I said, "You wanted me for something?"

"Well, the truth is, I don't know what it is. I was going through your father's things and I found this." She handed me a large brown envelope with my name on the front.

"I wonder what it is?" I said for no good reason.

"I don't know. It has your name on it, not mine. I suggest you open it and find out."

I smiled at her and said, "Of course." I ripped the envelope open and found a letter addressed to me and two smaller envelopes. The first envelope had the word 'Courage' written on the outside and the second envelope said 'Faith.' Both envelopes were sealed, so I looked at the letter for more information:

Dear Joe,

If you're reading this, it's because I'm no longer here. Don't be saddened by this, because I have lived an extraordinary life and for this I'm eternally grateful. I did a lot and saw a lot in my time on this earth and I lived a long time. I have regrets, as we all do, but mine are few and far between. I know that I did the best I could and I believe this is what satisfies me the most. The business success and the material items I've acquired have been nice, but my most important legacy is you, your brothers and your sister. I guess any father would say the same thing, but I mean it in every sense. You kids have meant everything to me, even if I didn't always show you the proper respect and love that you all deserve.

I am writing you this letter because I know my days are numbered and I want you to know how much our talks of late have meant to me. As the youngest, I fear I didn't give you the guidance you needed and you, being the sly one of the bunch, sought it out by asking me about my past experiences. Your siblings have probably heard my stories so many times that they've tired of hearing me drone on about a bygone era. You, on the other hand, seemed to derive a great deal of pleasure in hearing about my past. I can't tell you how much I've enjoyed having these talks and since I am no longer here to tell you about the events that shaped my life, I have written two more stories down for you to read. Of course I'd rather be telling them to you myself, but since that is not possible now I guess this will have to do. I've labeled each letter.

The first one is labeled 'Courage.' It's the story about one of the bravest men I ever met. Read it sometime when you feel like the odds are against you. My hope is that this story will bring you some perspective on what true courage is all about. It's about putting your life on the line for the people and principals that mean the most to you.

The second envelope is entitled 'Faith.' Faith in a higher being, faith in your fellow man, and faith that everything will be okay if you simply believe that miracles can happen. Read it when you are feeling spiritually depleted. It will hopefully redirect you and help you become whole again.

You will need both of these qualities to be a success in this world, and it is my hope that you will demonstrate both of them admirably. Don't stop trying to be the best you can be and don't ever stop asking questions of those who may know more than you. You are a special person and your legacy has yet to be written.

As for me, you are my legacy. I am proud to know that I have left you to speak and act on my behalf.

I love you son,

Dad

I looked up from the letter at my mother and my face must have said it all. She said, "Well, what did it say?" I had a lump in my throat so I simply handed her the letter.

When she was done I said, "Did you know he was writing a letters to us?"

"No, I didn't. Now I know what he was doing at his office."

"With his dementia, how was he able to write such a concise letter?"

My mother looked at me and smiled. "He had his moments. His brain wasn't always clouded. There were times when he was his old self, but it took a lot of effort on his part. It must've meant a lot to him to do this—I'm sure it took him a long time to write it."

Pain ripped through my heart when I heard her say that. Mom was studying my face and said, "What's wrong?"

I hesitated for moment then said, "He told me so much over the last few years and he's still communicating with me, even after his death. But I never told him how much he meant to me. I'd been trying to find out who he was, trying to know him better, and now he's gone."

Mom smiled, touched my shoulder, and said, "He knew how you felt, and you can still learn about a person after they're gone."

"Maybe. I just wish I'd told him how I felt about him when I had the chance."

For a minute we sat in silence until Mom asked, "When will you open the two envelopes?"

"I don't know, but I'm sure the right time will present itself soon enough."

From my days at UHI, I knew that starting my own business wouldn't be a cakewalk. When we opened up an agency, there were many tough challenges . . . not including Harvey. And UHI provided me with a bottomless pit of personnel and financial resources to get the agencies up and running. Now, I wouldn't have any of that. I was prepared for a steep climb and knew that the challenges I faced would eventually lead me back to the letters Dad had left for me.

Before quitting my job, per Dad's instructions, I spent a lot of time talking with experienced businessmen who knew a lot more than me. One of the men whose ear I bent the hardest was that old family friend, Tom Terry. Tom was incredibly intelligent and had achieved a lot of success in many different forms of business and he was the father of one of my best friends, Mike Terry. Tom knew me well and he gladly accepted the role of mentor after Dad's death.

Tom started out as a sheriff in a small suburb of Chicago, and then moved into the automotive business working side by side with Lee Iacocca in the early days of his career at Ford. After that, he was an important part of putting Browning Ferris International on the map. He then went on to numerous other entrepreneurial ventures in real estate and communications, achieving a great deal of success in everything he did. I respected him for his success, but beyond that I truly liked and appreciated the fact that he always had time for me. He'd helped me get going in my professional life after college by offering me a job in one of his warehouses and then later served as a reference, telling everyone what a special talent I was. I can't count the times when I needed advice or just someone to bounce an idea off of, and he made time, even on a moment's notice. He always shot straight with me, without being condescending or degrading.

One time, when I had an interview with a large marketing company in Dallas, I asked if he would help me prep for the interview. I thought a trial run with Tom would be a good way to prepare. He didn't hesitate in saying yes, even though he must've had a million other things to do that were more important. The first thing he did was hand me the company's annual report saying, "Welcome to ABC Marketing Joe. Here's our annual report. Can you please tell me what our profit for the third quarter of last year was?"

I fumbled through the report and then keyed in on a number and said, "$137,000."

He took the report back from me, looked at the number, and said, "You're $2 million off. Your number is only the profit from interest payments received in the third quarter. The total profits are $2.2 million. You need to be able to read a financial statement in your sleep. I'll write down some important numbers for you to key in on. They may not ask you any of this, but it's good information for you to know any time you are interviewing with a company. If they ask you anything about their performance and you don't know the answer, it won't reflect well on you. On the other hand, if their financial house is in disarray, then you probably don't want to work for them in the first place."

He said all of this to me as if I was his peer, not the dumb kid I was. This type of attention to detail is what made him successful and the lessons he taught me are what made me his loyal fan.

Before I started my business, Tom told me something that really stuck with me: "Joe, this isn't going to be easy, but you need to keep the doors open. Too many people give up on their dreams too quickly. The call that could put you over the top may come in at any time. You need to be open and ready to answer that call. Don't quit! When you feel like quitting, just remember that God is testing you. If you hang in there, he will reward you with an opportunity. Always remember that." I had no idea how valuable those words would be to me in the future.

I looked around for a great office, one that was close by and easy to get to, one with a great view. I also wanted an office with a low overhead, because Tom had pounded into me the mantra of conserving my cash. When I found it, I knew it was perfect. It was the second bedroom of my house. And the view was magnificent: my wife and daughter coming in to urge me on.

The first two things on my agenda were drafting the state-required policies and procedures and finding a way to fund my start-up, though not necessarily in that order. I'd learned that most start-ups are funded by family and friends. Fortunately, my mother agreed to let me borrow against a $30,000 CD she had sitting at a local bank. I figured that was just enough to get me going.

I applied for my state license, which would take about six weeks to process, and in the meantime I looked for a place to interview employees. Most of the employees would be women and directing them to sit on my bed while I asked a few questions seemed like a lawsuit waiting to happen.

I had a buddy whose dad had an old rundown office building near my house, so I worked out an arrangement where I could lease an *official* office from him for $200 per month. It was a dump, but what could I expect for that price? I got a lot done in those first six weeks and was excited to finally get a letter from the state of Texas telling me when my first inspection would occur. After this inspection—or *survey*—if I passed muster with their rules, I'd be awarded my license and could actually take on patients.

The first thing I had to do was find some staff to take care of the patients I didn't yet have. Finding good people is hard enough, but when you're hiring them to take care of the elderly—and you have a conscious—it's excruciatingly difficult. Keep in mind that in 'private pay' home care, I needed low cost employees to perform custodial work directly with the patients. These people needed to be honest, sweet, nice, detail oriented, and punctual. And they needed to be all of those things for no more than $9.00 an hour or else my business model wouldn't work.

Interviewing potential employees is like sales: you have to see a lot of people before you find one that is worth a darn. I spent hours interviewing dozens of folks and wasn't impressed with the caliber of the candidates I was meeting.

My first interview of the day was with a lady who appeared very together. She had solid experience, was well dressed, spoke well and even smelled good. The only problem was her nails—she had three-inch long press-on nails that were covered in sunsets and birds and other such things. To me they looked like stiletto knives sticking out from the end of her fingers. Yet she was very pleasant to speak to, so I just told her my honest thoughts to see if we could work through it.

"I'd like to hire you, but I'm going to have to ask you to remove the nails. It's not possible to provide personal care to elderly patients with nails like that. Is this okay with you?"

"Certainly," she said. "I'll take them off before I begin my first case."

"Great! Then welcome to the team."

When she came back to the office a couple days later for her orientation, I noticed she still had the nails on. I said, "Hey, weren't you planning on removing those?"

She nodded. "Yes, of course. But you haven't put me on a case yet, so I was just going to wait until you do, then remove them."

"Oh," I said. "Sounds good."

A few days later I received a call from a very nice family that needed care for their elderly father. I immediately staffed the case with this lady, even bragging a bit to the man's daughter about how impressed she was going to be with the quality of caregiver I was sending. On the day we started, I received a call from the daughter and she was not happy. One of the first jobs they had lined up for my caregiver was to give the man a bath. He got himself undressed and in the tub before he realized that the woman was about to clean his private parts with blades on her fingers. He went berserk (and for the record I can't blame him). He wouldn't let her touch him, which kind of defeated the purpose of her being there. The daughter bent my ear for twenty minutes wondering why in the world I would hire someone like her to provide personal care. I didn't have a good answer for her. I had trusted this woman and she'd lied to me. But it was my company and therefore it was my mistake.

When I finally got stiletto nails on the phone, she said she'd never agreed to take off her precious nails, "They're an artistic expression of my soul and I wouldn't take them off for anyone."

I sighed with heavy frustration and said, "I perfectly understand. In that case you're fired and I'll mail you a check for the thirty minutes of time you were on my clock."

She told me that I was a very bad man and called me a few other choice words before hanging up on me. Needless to say, my little company lost some business as a result of this episode. I was mortified to not only lose the business, but also to find out that this type of episode could result in all kinds of bad publicity. A case that goes well results in the family telling a few other families of the nice experience. A case that goes badly results in the family telling everyone that they know to never use *that* company. Yes, in this business so many things could go so wrong, not to mention the time she had wasted.

About the time I got over Ms. Nails, the door to my office opened and in walked a lady that was the epitome of what a classic nurse looked like. She had this little white hat, a white nursing dress, white leggings, and white shoes. She really looked the part and seemed intelligent too. After the interview, I told her I required all of my caregivers to pass a criminal history check and a drug screen. She didn't miss a beat and even told me how responsible I was to run such checks. I ran the criminal check in the office before she left and she was clean as a whistle, so I gave her the form to go have her drug screen done and then sat down to give myself a nice long pat on the back. Finally, I was getting the break I needed.

In a couple of hours the drug screening clinic called to tell me this lady's pee was so toxic that they were afraid to flush it down the toilet. She was on everything from marijuana to Black Molly's. I didn't actually know what a Black Molly was, but I assumed that being on them was not conducive to provided quality care to the elderly. So, I picked up the phone and called her.

"Ma'am, the results of your drug screening came back and you have a host of illegal drugs in your urine and thus, you're completely unemployable. I'm really sorry."

To my amazement she was shocked. "What? Surely you're joking sir. There's no possible way. I'd never do such a thing. They must've mixed up the urine somehow. You must test me again. You must!"

Well, I wasn't expecting that response. And I really wanted her to be clean. "Okay, go back down there and take another test. A few hours later my phone rang.

"Hey dude, did you not hear me clearly the first time?" It was the drug screen clinic manager. "Why do you keep sending this person back in here? She came in here while I was at lunch and my people tested her again. With the level of smack in her system, I'm afraid she's gonna lose her mind while she's in my clinic and hurt someone. Don't *ever* send her back here. I don't need the business that bad."

I assured him I was done with her and hung up feeling like a fool. When I called her back I was mad as hell. "Why did you demand another test when you knew you wouldn't pass?"

I heard her chuckle. "Well, you can't blame a girl for trying, can you? It's worked before."

I slammed the phone down and kicked myself for being so desperate. And she'd wasted $60 of my precious startup money. I wasn't happy. Sadly, I'd learned a valuable business lesson: it's a cold, cruel world out there.

Later that same day as I cleaned up the office and was about to call it a day, the office phone rang. I could've let the call roll to the answering service but because I was a new entrepreneur, I didn't want to miss a possible referral. So, I snatched up the phone, gave the best greeting I could muster, and said, "Good afternoon, can I help you?"

There was a brief pause then the person on the other end said, "You got a job?"

I was completely deflated by the question and in a deadpan voice, my reply was short and sweet, "Yes I do, thank you for your concern." I hung up the phone and left the office as fast I could, hoping the phone wouldn't ring again before I could shut the door.

All licensed home care agencies are required to have a registered nurse on staff. Since I couldn't afford to pay a nurse full time, I needed to find someone who could work on an as-needed basis. Under state regulations, this was allowable. So I called a nurse, Sarah, who'd worked with me for a short time at CTS Care. When I told her about my situation, she was more than happy to help out.

Sarah was young, energetic, and had a pleasant personality. She was married with two kids, and couldn't afford to leave her current job, but could use the extra income. And she was a good nurse who really cared about the elderly. During those early days, I trusted her to handle any situation.

Slowly, my company added patients. As it did, I was surprised to learn how connected some patients wanted to be with me. These elderly folks not only knew who I was, but also wanted me to interact with them on a regular basis. I thought it was a good thing, but at first I didn't truly understand the concept. In my mind I was just the guy at the office creating schedules and cutting paychecks. More than anything else they seemed to take an interest in me because I was the owner of the company. Their generation was used to interacting with the person in charge. It was important to them, like my dad knowing the waiter at his favorite restaurant. Yet usually, because I wasn't a caregiver or a nurse, I rarely saw them. I just never took the opportunity to drop by and catch up with my patients because I was in the business side of things, not the clinical. Until a woman set me straight.

One day I received a call from Margaret Harrison, a slightly annoyed patient. We provided care twenty-four hours a day and that was (and still is) a big case. Mrs. Harrison told me how she was underwhelmed that I hadn't called her to wish her happy birthday. I knew my field staff was pretty good about notifying me of things like that and they probably would've called later in the day to inform me of her special occasion. But that wasn't good enough. She felt that because of our relationship, I should've called her first thing that morning. And, of course, she was right. I apologized to her and then an hour later showed up at her door with flowers. I wasn't sure if she remembered calling me that morning, because when she saw me with those flowers, her face reflected complete and genuine surprise. And she was giddy—downright ecstatic—to receive a visitor.

"You are quite the Casanova," she said. "I haven't had a gentleman caller in quite some time." I wasn't sure if Mrs. Harrison had the wrong idea, but I was even more unsure when she invited me to sit with her in the 'parlor.' My caregiver was present and got quite a kick out of this little exchange. Eventually I was able to explain that I only had time for a brief visit before wishing her a very happy birthday and making my exit.

When I got back to the office, Sarah wanted to know all about the parlor visit. She said, "You know, in all the times I've been to see Mrs. Harrison, I have never once seen her parlor."

"Very funny," I said. "Don't you have some work to do?" My company ended up taking care of Mrs. Harrison for many years. She was a sweet lady who expected a lot—from all of us. I think we did pretty well by her, and I never missed her birthday again.

It was after this occasion that I decided to make myself more available to the people that my company cared for. I loved them, respected them, and enjoyed their company as well as their counsel. I needed them and because of the respect I had for their generation, I think they needed me. Everyone needs respect, but I've always felt this group truly deserves it.

At that time, I was marketing my company by sending direct mail into the homes of the wealthiest neighborhoods (this was the demographic that could afford our services). I'd managed to get my hands on a few directories from the local country clubs, so I sent them letters describing what my company did. The process was slow because I did it by myself, and the response was slow since only about 1% of direct mail ever finds its mark. Even so, it worked well enough and my business slowly gained momentum. Truthfully, if I'd received a larger response I probably couldn't have handled all of the business anyway, so in the end it worked out fine.

I was still so small that I wasn't paying myself much and this was a problem for my family. My wife was very supportive and earned a good living, but by this time we'd added a son to our family and she really wanted to stay home and be a fulltime mom, which I wanted too. I began looking for another agency to acquire so I could have some critical mass. To find another company, I hired a college kid to sit on the phone for hours at a time and call small companies like mine in hopes they may be interested in selling. He called all of the local agencies and managed to come up with some leads, one of which looked promising. It was located in Plano, Texas just north of my existing Dallas office.

To purchase this little company, I intended to get an SBA loan. The SBA required that I come to closing with $150,000 dollars. Since I didn't have $150,000, I went out to my friends and family to see if I could find some investors.

One of those investors was my old friend Tom Terry. When I approached him about a small investment in my new home care company, he didn't hesitate. He said he was happy to support me and pleased that I had landed in the health care profession. As he handed me his check, he said to me, "You're earning a living by taking care of others. There's nothing more noble you could be doing with your life and I'm proud of you."

Hearing those words from a man I respected as much as Tom was very special to me. I kept in touch with him regularly as my company grew and evolved. He was always available to me, never turning down an opportunity to help me conquer my latest challenge.

The Plano agency came with a nursing director, Bonnie. She was very nice and very capable, which was good, because the patients in this agency were more rural. Not as bad as Hillsboro, but not without some interesting challenges. One day, Bonnie was out making rounds and visiting patients.

She stopped by one lady's house to check up on her and see how our care-givers were doing. For many of our patients, it was standard procedure to leave the door unlocked when they were expecting our nurse to drop by. Knowing this, my nursing director simply walked in and began calling the patient's name to let her know she was there. She continued calling out as she slowly walked through the home, trying to find our patient.

Many times, it's the home care nurse who finds the patient in a difficult position and saves the day. More than once my nurses have found patients who have slipped in the bath or the backyard and been unable to move or call out loud enough to get someone's attention. On other occasions, my nurses have made grim discoveries that have led to a visit from the coroner. In this case it seemed no one was home, so Bonnie retraced her steps and headed out the front door.

Once back in the car, her cell phone rang and on the other end was a male voice. Until that moment, it had always been our understanding that the patient lived alone in her house, but the person on the phone told a different story.

The man started out by telling her she had a very pretty red dress. At first she was confused, having no idea who the person was or when he had seen her. But as the man continued to talk, Bonnie began to fully under-stand what he was telling her. He was the son of our patient and he lived with his mother. That someone other than the woman lived in the home was a surprise, but not a monumental one, because he could've been at work when our staff made their visits. But this wouldn't explain how he knew what she was wearing. Bonnie continued to ask the man questions, trying to figure out how he knew she was wearing a red dress. He explained he worked at night and was home every day. Yet if he was home every day, why hadn't anyone ever seen him before?

This guy was talking a lot, but saying nothing. Bonnie was beginning to get frustrated by the whole confusing call and finally, said, "Okay, how do you know I'm wearing a red dress?" Bonnie wasn't expecting this answer.

"I'm a vampire. I live in the attic during the day and come out to feed at night. I have tiny openings where I see everything and I've been watching you while you looked for Mother. I've been watching all your nurses that have come here."

Bonnie dropped the phone and couldn't get her car moving fast enough. We called Adult Protective Services who soon moved the lady out of the house entirely, leaving the attic dweller to his own devices . . . and I guess, own feeding schedule.

Soon after that, Bonnie turned in her two-weeks' notice. I didn't blame her. Home care isn't for everyone. Because I really liked her, we threw her a nice party on her last day—a Friday. She loved the party and was misty-eyed that we cared so much. I wouldn't have thought of losing her without having a going-away party. We hugged and I wished her well as she walked out the door.

The next Monday, my phones lit up like a Christmas tree. Every one of our patients had received a call from Bonnie trying to get them to come to *her* new home car company, one she had just set up. Now, she was working hard to take all of my patients. Soon, my best employees were getting offers. It was outrageous! She'd signed a non-compete agreement when I bought the company. This document forbid her from approaching my patients, employees, or referral sources for a period of three years after she left my company. That afternoon I hired a lawyer to threaten her to stop doing all this. Bonnie immediately agreed to stop and went away.

The next day, I was approached by one of my filing clerks. She was an outspoken older lady who wasn't shy about voicing her opinion. She said, "You know, she filled out all of the paperwork for her company's license in the middle of the day sitting right at her desk while you were paying her to work for you. *And*, she had the license mailed to this office. I signed for it myself. You've been taken advantage of and I hope this teaches you a lesson that you can't go around trusting people the way you do."

I was stunned not only with this information, but by her attitude. I said to her, "I want to grow my business and to do that, I have to attempt to hire the most qualified people and then trust them to do the job they are paid to do. I'm not going to stop trusting people due to the actions of one person. But since you brought it up, why don't *you* explain to me why

I should ever trust you again? Obviously you decided not to tell me about her inappropriate actions, knowing she'd be hurting the very company you work for. Isn't that the same thing as aiding and abetting the thief?" With this, she was tongue-tied. I don't know if I insulted her or what, but she resigned a few days later.

Bonnie was my first real taste of bad behavior in my new role as owner, but it wasn't going to be my last. I just wondered if I had the ability to hang on for the rough ride ahead.

11

With the Bonnie mess out of my life, my business was doing okay. I certainly wasn't going to threaten UHI's stranglehold on the home care business yet, but I was waking up each day not worrying about surviving, either. Instead I woke up thinking about how to better serve my clients. This had a nice benefit: making me happy while making my clients happy at the same time (which of course, caused them spread the word, bringing us even more business). It was a win-win situation. Still, it was up to my staff to carry out my directives and with the past issues I'd had with some of them, I often wondered. And then something surprising happened.

I received a call from the daughter of a man, Walter Foran, who had a brain tumor. He was slowly dying and his wife, on top of being an emotional wreck, was working herself to the bone taking care of him. The daughter, with the support of her siblings, was trying to help.

Since this couple lived in a two-story house and the master bedroom was upstairs, the family had put Mr. Foran in the downstairs living room to better access him. As expected, Mr. Foran died shortly thereafter. The day it happened, Joyce, my caregiver, took it upon herself to call the medical equipment company and ask them to come get the hospital bed he'd been using. She waited for the company to arrive, retrieve their bed, and leave, before completely cleaning the living room and putting it back to the way it was prior to his illness. When she was done, she helped the family by serving the visitors who had started streaming in. It was truly above and beyond the call of duty.

The next week I looked at her time sheet and saw that she never turned in that extra time. I pulled her aside and asked her why she hadn't turned in her time. Her response hit me straight between the eyes. "I stayed to help because that's what good people do."

Those were the exact words Tom Terry had used when he gave me his check months before. I knew if I were to ever have true success in this business, it would be because of people like Joyce. I took it upon myself to manually enter her time for that day and when she received her check, she called me to protest. I eventually got her to take the money by explaining that if she didn't take the money, the people from the labor board could put me in jail. She finally laughed and said, "I think you're pulling my leg, but since I don't know anything about any labor board, I'll take the money. I don't want your daughter to have a daddy in jail on my account."

Believe me, it's hard to fail at any business when you have people like that!

My mother-in-law was a good friend of the Foran family, so when we stood in the receiving line to pay our condolences at Mr. Foran's funeral, my mother-in-law was in front. Yet when Mrs. Foran saw us next in line, she hesitated for a moment and then lunged at me, throwing her arms around my shoulders. She kissed me, thanked me, and told me what a great job we had done. I was humbled by the fact that, when faced with her dear friend and the guy who owned the company that had cared for her husband, she chose to thank me first. As we walked away, my mother-in-law said, "You must've done quite a job caring for Walter."

I just smiled and said, "Yeah, we did alright on that one."

The next few weeks passed without incident, so I relaxed and assumed I was past the worst of my employee-related challenges. Wrong! We began caring for a nice lady, Margaret Rawlings, who had fallen and broken her hip. She didn't have dementia and just needed someone to help her throughout her day, since she couldn't get around very easily. This should have made her a very easy case for any caregiver, because all they had to do was show up on time and do what they were asked until it was time to leave. Simple. Our aide started out well, doing everything Mrs. Black required and she was very pleased. Then something happened—something awful.

One day our aide came across Mrs. Rawling's checkbook and it was full of checks. Apparently the temptation was too great for this lady so she took a few of the checks for herself. I have to assume that she had never done this before because she had passed a complete and thorough background check. Or perhaps she had just never been caught.

So here she is, with these checks in her pocket. She knows she can't go and cash them or she might get caught, so she enlists her friend to help out. Her friend is a young 400 pound woman wearing mustard colored stretch pants and a multi-colored moo moo from Wal-Mart, while Mrs. Rawlings wears Prada or Versace and is a frail, ninety-pound, seventy-three-year-old. And Mrs. Rawlings banks at the Northern Trust Bank located in the tony Highland Park Village, quite near where the Rawlings lived. There are many rich people in Dallas, but the richest live near Highland Park Village. So, this woman goes to Northern Trust, with its beautiful marble floors and opulent interior, hands the teller a check for $4,500 made out in cash and signed by Mrs. Margaret Rawlings, then says with a straight face, "Hello, my name is Margaret Rawlings and I would like to cash this check."

The teller takes one look at the check and the lady who has presented it to her, smiles, and says, "Of course, Mrs. Rawlings, if you'll excuse me one minute I'll get your cash." I'm sure the new Mrs. Rawlings was smiling at that moment, thinking she was just seconds away from winning the home care lottery and dreaming about all the cool stuff she was about to buy when a myriad of officers approached her from the rear and forced her to the ground, guns drawn. They made her lay spread-eagled as two sets of handcuffs were joined together to make it all work.

When I learned about this I called my aide to fire her but was unable to reach her. She could have been headed for Mexico, for all I knew, but I took a chance and showed up to at the Rawlings' home at the time her shift was to start. Unbelievably, the aide showed up right on time. I confronted her in the driveway and she denied everything, but at least she left without incident. I later learned that the criminal at the bank was our aide's aunt and when questioned by the police, quickly spilled the beans. My aide soon went to jail where she was tasked with taking care of the geriatric inmates, so I guess everything worked out.

Some weeks it seemed like the moment I put one fire out, another popped up. One such fire came up when we were called upon to admit a new case in a tough part of town. We always took precautions in those situations but it's hard to prepare for every eventuality.

When going into the bad areas of town in early days of home care, nurses and doctors were instructed to wear their medical attire complete with a big red cross on their lab coat. The theory then was that if people knew someone was coming in to take care of one of their own, the professional would be left alone. By the time I entered the business in the early nineties, things had changed: drug use was much more commonplace. The users in those areas saw the medical personnel as repositories of a cornucopia of goods. They sought to rob them of syringes, pills, or anything else they could get their hands on. As a result, I was always taught to dumb down the appearance of my workers so they looked less medical. This way the bad guys wouldn't be alerted or tempted. Unfortunately, there wasn't much more we could do when we accepted a case in these areas.

As a precaution, we always told our nurses to not carry any more supplies than they absolutely needed, since a big medical bag was nothing but a target. Unfortunately however, like a lion waiting by a watering hole for prey, the bad guys not only knew which people received home care, they usually knew the schedule too.

On this day the nurse we sent was a cool customer and tough as nails. And sure enough, on her first day on the new case a man approached her as she was getting out of her car. "Whatcha got in that bag, missy?"

She said calmly, "Very little. See?" She opened her bag so the would-be assailant could look in. When he lowered his head to get a better look, she used her other hand to fire some pepper spray directly into his face.

"*Aaaaiiiiii!!!*" he screamed. This attracted the attention of his companions who came running.

My nurse realized it was time to go and scrambled back into her car. She had just started the engine and was putting it in drive when glass shattered everywhere. One of the criminals had thrown a brick through her rear windshield just as she had pressed on the gas. Her car fishtailed away squealing rubber and leaking glass everywhere as the angry mob chased her down the street.

When she got back to the office, we had to perform an emergency discharge of the patient, a patient who really needed our help. We alerted Adult Protective Services to look in on the patient, but there was nothing more we could do. The incident had proven that the patient's area was too dangerous for our staff. Of course, I had to pay for a new windshield, though honestly I was thrilled I wasn't paying for her medical bills or talking to her next of kin. It had been a very close call.

Incidents like these gave me pause and made me question what I was doing. I've known a lot of people who have operated in business at a high level, yet here I was dealing with criminals and people who had little or no common sense. Folks who thought nothing of stealing from me or my patients. It was not just frustrating, but also deeply depressing.

Having trouble dealing with all this, I wanted desperately to read one of the letters Dad had left me but for some reason I just didn't feel like I was ready for that. Instead, I settled for something very close: I went to see my mentor, Tom Terry. When I told him the story I'd expected him to gasp and say that he'd never heard of anything so crazy, but he didn't.

Instead, he leaned back in his chair, smiled and said, "What you're doing now is creating momentum, and that's by far the hardest thing any new business owner has to do. Think of it this way: have you ever heard of someone who stepped into a family business and done really well? I know of many cases where a smart guy or girl takes a $10 million ongoing concern and makes it a $20 million business. I find this to be much less impressive than anyone who starts with nothing and creates a $1 million business. And that's what you're doing, Joe."

"So you're saying making $10 million is easier than $1 million?"

Tom leaned forward. "Think about it. The guy who starts with a $10 million dollar company has a platform in place. The company already has processes and procedures, operational and accounting policies and customers and cash flow. If the person who steps in is good at marketing and sales, they can garner some new accounts and the next thing you know the company has a lot more revenue and the new leader is praised for being a genius. The guy who starts from scratch has nothing. *Nothing!* He must figure everything out on his own and create momentum out of thin air. It's a hard, hard thing to do, as you're learning now."

Then Tom looked away for a moment and I could tell he was thinking. When he turned back towards me he had a stern look on his face. "Look" he said "This is hard, no one knows that better than me, but you also need to keep your perspective in check. Perspective is a powerful tool to keep in your tool box Joe."

I was a little lost and replied, "Perspective, what do you mean?"

Tom's look softened a bit then he said, "You have your health, a great family and a bright future, don't forget how lucky you are and take these setbacks for what they are - unpleasant distractions that can be overcome. It is important to always keep things in perspective."

Tom hesitated, stared at me for a moment, then said, "May I make an observation?"

"Sure," I said.

"I think you need to put more emphasis on the people you're caring for. I know you want to be a successful businessman, but it seems to me that a person like you only ventures into a business like this for one reason: the patients themselves. I think you need to make a concerted effort to spend more time with the end user of your service. That's why you're doing what you're doing and spending time with them is what's going to give you the most satisfaction. Get to know your patients and the rest will work itself out. Hang in there, Joe, and remember . . . never quit."

I smiled, thanked him, shook his hand and left, thinking about all that he had said. Once back at the office I took a deep breath, slapped both cheeks and decided to follow Tom's advice. I was quite certain that he knew a few things I didn't.

As I sat down at my desk, my receptionist called out, "Joe, line two."

I picked up the phone. "Joe speaking."

"Joe, this is Margaret Rawlings, remember me?"

My heart skipped a beat. Instantly a visual of my caregiver's aunt spread-eagled on the floor as the police trained their guns down on her popped into my head. Fortunately, the Rawlings hadn't fired us and we spent several months getting Mrs. Rawlings' hip healed and back on her feet. Still, my first thought was negative: more stolen checks had been passed and I'm going to have to pay for them. Forcing myself to smile, I said, "Of course I remember you. How are you doing, Mrs. Rawlings?"

She sounded down. "Oh, I'm doing fine. But it's Leo. He needs your help."

In a split second my negativity and frustration washed away. "I'm sorry to hear that Mrs. Rawlings, but I'm so glad you called me. After all that's why I'm here—to take care of folks like you and Leo."

12

I got in my car and drove to their house immediately. I had spoken many times to Mr. Rawlings, but didn't really know him. Before it had been all business. I'd smile, say hi and move on. Now, with Tom's advice rattling around in my brain, I needed to 'get my mind right' and I needed to get to know my patient. Leo, like my father, could teach me a lot so I committed myself to mentally getting to know him.

When I arrived, Mrs. Rawlings said that her husband was napping so I sat with her and learned about who Leo Rawlings was. He was born in Montgomery, Alabama in 1917. He graduated from high school in 1934 then he worked his way through Princeton University before attending Harvard Business School. After school, Leo joined his father's construction business, but left after Pearl Harbor to join the Navy SeaBees when World War II broke out. He was sent to Europe where he built roads and bridges all over the continent. After the war, Leo returned to Dallas and rejoined his father's business, eventually becoming president upon his father's death. When we were done talking I was amazed and impressed. I already knew Leo had turned his father's construction business into a global icon in the industry and that he was tough as nails on the job, but understanding his background gave me a great dimension to his personality.

When Leo woke up from his nap, Mrs. Rawlings, Sarah and I went in to talk with him to begin discussing his health. He was frail and suffering from congestive heart failure. He also had a skin disorder resembling shingles, which caused him a lot of pain and discomfort. Yet despite these issues, he was upbeat and pleasant to be around. The aspect of Leo that I admired most was his ability to make light of the situation. Unlike many people his age, his issues were almost 100% physical. Mentally he was all there, snapping off witticisms in the blink of an eye. And he was genuinely funny, too. While I was finishing up our discussion, his attractive daughter-in-law walked up and asked him if she could get him something to eat.

He didn't miss a beat and said, "You know darling, when you're around I'm not thinking about food." The daughter-in-law and I fell out laughing and then, when we noticed Leo was laughing just as hard as we were, we laughed again. As I left their house, I felt different, like I really knew my client. And this made it easier to staff, because I was already dialed into both his personality and his needs.

A few days later, after our staff was in place, I went to visit with Leo to see how things were going. He was very happy and liked each of the caregivers we'd assigned him. Normally, this is the point where I would've nodded, smiled, and said goodbye, not seeing them again. Instead, I pulled up a chair and said, "Okay Leo." He'd insisted I not call him Mr. Rawlings. "I'd like to learn more about you, can you share some of your past experiences with me?"

"Well, I'll do my best. Let's see, here's a story for you. It was the early fifties and we were focused on commercial construction when one day I got a call from a TV producer.

He said, 'Are you boys able to build a house real quick so we could show it on TV?' When I heard that I thought for a second. Our business could be very monotonous at times, a grind. Even though it was out of character for me, I told this fellow that I'd talk to my people and get back with him.

"The next day we had a meeting and I told my staff, 'Now listen here, we've been asked to build a house in a very short time for TV. They're going to have cameras everywhere and it will give us some good publicity. But we've got to tell them how quick we can do it, because they're calling our competitors and asking them the same thing. So how fast do you think we can build it?'

"At this time we were a good-sized company, but we didn't have a lot of extra resources to call on for something like this. Of course, neither did any of our competitors. Because of this, most of our competitors called back and said they could do it in a week by using crews after their various shifts were over. My staff suggested the same thing. That's when I told my staff, 'We don't need this project lingering on for a whole week. If we're going to do it, let's get in, get it built and get out. I'm gonna tell them we can build that dang house in twenty-four hours.'

"My staff looked at me as if I were crazy. 'There's no way a home can be built in twenty-four hours. No way!' I laughed at first, because I thought their reaction was funny, but after a few minutes of being told what *my* company could *not* do, I got pretty mad at them. Finally, I said, 'I'll decide what we can and can't do. Now, I'm gonna call that TV producer and tell him we'll build them a house in twenty-four hours. And you folks need to get busy planning it all out.' They sat perfectly still and stared at me, until I slammed my hand on the table and said, 'Do it! Now!' That woke them up.

"The TV guys were thrilled. They didn't think anyone would be dumb enough to try that. My people began laying out the plans for the house and calculating exactly what supplies would be needed, right down to the last nail. We didn't leave anything to chance, going over the plans in detail for weeks before the day of the build.

"For the necessary manpower, I halted two of our projects for forty-eight hours. It wasn't a big deal for those projects to be delayed for such a short time—we were already ahead of schedule on both of them. Plus, I promised both the customers some good press once the twenty-four-hour house was completed.

"When the day of the build came my guys worked like greased lightning. We started at 8 a.m. and had the house fully framed out by 11 a.m. When one section was finished we had the next set of workers come in right behind them. At 7 a.m. the next morning we were wrapping up the details and by 8 a.m. we were completely finished. We capped off the completion of the house by sneaking a model dressed up as a housewife in the back door and at 8 a.m. when the cameras were rolling and I was giving my interview at the front door, we had a traveling salesman approach the house. The emcee of the show and his whole crew stopped what they were doing to watch this guy walk up the sidewalk right past all of us and ring the doorbell. To their amazement a June Cleaver lookalike opened the door, pearls and all, greeted this young man gracefully and then started buying products. It was great! They all cheered and the whole project was a huge hit. After that, my staff didn't question me a whole lot when I told them what I thought we could accomplish."

I was speechless. A story like this was simply awesome to me. Leo had broken new barriers with his intelligence and creativity. Even though he had lived in a time where most things seemed pretty black and white, Leo saw plenty of grey. Several times, he said "They told me I couldn't do this or that and I always responded the same way, 'Why not?' " I loved his approach to life and I really began to click with Leo.

After one rough week at the office, I went by on Friday afternoon to see Leo. When I arrived at his bedside, I said, "How are you Leo?" He was in a good mood so I decided to ask him more about his past. "I enjoyed hearing about the twenty-four-hour house. How about another story from your glory days?"

He laughed for a minute or so and then calmed down and started talking. "Let's see, well what do you want to hear about?"

"Well, how about that shelter I heard you talking about the other day?"

Leo grinned and said, "Oh yes, I love talking about that." Then he got comfortable and said, "Well, I was walking through downtown Dallas one day heading to an appointment, when I saw a homeless man on the sidewalk. It was a pretty cold day and I was concerned that he didn't have any place to go. I was in a hurry so I gave the man twenty bucks and kept walking, but I didn't forget about him. When I arrived back at my office, I called the mayor. He was an old friend of mine and someone who I thought would have information on the city's homeless population. I said, 'Rob, I saw a homeless man today and I was wondering what the city has done to help these people?'

"He paused a moment and said, 'Help them? How do you mean?'

"Well, this was in the 1970's and I guess homelessness wasn't really in the forefront of most folks minds yet, but it still really bothered me. 'Rob, we have a bunch of homeless people wandering around this city and I think we should do something about it, don't you?'

"He gave me the typical bureaucratic response, something like, 'Well, you know funding for something like that would be difficult, because it rained last Tuesday and, blah, blah, blah.'

"I got so mad at him, I said, "That man is still on the street and you're probably getting ready to go have a steak lunch on the taxpayer's nickel. I hope you eat well.' Then I hung up."

"How these people fed themselves was my biggest concern. I just couldn't imagine what it must be like to be hungry all the time. My next call was to an old friend of mine who'd been involved in numerous charitable endeavors. I knew he'd have some thoughts on the matter. He told me there were a few shelters around, but that they were all poorly run and offered very little in the way of food. I'd heard enough. A bureaucrat couldn't get done what I wanted to get done, so I called several other businessmen who were friends of mine and within a few days, I had enough help pulled together to fund the purchase of a building in downtown Dallas that would serve as our shelter."

"Once we found a nice couple to run it, we were off to the races. The focus was to give these people a nice, clean place to go if they needed shelter and a good meal. Today that shelter houses and feeds hundreds of people every night. The best thing about it is that it takes no government funding of any kind. It's run by donations from private individuals and private companies. That shelter is truly one of my greatest accomplishments."

I sat there staring at this man, forgetting my problems. This was simply awesome to me. Someone who saw a problem like that and just got it done. And I wondered how many people knew all this? A few days later I returned. As I walked into his room he appeared to be sleeping. I remember thinking how frail he looked, just laying there in bed. I started to turn and quietly leave when he said, "What does someone have to do to get a sandwich in this place?"

I chuckled and said, "I'll get you a sandwich Leo. What kind would you like?"

He said, "Anything will do, just get it quickly, I'm starving!" I hustled off and made him a turkey sandwich, then brought it back and we talked while he ate. It's such a simple thing to sit and chat with someone while they eat. We didn't solve any of the world's problems that day, yet I remember how much fun we both had. And he was always straightforward with his thoughts. A person always knew where he stood with Leo.

When he was done with his sandwich, I was going to leave, but for some reason decided to ask a throwaway question, "I know you were doing a lot of construction in World War II, so I don't suppose you have any good war stories do you?"

"Hmm, the war," he said, sighing deeply. "Boy, no one's asked me about those days in a long, long time." He started breathing heavily, so I figured he was done talking and wanted to sleep, but I was wrong. "Let me think. Well, I think the part of my service that makes me the most proud is the time I spent building bridges in the spring of 1945. The bridges were needed so that our troops could keep advancing towards Berlin to get that bastard Hitler. As the Germans were being pushed back, they'd destroyed many of the bridges and roadways. Our guys needed a way to get their equipment through France and into Germany quickly, so it was our job to rebuild as many of those structures as we could. I'm most proud of my involvement in the building of one of the first bridges over the Rhine, which Patton and his boys used to cross into Germany and give the final knockout punch to the Germans.

"I remember one young brash lieutenant named Fred who showed up just before the bridge was finished. He was talking up a storm, telling all of us what he was going to do to the Germans if we would just hurry up and finish that damn bridge. He bent my ear the most, because he was also from Dallas and he thought that made us buddies. I got so sick of hearing him jabber that I began to avoid him at all costs. He'd just graduated from Texas A&M and definitely thought a lot of himself. In those final days before the bridge was completed, every time I took a break from my job there'd be Fred, talking. Always talking. That guy could talk a blue streak, but he usually wasn't saying much. Anyway, we got the bridge built and off all of the men went, including Fred, to give Hitler hell.

"It was a proud day for us Seabees, watching those men march off into Germany. We knew they were going to deal the final blow that would end the war in Europe. A few months later we were putting the final touches on a new base we were building when the same platoon of men who'd been waiting on us to finish the Rhine bridge came marching into camp looking for a place to stop for the night. This time it was me seeking out that young lieutenant from A&M—I wanted to hear about what he'd seen.

"I found Fred in the officer's club and he was as quiet as a church mouse. I mean that guy, the same guy that wouldn't shut his mouth three months prior, wouldn't say a thing. We had a few drinks and finally he started opening up. They had marched all the way across Germany and into Austria. Then they had assisted with the liberation of Dachau prison camp - Fred was in a state over what he had seen. I had to get him pretty well liquored up before he'd open up, but eventually he began to tell me what it looked like. The scene had humbled my friend, to say the least. When I thought he was done talking, I began to say something but he stopped me. I'll never forget what he said. 'You know Leo, you guys did a great job with that bridge and if it weren't for you we wouldn't have been able to do what we did in Germany. That was some good work and I appreciate the part you played in getting us in there.'

"I was floored and touched at the same time. We proposed a toast to all of the newly liberated men and women and then proceeded to drink ourselves into a stupor. We laughed and cried many times that night and the next day, before he left, Fred came and found me to say goodbye. I was working with my crew when he approached and asked if he could talk with me. We stepped to one side and he hugged me. I was surprised by his show of affection, because back in those days men didn't hug like they do today. He said he was leaving and thanked me again. I told him to be careful and we'd talk again one day when the world was a calmer place. He agreed, we shook hands and off he went.

"When I got back to my men, one of them said, 'What the hell was that all about? Are you and that asshole sweet on each other now?'

"I looked at him and I said, 'If you ever speak of that man again in anything other than a respectful tone I'll knock your block off. Am I clear?'

"The man was an ensign so I outranked him, but he was twice my size. He looked confused but said, 'Yes sir,' and that was the end of it.

"Fred and I did get together after the war ended and to this day he's one of my dearest friends in the world."

As Leo wrapped up his story, I noticed his eyes were moist. To my surprise, I realized mine were too. I choked out, "Thanks for sharing that with me, Leo."

He said, "Thanks for asking. That's a good memory, one I hadn't thought about in quite some time."

Over the next few months he declined to the point where he had to be transferred to the hospital. One morning I received a call at 6 a.m. from his wife. She was upset and told me Leo had just passed and would I mind calling his daughter—her step-daughter—to break the news. I said I'd do anything to help. As I dialed her number I was thinking of how I would phrase it when she picked up the phone and said, "Hello?" Suddenly my throat clenched and I couldn't speak, not one word. "Hello?" she said again.

I was about to lose it, but somehow, Leo showed up to give me some help. "We lost your father last night." Of course she got emotional, then I got more emotional. Eventually we hung up and I had to sit down and collect myself. It was then that I realized how much I had truly come to care for that man and how much the world needed great men like Leo Rawlings. He was eighty-nine years old.

13

Within a few months of Leo's death, I received call from a family who needed some help. I wrote down the name and address, grabbed my briefcase and out I went. When I arrived at their house, I was escorted in to see an eighty-eight-year-old man suffering from congestive heart failure and definitely in need of some help. I sat down and began taking some background information and finding out more about my new patient.

"Okay, Mr. Lambert, how did you hear about our agency?

"First, you can call me Fred. Everyone else does. And I heard about you fellows from my good buddy Leo Rawlings, before he passed away."

I blinked several times. "Uhh, Leo Rawlings?" as if I didn't hear him the first time.

"Yeah you heard me. Are you the one here that needs hearing aids?"

"No sir . . . I mean Fred. That's wonderful. Leo was a great guy."

"Yeah he was, now back to me. What do you want to know?"

I realized Fred was going to be another real character. I started in on his birth and worked forward. Fred was born in Dallas in 1923 and apparently was a feisty young man with more energy and smarts than his parents could handle. He was so with it that on most days his schoolwork was completed ahead of schedule and he had plenty of spare time on his hands. This usually led to trouble.

To burn off some extra energy he jumped into athletics, becoming a respected football player. He wasn't gifted with unique athleticism, but his effort was always one hundred percent, which more often than not, led to him being at the right place at the right time. This earned him quite a bit of favor with the coaches. When he graduated from high school he wasn't good enough to receive a college scholarship, so he decided to walk on at his beloved Texas A&M. Fred's father had been an Aggie and had raised Fred to be an ardent fan, but Fred didn't know if he would—or could—make the team. But his father's immense pride at seeing him try was enough motivation for him to give it a go. Fred worked hard during tryouts, but he just didn't have enough ability to play college ball. He was extremely disappointed when he was cut from the team.

His parents were worried about how he would take being cut, so his father drove to College Station to have a chat. The purpose was to console Fred, but when his father pulled on campus and saw the Corp of Cadets marching in the quadrangle, a thought struck him. So he suggested that Fred join the Corp. The thought hadn't occurred to Fred until that very moment, but the minute he heard the words come out of his father's mouth, he knew that the Corp was his future. Fred needed to be a part of something and he had A&M in his blood so he became a proud cadet.

Fred loved the Corp and threw himself into it with gusto and when he graduated, was enlisted in the Army and commissioned as a second lieutenant. We stopped the story there because I could tell he was getting tired. I made my goodbyes and left his house, heading back to the office to find the right staff for him. But I was soon to find out my new client was tough customer. He liked whom he liked and he didn't give a damn about any regulations I had to abide by. I've always believed the old saying that the customer is always right so it was hard for me to tell him I couldn't do what he wanted, but I had to. It was either that or risk my business. On a couple of occasions he became quite upset with me for not honoring his wishes. The good news was, he never held a grudge for very long.

The biggest problem I had was that Fred had a caregiver he loved—he really thought he couldn't do without her. And Mable was indeed great at providing patient care. She was also great at playing the game between patient and agency as well. Fred wanted her to work sixty plus hours each week, which she also wanted, as it would mean lots of overtime and a big fat check. I explained to Fred that this wouldn't be possible unless he paid for the overtime associated with the extra twenty hours. Fred, however, didn't want to pay. Mable lobbied him hard for the extra hours stating that

I should eat this cost for him and this caused Fred to blow up my phone with calls asking me to reconsider.

Finally, I had to bring Mable into the office and tell her if she didn't stop pushing him for the extra hours, she'd be pulled from the case. I couldn't have our field staff trying to manage cases from the field, especially when it was in a manner detrimental to the company. I also didn't want our caregivers leaning on their patients for anything. Their job was to show up and do everything in their power to make life better for the patient, not themselves.

After my talk with Mable she went right back to Fred and told him everything we'd talked about. He called me and gave me an earful. I'd figured this might happen, so I'd already prepared my response well ahead of time. I calmly told him, "Mable has left me no choice Fred. I'm going to have to pull her from your case and terminate her from the company."

I held the phone away from my ear, expecting him to start screaming and telling me he'd be finding another company to provide him with the care he needed. Instead, he paused a moment, and said, "Leo said you run a tight ship. I'll miss Mable, but I understand your decision. You can't have the tail wagging the dog, now can you?"

I was floored. And when I regained my composure, I said, "No sir, you cannot. A tight ship indeed, one I know you can appreciate." I couldn't finish my conversation fast enough. I hate to admit it, but I felt a good deal of satisfaction telling Mable that she had lost the game.

After this, we got into a good groove with Fred and I was able to get to know him without all of the drama going on. I visited him regularly to see how things were going and we talked about a myriad of things. His mind was still sharp and thankfully he wasn't suffering from any memory loss. During one of our visits I pulled up a chair, and said, "Leo told me about building the Rhine Bridge in Europe and the way you met. Can you please tell me about your time in the Army?"

Fred stared at me for a moment with a strange look on his face and said, "Why do you want to know about that?"

"Well," I said, "My father was in the Navy and he used to tell me stories about what he'd experienced. I really appreciate hearing about those times and have a great deal of respect for all you guys did. To me there's nothing better than hearing about history through men like you."

Fred studied me for a moment longer, took a deep breath and said, "Okay, but would you get me a sandwich first?"

I laughed out loud. "What is it about you old guys and sandwiches? Leo had me do the same thing before he told me his story."

"Really!" Fred said. "What kind of sandwich did you make Leo?"

"Turkey."

"Then make me a turkey sandwich, too," he said with a large smile on his face. "I like to emulate Leo any time I can."

"Yes, sir," I said. "I'll be back in a minute."

When I came back in Fred ate his sandwich and then he began to talk.

"I'm an Aggie. Did you know I was an Aggie?"

"Yes sir, I did."

"Really, how did you know that?"

I chuckled and said "Well, where do I start. Your car is maroon and covered in A&M stickers. The maroon carpet in the entryway has an A&M logo on it. Your drinking and coffee cups have the A&M logo on them. You have the Aggie War Hymn framed on the wall over there. Your cadet boots have been bronzed and are sitting over in that corner. And your dog is named Reveille."

He smiled and said, "Subtlety was never my strong suit."

We both laughed and then he began to speak, not stopping for quite some time.

"I was going to play football at A&M, but I didn't make the team. The truth was that I didn't have any business being on that team but, boy, did I want it back then. When that didn't work out, I was heartbroken, so I joined the Corp. Once I joined, I knew I'd found a home. I jumped into the routine and the fall flew by. Then the damn Japs bombed us at Pearl and the world changed.

"My classmates and I were ready to drop everything to go fight, but we were told by the higher ups that the war was going to last a while and that the Army was going to need officers. They encouraged us to stay put and finish school. We did what we were told, but it was painful having to read about the war and not participate.

"I managed to knock out my coursework in under three years and graduated early. Because of my Corp training, the Army took me in as a second lieutenant. At that point I thought I'd be heading straight into the action, but the Army had another idea. They sent me to Europe where I was stationed in London as a supply officer. I immediately began putting in requests for a transfer, but ended up stuck in that boring job for three months.

"Finally, a new group of young officers arrived which allowed me transfer out. My wish was finally granted: I was going to fight Germans. I was deployed to France where I joined Patton's 3rd Army, which had already made its way across half of France. When we got to the Rhine we were held up—the bridge we were supposed to cross was still under construction. I hadn't done a damned thing yet, but thought I was Patton himself in those days. I was so cocky and full of myself that I asked, well *demanded* is a better way to put it, to speak with the project supervisor. They wouldn't let a loud-mouthed second lieutenant talk with a man like that, but they did hook me up with one of his project supervisors, and that was the first time I ever met Leo Rawlings. He was clearly not excited about having to explain himself to me, but he was always a gentleman and extremely professional. We quickly figured out that we were both from Dallas and knew a lot of the same people. That was nice because, even though I hadn't been in Europe that long, it was good to connect with someone from home.

"Despite the connection we had, I think Leo still tried to avoid me most of the time. I'm sure he had better things to do than to constantly provide me with updates on the bridge's progress. When I look back on that time I can hardly blame him. I thought I was really something special and I ran my mouth constantly. The Seabees were doing great work under very difficult circumstances and sure as hell didn't need my supervision.

"The day came when the bridge was finally finished and we received orders to head out. I'll never forget that day. All of the men on the construction crew lined the bridge and clapped as we made our way across the bridge and on to our destiny with Hitler.

"For the first week we didn't receive any resistance as we made our way into Germany. The Germans were nowhere to be found, so I think all of us got a little relaxed. Then one day a sniper from a hillside pillbox attacked us. This was my first exposure to actual combat and it was a tough way to be introduced to the horrors of war. The very first shot hit a good buddy of mine who was standing no more than ten feet away from me. The night before I'd been playing cards and laughing with him. Twelve hours later I was helping a medic tend to a gaping wound in my friend's chest. He died right there on that hillside. His name was Dexter Williams, but we just called him Dex. He was an outspoken, brash kid from the Bronx, always running his mouth. Sound familiar? I guess that's why we got along so well, even though I was an Aggie from Dallas and he was a Yankee from New York. That incident made me focus on the reality of what I'd signed up to do. It brought me back down to earth and knocked the edge off my cocky attitude.

"In early April we managed to advance all the way into Austria. Then, a couple of weeks later, I was instructed to lead a small group of men back into Germany to assist the 7th Army since they had just liberated Dachau prison camp just outside of Munich. We knew the Germans had a bunch of these camps, but had no idea what was going on inside of them. What the men found when they went in was beyond comprehension.

"By the time I arrived with my group of men the camp had been partially cleaned up but there was still a lot of work to do. The first thing I noticed when I approached the gate was the smell. It was truly awful. A combination of death and excrement filled our nostrils. The smell was so thick you could cut it with a knife. Just inside the gate I passed a few of the men who had walked in before me and they were retching. Inside the gate the smell was so bad I had to put a handkerchief over my nose and mouth . . . and then I saw the bodies. Just inside the front gate there were bodies stacked five high and not a one of them could've weighed more than ninety pounds. I was so taken aback that I think I was drifting towards shock. One of the men who had been there a while saw us and directed us to the makeshift headquarters so that we could be given our orders. We learned that we were needed to debrief any prisoners who were still able to communicate.

"These guys hadn't eaten any more than scraps for months and in some cases, years. As a result we set up shop in the makeshift cafeteria which was running twenty-four hours a day to feed the prisoners. The officers divided the men up and interviewed as many as we could. Some were not in any condition to talk, but others had enough strength to tell us about what they had been through. I'll never forget one man I spoke with named Victor Ivanovich. He was a Russian from a small town outside of Moscow and spoke very good English. He told me that he'd been a prisoner since his capture in occupied France in the spring of 1943. For two years he'd been beaten, starved and forced to watch as many of his fellow prisoners had died. Victor was so full of life, now that he was out of the camp, that he couldn't stop asking me questions. My heart went out to this nice guy who, on top of his poor physical condition, really needed some mental nutrition as well; he just wanted to know what was going on in the world. I couldn't blame him, so I did my best to fill him in.

"Victor especially wanted to know everything that was happening in the war effort in the European Theatre and in the Pacific. But he also wanted to know such cultural things as the Tigers winning the World Series and the new models Ford, Buick and Chevrolet were putting out. Victor wanted to know everything he could, so I told him, at least to the best of my ability. When he asked me who won the Miss America pageant I had to admit that I didn't have any idea. When I said this, he laughed and I realized that he was just having some fun with me. Can you imagine a man like that being able to joke around just hours after leaving a place like Dachau? I admired him very much and I checked in on him every chance I could.

"A couple of weeks later was VE day which marked the end of my time in Germany. The army wanted me back in London to help with some administrative clean up before they would decide what to do with me next. A company of men—all in the same boat as me—headed back the way we came. All of us were changed men because of what we had seen. There wasn't the same bravado as there had been before. Now, we were all business.

"As for me, I was probably the one that changed the most. Aggies are a very confident and enthusiastic group, and I'd been their poster child. After what I saw in Germany, that enthusiasm left me for a while. I got it back eventually, but my experience over there had made me a different person. I gained the reserved temperament and maturity of a man who has seen all that the world has to offer, both good and bad.

"When we reached France, we needed a place to stop and were directed to a base that was just being completed. There we ran into many of the same Seabees who'd been working on the Rhine Bridge a few months earlier. It was late in the day when we arrived and some of the guys said they were going to go get some chow. Personally, I didn't want any food. I told them I was going to go find a drink. I headed to the officer's club, ordered a drink and did my best to make the last several months of my life go away. I had downed two drinks when in walks Leo Rawlings. The minute we locked eye's I figured Leo would head in the other direction. Since the first time we met I'd been such a pain in the ass, I assumed he wanted nothing to do with me. But Leo headed straight towards me and sat at my table. The first thing he said was, 'Fred, I heard you were back and I've been looking for you.'

" 'Why,' I said.

" 'Because you boys went and won the war for us and I want to hear all about it.' By that point, with the fate of the war in Europe having already been decided, everyone was in a pretty good mood, including Leo. I said I hadn't done anything worth a damn and didn't have much to talk about but Leo didn't let up. 'Come on Fred, I've never seen you at a loss for words, tell me what happened.'

"Finally I said, 'Okay but let me polish off a few more drinks and then I'll talk.' Leo agreed and we both sat there and drank our troubles away.

"Over the course of the night I told Leo what I'd seen and I also told him how it had affected me. He could see that I was reeling and offered his support. I told him we couldn't have gotten there if it weren't for the Seabees good work on the bridges. We sat there for hours and had way too much to drink. I think we both just needed to blow off some steam. The next day my company headed out, but before we left I found Leo and we said our goodbye's. He told me we'd reconnect when the war was over, but I wasn't so sure about that. We left the camp and headed to London where I spent a few months before transferring back to the states to work in Army intelligence until the Japs finally surrendered. Shortly after that I left the military and that's the story."

Fred shrugged his shoulders the way a kid would do when he didn't know what else to say. He seemed almost childlike for a moment, lost in thought, and he looked exhausted. Still. I had one more question to ask. "Did you ever communicate with Victor again?"

The question caught him off guard. "What?" he said.

"Victor, from Dachau, did you ever communicate with him again?"

Fred smiled and said, "As a matter of fact I did. I remembered that he was from a small city called Yurlovo so when I arrived back in the states, I sent him a letter. I had no idea if he would ever receive it, because I didn't have a specific address for him. I was hoping that, like any small town in America, it would eventually get to him because everyone knows everyone else. I didn't hear back from him for at least eight months. By that time I'd assumed he never received my letter. But then, out of the blue I got a reply. It had taken weeks to get to me, but the Army is pretty good about making sure that all mail eventually finds its mark.

"Victor wrote to congratulate me on America's great victory in the war. He also told me he was eating well, had gained thirty pounds and was back at his job as a butcher. This, he joked was 'helping him in his quest to re-gain his old form.' I wrote back, hoping to keep the communication going, but I never heard from him again."

Again Fred looked to be lost in thought and very tired. I knew he'd reached his limit for the day so I said, "Fred, thank you for telling me that amazing story. You're a real American hero."

"No, I'm not. So many people did so much more than I did."

I smiled and said, "Let me rephrase that then, you are a real hero to me."

He reached over and patted me on the hand, smiling. One month later, almost to the day of our visit, Fred died in his sleep. He was eighty-eight years old.

During the funeral many stories were told about Fred and all that he had done in his life. I sat in the back of the church and smiled because I'd heard many of those same stories from Fred.

I truly felt privileged to have heard those stories from the man himself and I felt pride that I'd been considered one of his friends. Fred was an-other great man who had been lost to the ages.

14

By now we had added another daughter to our growing family. Around my wife and children, I tried hard to always maintain an upbeat attitude. But one night, after they had all gone to bed, I stayed up wallowing in my misery. It was difficult to lose people who'd meant so much to me and I wasn't handling it well. I sat slumped in my chair watching some movie for the fifth time, hoping to place my mind on autopilot. It was a war movie, which got me thinking about my dad. With that, a thought hit me and I bolted upright, walked swiftly to my dresser drawer and pulled out the two envelopes Dad had left for me. I took them into the living room and sat on the couch. I looked at the words written on them, 'Courage' and 'Faith,' wondering which one to choose. I thought for a moment then decided I needed some courage to deal with this setback. So I opened the envelope and began to read . . .

Dear Joe,

In November of 1944, I took part in the Philippines Campaign. My squadron's job was to make strafing and bombing runs on the island of Zablan. One mission from that campaign changed my life.

My wingman was a fellow I was quite fond of by the name of Jack Harrison. Jack was from Nebraska and was a farmer's son. He was as straight-laced as anyone I'd ever met. Square jawed with a dimpled chin and he kept a crew cut at all times. He never drank and it was his intention to marry Margie Wilson, his high school sweetheart, the moment his tour in the South Pacific was over. We used to joke that he should be on the posters the Navy used to attract new recruits. We were quite different from one another, but we played off of each other well and we enjoyed each other's company. By the time he was assigned as my wingman for this mission I loved Jack like a brother.

The only thing that Jack ever did that got him into hot water was to slightly alter the appearance of his corsair. He didn't think it was fair that the Army Air Corp boys flying the B-17s were the only ones allowed to paint pretty girls on their planes, so Jack took it upon himself to paint his fiancée's name on the side of his plane. This was not Navy protocol and the CO got pretty upset with him. He was ordered to remove it, but Jack told the maintenance guys to leave Margie's name where it was. He knew he only had a few missions left before he was done and he thought that it'd bring him good luck.

The friendship I had with Jack was quite common among pilots, because despite all of our many differences we had one thing very much in common: we were Navy fighter pilots. Don't get me wrong, there were many pilots that guys like Jack and I didn't get along with. Some were hot dogs who thought each mission was an opportunity to show off or gain personal glory. Others were so scared they'd fold under the pressure of a tough mission. Some were even caught with flasks in their cockpits to ease their nerves when the pressure got too much to bear. Guys like this weren't our friends because they jeopardized their lives and ours. We tried to run them off as quickly as we could.

That day, eighteen planes in my squadron took off at 0700 for our mission. We were prepared for enemy resistance from the ground, but weren't anticipating much resistance in the air—the stock of Jap pilots had been pretty well depleted. When we got close to the island we received a big surprise: an entire squadron of zeros.

By that point in the war we had confidence in our ability to overcome most obstacles. When the trouble started, we were out over open water approximately fifteen miles due south of Zablan and flying in formation, keeping our eyes peeled despite the fact that we thought the mission wouldn't receive a great deal of opposition. All at once I heard the radio crackle, but the pilot talking was speaking so fast I couldn't understand what he said. Neither had a number of the other men, so several of us asked for him to repeat himself.

"Enemy fighters at eleven o'clock!"

My heart started pounding as I looked up to the left squinting hard. What I saw made my blood run cold. There must have been forty zeros. One by one they were banking left to engage our squadron. I had been in dogfights before, but never against such an overwhelming force. The squadron leader told us to break up and engage. Although splitting up our larger formation, each man and his wingman were to stay together and fight as a unit so that we could watch each other's back.

"Jack," I said. "I'll lead the way, we're going to hit the deck and hope to bring some of them with us."

"Roger."

More than fifty planes dancing across the sky at one time can be treacherous, so my hope was to pull them away from the group and pick them off one at a time. It worked! A lone zero banked hard and headed right towards us. I was at five thousand feet, so I pushed my stick forward all the way and headed right to the ocean. When I did this the zero keyed on me like I hoped he would, while Jack banked hard left so he could loop back around. As I approached fifteen hundred feet, I could see the ocean boiling below me. I realized that it was the zero's machine gun fire as he tried his best to send me to my grave. Just then I heard Jack scream, "Break right Vince!" I did and heard Jack say, "One down!" I turned and saw the zero heading into the Pacific with flames coming from its engine.

We headed back up and into the fray. We keyed in on a zero that was trying to pick off our guys who were engaged with other zeros. We fired at him to get his attention and sure enough he turned and engaged the two of us. Once again we led him away from the pack so that we could lessen the chance of an air-to-air collision or the possibility of accidentally shooting down one of our own guys. This time the guy keyed right in on Jack so it was my turn to bank up and away then loop back in for the kill. Jack took him low just as I had done and I set a course just off center of the zero. Then, as he had done with me, I told Jack to break right. The minute I saw him begin to make the turn I began firing the machine guns located in the wings of my corsair. When the zero turned to pursue Jack, he turned right into my line of fire. My rounds entered the zero at an angle beginning at the front of the fuselage tracking back to the tail section. The engine burst into flames and the plane took a sharp angle downward to the sea. Two zeros down.

In the split second it took to observe what I'd done, I had another zero on my tail. By the time I realized he was there, he already had a line on me and began firing. His shots hit my plane in the engine and grazed the belly. At first I thought they were just glancing blows, because the plane was still functioning. But a few moments later the engine began to lose power.

I didn't realize it, but while the zero had been engaged with me, Jack had looped back around and was giving him a taste of his own medicine. Jack ripped him apart and then flew down to check on me. He asked how I was doing and I told him I was going into the drink. Jack told me he was going to escort me down to make sure that none of the other zeros got any big ideas about finishing me off. When I was below a thousand feet Jack said, "Be careful Vince, there are sharks in those waters." I told him that I was more worried about the sharks in the air and told him to also be careful.

After an uneventful water landing, I managed to crawl out of my plane and into my tiny rubber raft. Then all I could do was sit and watch the intense fighting going on over my head. My squadron put up a hell of fight, but there were just too many Japs that day. Some good men went down and not all of them were as fortunate as me. The remaining few who were still flying eventually headed up into the clouds to make their getaway so they could fly another day. I couldn't keep up with Jack so I didn't know if he had made it or not.

All but two of the zeros left the area. I assumed the two that stayed were the ones with the most fuel. With nothing else to shoot at, those two remaining zeros began making low passes over the water. I presumed this was to see if there were any survivors and in a matter of moments, I realized to my horror, that my suspicion was correct. After one low pass I saw the zeros pull up and away then come in low again over the same area, but this time they strafed the water with machine gun fire. They were at least half a mile away from me so I couldn't see their target, but it didn't take a genius to figure out what they were doing. Those bastards were killing American pilots as they sat helpless, floating in the sea.

The passes they made were bringing them closer and closer to where I sat, so I assumed my time would eventually come. My only chance would be to jump in the water and hope they didn't see me. I was contemplating this strategy and assessing the water for sharks when I suddenly heard another plane engine overhead. It was faint at first but as it became louder, I eventually found the source of the new sound: it was a lone corsair. It had just broken through the clouds and was headed straight for the zeros. I watched in awe as the pilot took an angle to intercept the two Jap planes just as they made another strafing run at some poor, helpless pilot. Before they reached their target the corsair pilot opened fire and scored a direct hit on one of the zeros. The plane was practically cut in half by the fire and then crumbled into the sea with a splash. The second zero banked up and away and immediately turned to engage the corsair. The American turned sharply to his right, banking hard over my head. As he flew over me, my blood ran cold as I clearly saw the name Margie written on the side of the plane. It was Jack. He must've been hiding in the clouds in case he was needed and then come out when he'd seen what the Japs were up to. I knew that by now he must be running on fumes and was probably dangerously low on ammunition. Sticking around was a gutsy thing for Jack to do and I was confident that it was his idea alone. I knew he was most likely ignoring a direct order to return to the carrier.

All I could do was sit and watch as Jack tried desperately to shake the zero from his tail. He was having a hell of time getting away when I saw him employ his tried and true tactic of heading straight up and into the clouds. The zero went into the clouds as well then after a few moments came out alone and headed back downward towards the ocean.

I thought Jack must have used his good judgment and headed back towards home, though I doubted he had enough fuel to make it. Either way, it would at least put some good distance between himself and the enemy.

As for the zero, if he had enough fuel I assumed he would resume his strafing runs. Sure enough, he came right back down to the ocean's surface and he was headed straight towards my position. First he made a low pass over the ocean about five hundred yards to the north of me. He didn't know I would be there—it was just a lucky guess on his part. When I saw how close his pass was going to be, I slid into ocean and hid underneath my raft. I hoped he would think the raft was abandoned, but unfortunately he wasn't buying it. I watched as he pulled up sharply after his low pass and then he began a sweeping left turn and prepared for his strafing run on my raft . . . and me.

At that moment I realized I was going to miss my Dad. There was so much I wanted to tell him, so many words left unsaid. Mom would be forced to have a memorial service for her son without a body to bury. And it's funny, but I even wished I was back in the ring with Gene Tunney getting my bell rung. All this in the blink of an eye.

I watched as the zero made his run to kill me, then I again heard a familiar sound. Here came Jack screaming out of the clouds and descending straight towards the zero just as he'd done the first time. Jack had had the element of surprise, but as he approached the zero and opened fire, he missed. Still, his actions had saved my life because the zero broke off his strafing to reengage Jack. As the zero banked to his right Jack fell in behind him. He was pretty low when he passed over me and I saw him through his canopy and he was looking right back at me. I gave him a quick salute before he began firing at the zero. He only got off a few rounds then I heard silence. He was out of ammunition.

Jack now only had one option if he was going to survive: he could chase the zero until the Jap pilot was dangerously low on fuel and then allow him to make a run for home. But Jack was low on fuel too. He knew he could be on the tail of the zero and his engine could die and he'd have to ditch in the water. That meant certain death because the zero would simply circle around and finish him off. It was a cruel war.

I watched as Jack pursued the zero across the sky without firing a shot. The zero clearly understood what was happening because his evasive maneuvers became much less dramatic. He was simply trying to wear out Jack until he found the right time to make his move. That time came a few moments later when the zero abruptly dove hard to the right. What I saw next is something I'll never forget, no matter how clouded my brain becomes in old age. Jack angled hard matching the zero's sharp turn. Then, as both planes banked sharply, Jack closed the gap between himself and the zero and crashed his corsair into the enemy plane. There was a sickening sound of metal on metal before both planes plummeted towards the ocean. I watched in horror as Jack's corsair and the zero violently crashed. I knew in an instant it wasn't a survivable crash. I sat in silence and thought about what my friend had just done for me and the rest of the surviving pilots. He'd given his life to save us when there would've been no shame in heading home, finishing up his few remaining missions and going home to marry his beloved Margie.

I sat in silence, the water lapping against my raft, and knew there was nothing I could do to repay such a debt. I made a promise to myself that I would retell the story of Jack Harrison, but until now it's been very hard for me to do. I also knew that I needed to go see Margie and tell her why I was still alive, but her fiancée wasn't. I needed her to know what a hero Jack had been on that day and how many American lives he'd saved, mine included.

Later that day a supply ship swept the area and picked me up along with four other downed pilots from my squadron. It took a couple of days to get all the way back to the Ticonderoga, but when I did my CO immediately brought me in and inquired about Jack. When I walked into his office he said that he needed to have a better understanding of the events of that day because, as I suspected, Jack had ignored a direct order to return to the carrier. I told him the story of what Jack had done and when I had finished the CO sat there in silence for quite a while. Then he *smiled the slightest bit and said to himself, "Whoever heard of painting your girlfriend's name on the side of a fighter plane?" Then he chuckled a bit and was silent again.*

I said to him, "Sir, I don't mean to make inquiries that are above my pay grade, but may I ask a question?" The CO looked up at me as if he had forgotten I was there then said, "Yes lieutenant, what's on your mind?"

"Well sir, if it wasn't for Jack, I'd be fish food right now. He saved my life, and he saved the lives of all the other downed pilots that day. He's a hero of the tallest order, but your inquiry sounds like it's just focusing on the fact that Jack disobeyed a direct order."

The CO waved me off and said, "That's for the brass to decide. Not me." With that he smiled, albeit a pained smile and continued muttering, "He only had a few weeks left. I wasn't even going to press him about the damn name on the side of the plane." Then he stopped and looked at me as if he was shocked I was still there. "That'll be all, lieutenant."

I said, "Yes, sir," and left.

I wrote Margie a long letter that day. After the war ended and I was able to scrape up some extra money, I made the trip to see her. I knew instantly why Jack had fallen in love with her—she was a special girl indeed. We sat in the sunroom of her parent's house and at her request, I told her everything that happened on that fateful day. As I told her, she sat there and quietly wept. I think she needed to hear it so she could truly begin to heal. It made me feel better, too. When I left, we hugged and she thanked me for coming to see her. I had a strong sense that she was going to be okay, because I could tell that she, like Jack, was a fighter.

Son, I want you to understand how special the human spirit can be. When brave men are put in situations where the deck is stacked against them, they have the ability to achieve extraordinary things. Jack proved it on that day in the South Pacific and it's a lesson I never forgot. My hope in sharing this story with you is that you'll tell it to others. People need to hear about the two traits that define a true hero: courage and selflessness. These two amazing human traits are rarely witnessed the way I did all those years ago. I hope you'll display both of these traits in your life. It's also my sincerest hope that you won't have to give your life in the process. Love Always, Dad

My father, from the grave, had succeeded in bringing my situation into focus. Once again, I sat in awe of the great generation that fought and sometimes died all those many years ago. In that moment, I remembered the words of Tom Terry, "Never quit!"

I carefully folded the letter and placed it back into its envelope. Then I wiped my eyes and wrote out my game plan for the next day, knowing I had the courage to face whatever I had to face with enthusiasm and Dad as my wingman.

15

I went to work the next day feeling much better and out of my funk. I felt I was ready to deal with anything, and next on my plate was Ruby, one of our caregivers. That morning I received a call from the daughter of a nice elderly couple we'd been taking care of for quite some time. She'd discovered both of her mother's wedding rings missing and suspected Ruby. I leaned back in my chair with the phone still at my ear thinking about all the trouble we'd already been through. I was on the verge of stepping right back into that funk when I decided to see that problem the way Jack Harrison would've—as just one more obstacle I needed to overcome. I was going to tackle this head on. "Alright ma'am, I'll help you sort this out. Let me know your thoughts on the matter and I'll be more than happy to begin an investigation."

What she gave me was pretty thin. All she really knew was that they'd been missing for perhaps a week or two. Our caregiver Ruby was in the home all day, every day and she was the only one we had staffed on the case. Since I knew where the investigation had to begin, I called Ruby into the office and informed her of what she was accused of.

Ruby insisted that she hadn't stolen anything, even offering to take a polygraph test to prove her innocence. Something about her extreme conviction made me tempted to believe her, but somehow I had my doubts. Still, Ruby did have an excellent track record with our company and since we had no proof of any kind of her guilt, I chose to believe her. Even so, I still had to document the episode by putting a verbal counseling form in her file. She wasn't happy about it.

"Sir, I didn't take the rings and your form suggests I did," she said pleading with me. "Why counsel someone for something they didn't do?"

While I could understand why she felt that way, I still had to cover my bases. "Ruby, that's the way I'm going to handle the situation for now, but if anything happens to prove your innocence we will certainly revisit the issue."

This was a blow to Ruby and it only got worse when I had to tell her that the family didn't want her back on their case. I think that hurt her the most, since she really loved the little old couple. As for he family themselves, they were absolutely devastated about the loss of the rings, but decided to give my company 'a second chance,' since the care they had received up to that point had been exemplary.

A month later we received a call from the new caregiver on the case telling us the family had been doing some cleaning at their mother's and father's house when they found both rings hidden in the back of her closet. The mother, who had some dementia, had hidden the rings to keep them safe and had simply forgotten where they were. The current caregiver on the case, who had been helping them clean, listened as the daughters realized in an open conversation that they had falsely accused my company—and more specifically Ruby—of theft. Our caregiver was calling to tell us that she had seen firsthand how horrible the daughters felt about the false accusation. I breathed a sigh of relief and waited for their call to apologize and make sure the record was put straight.

The more I thought about it, however, the more my relief was tempered with regret—I'd counseled someone about a theft she'd hadn't committed. I personally placed a call to Ruby and asked her to come into the office so we could talk. On the phone she acted like she was probably going to get in trouble again, sighed, and said she would come in that afternoon. When she arrived I told her what had happened and I gave her a heartfelt apology. I also took the counseling form out of her file and ripped it up in front of her. Ruby was so happy and relieved, that she cried and hugged me so hard I think she cracked one of my ribs. I told her I would let her know what the family said when they called and she went back to work a happy woman.

I waited for the phone call that day and the next day too, but it didn't come. A week later, I still hadn't heard from the daughters. A month later I realized they were never going to call. The reason is this: it's very hard to admit your guilt when you don't have to.

The work place is a strange environment and it was one I didn't always have a firm handle on. However, I did feel I had a handle on my sales reps. These folks were out of the office 95% of the day calling on doctors and homes to generate leads, like I had done with The American Coupon Company. They had a lot of leeway with their time because sometimes, they had to meet potential referrers in the evening. As such, I kept an eye on them but gave them a lot of freedom too. Then another issue materialized and her name was Piper.

Piper started work for the agency as a marketing rep and after six months still wasn't having much success. In that time she'd only generated five referrals. (A good rep will generate ten referrals in a slow month and forty in a good month.) In fairness to Piper, it does take several months to get plugged in and start getting referrals heading your way. But one thing a sales rep has to get used to is rejection, and that was one thing Piper had a really hard time handling. Concerned with her performance after six months, I decided to look into it. When I looked at her weekly reports they showed her spending a lot of time at one particular senior center visiting the facility's activities director. When I asked Piper about this she said this lady was a 'gold mine' and that she was trying to establish a really solid relationship with her.

That answer might have flown, except that her reports indicated she was spending multiple hours a day with this woman. On top of that, I received a call from the manager of that senior center a few days later. He was very upset, explaining that his employees had better things to do than sit and chat with their buddies all day, every day. I knew who he was talking about, but asked him to elaborate on what he meant by 'buddies.' He went on to explain that Piper and his activities director went to church together and were old friends. This information had come out when he'd sat his employee down for a meeting and told her she was going to be fired if she didn't tell him why she and Piper were joined at the hip each day. The girl spilled the beans that they were just friends hanging out while getting paid to work and promised to stop the daily meetings. I apologized to the man and told him that the meetings were over.

When I called Piper in she was as wide-eyed as anyone I'd ever seen. I proceeded with a written warning on the off chance I could salvage an employee whom I had a six-month investment in. I told her to get back out there and generate some referrals this week. It was pretty cut and dry. No yelling or screaming and no threats of termination. And certainly no mention of what an unacceptable job she had done so far. She left the office and went back to work.

The next morning Piper walked into my office with tears in her eyes and handed me a piece of paper. "I'm resigning. Last night I had a miscarriage. I can't work for a company that would put so much stress on me that I'd lose a baby, one I so desperately wanted." As I sat there stunned she turned and stormed out of my office.

About five minutes later Sarah came into my office.

"Sarah, did you know she was pregnant?"

Sarah said, "No, and I'm not sure she knew, either." She paused. "You know, Joe, you're too nice. You give people a long rope to hang themselves on, and then they end up hanging you with it. Let me handle the day-to-day around here and you go out and see the patients. They like you and you like them. It's what you're good at. It's what you're here for."

Sarah was saying the same thing Tom Terry had said and I knew she was right. I'd let myself become distracted by the day-to-day minutia. Ten minutes later, almost on cue, I received a call from Mark McAlister, a friend whom I'd known for several years. He wanted me to meet with him at his mother's house to discuss home care options. His mother had been a friend of our family for years, but she'd always been Mrs. McAlister to me, at least until we admitted her to our service. Then she became 'Aunt Edna.'

When I arrived at her home for the initial meet and greet, Aunt Edna met me at the door with a hug. Mark was running late so she and I sat down to discuss the situation. Surprisingly, she was open, honest and fully understood what was happening to her. I'd known she was sick, but until this moment, I didn't grasp that she was fighting for her life. Her emphysema had reached a critical stage and she was barely staying on top of it. She had a lot of questions about how everything would work. I answered them and promised her that I would be personally involved in her care for as long as she was using our service. Although I'd known her for years, it was fairly obvious our relationship was about to change. I'm pretty formal with most patients, but with some, I'm informal and even personal. Aunt Edna would be the latter. And we both understood the fact that I would be with her until the bitter end.

At this point, I'd been there a while and I was growing concerned that all of the talking we'd been doing was wearing her out. I began to excuse myself so I could let Sarah step in and fill out her admission paperwork, but as I stood up, Aunt Edna motioned me over to her bedside. She took a moment to get her breath then she looked at me directly in the eyes and said, "Whatever you do Joe, don't screw this up."

She was very direct and always got straight to the point. I grabbed her hand and said, "I will *not* screw up this case, Aunt Edna."

She smiled at me, but didn't say anything. She also didn't let go of my hand. After a few seconds I realized she was catching her breath so she could ask me one more question. "Joe, you miss your father, don't you?"

The question had come out of the blue and I was a little taken aback. "Yes," I said. "Very much."

"You know that we were very good friends, don't you?"

I smiled at her and said, "I know you were, how many years did you know him?"

She said, "Oh, probably forty-five. Remind me, how long ago did he die?"

"About four years ago, why?"

"Well, I was just thinking about Vince and how you remind me so much of him."

I smiled, though I was suddenly overtaken by a huge wave of sadness. For a moment I felt as if I'd lost Dad just yesterday. I sat there for a moment, but despite my best efforts, I could feel my face flushing. Edna looked at me, but didn't say anything. She just studied me.

To move the conversation in a different direction I said, "Aunt Edna, the nurse has a few questions to ask you, so I'm going to get out of your hair. Now, you know you can call me anytime you need anything at all, right?"

She looked at me and said, "I know dear, and since this nurse is going to start asking me questions about my health, I'm going to ask you for something right now."

"Of course, what can I do for you?"

"Go to the bar, pour me three fingers of Dewar's over ice, splash some water on it, and bring it back to me. And please, don't screw that up either." She chuckled, let go of my hand and pointed to the bar.

As I was pouring the drink, Mark showed up, took one look at me and fell out laughing. "Either she already has you making her drinks or she's already driven you to drink. Which is it?"

We laughed and I told him we were wrapping up and that she needed her nightly cocktail before dinner. After I handed her the drink, Mark and I sat down and talked for a while. He confirmed that this care was going to take her to the end. The doctors had told them she probably only had a few months more to live and that movement of any kind would become progressively harder for her as the emphysema ate away at her lungs. He was sad, but realistic about the whole situation. He knew he was losing his mother in a tragic way and his primary goal was to make her as comfortable as possible.

This sentiment is common among kids with dying parents, but unfortunately many cannot afford twenty-four hour care. Mark and his family could, so they were going to do whatever it took to provide the best care for their mother. By this point, the size of my company prevented me from being personally involved in every case we managed, but I made it abundantly clear to my staff that I'd be involved in this case every step of the way.

When I got back to the office, Sarah and I set the schedule for our selected caregivers and got them in place for the next day. We had to juggle caregivers around a couple of times to get the group we wanted, but within a few days we'd found our groove. Unfortunately Edna's deterioration started almost immediately and the case quickly escalated, becoming quite a bit more complicated.

I found it hard to come by to visit her after the comment about my dad. I told myself I was busy, but it was more likely that I just didn't want to feel sad all over again. Then I got call from Sarah letting me know that Edna, who was on oxygen, was sneaking into the bathroom to smoke while the caregivers were off making her meals. I called Mark and explained what Edna was doing and his response was somewhat relaxed, "You know, she's in her current situation because of that damn smoking and I hate it, but at this point, with the end so near, I don't know that it matters much if she has an occasional cigarette. If she wants to smoke then I'm inclined to let her do it."

I said, "Mark, I know where you're coming from, but I have to consider the safety of my employee. If she gets a flame too close to that oxygen then she's going to blow up not only herself, but the house and my employee with her!"

Mark was startled. "Oh my gosh, I hadn't considered the oxygen. I'll get over there right now!"

I'd seen this situation before, the addiction is so great that despite the risk of it slowly killing them, smokers simply have to do it. Even the risk of igniting an oxygen tank isn't enough to get them to stop. As a result, many of them have blown themselves up. Most smokers at least make an effort to keep the flame away from their oxygen tube, but sometimes it's just not far enough. When I worked at UHI, one gentleman we took care of had his oxygen hose catch fire. It ended up dripping molten rubber all over his face, while the flame shot up his nose giving him third degree burns inside his nostrils to complicate the third degree burns on his face.

We were able to stop Edna from smoking in the bathroom, but when she heard from her son that I had told on her, she wasn't happy with me. A week after this episode, I finally decided to go by and check in on her. I was afraid she might still be mad at me for ratting her out, but on this day she had something else on her mind and was all smiles. She took one look at me and said, "Hello Joe, have a seat."

I walked over and sat next to her. Neither one of us said anything for a few moments. Then Aunt Edna propped herself up in her bed and said, "Do you remember the first day my care started and I asked you about your father?"

"Sure," I said. "I remember. Why?"

"Well, I've thought a lot about that and I wanted to talk with you about your reaction."

I stiffened a bit. "What reaction?"

"You got sad, dear."

I wasn't sure why she was so intent on talking about this subject. "Sure I did, I miss him."

"I know you do, dear, but years after they're gone is a long time to be visibly saddened over the loss of your father in casual conversation. Don't you agree?"

I nodded and looked away.

"I saw what you were going through that day at the funeral and I've seen you agonizing over his loss ever since. You didn't have to tell me what was going on—it was written all over your face. Your father was a good man, but he was old, like me, and it was his time. I know you probably have some regrets about things you wish you'd said or done—everyone who suddenly loses a loved one does—but you need to move on. Your father would want that. There's no point in harboring sad feelings indefinitely. Save those feelings for the loved ones who are still here. Tell *them* how you feel."

I knew she was right and was amazed at how astute her observations had been. The silence that followed was rather uncomfortable. Finally I said, "Okay, I see your point and I want you to know two things."

She furrowed her brow. "What would those be, dear?"

"Well, first, you're right about me. Everything you said was true. There's nothing I can do to change what did or didn't happen before Dad died. I realize that now and I'll move on. Two, since you're still here, I want to tell you that you are often as hard-headed as a mule, tough as a boot, and can be a real pain in the ass, but I love you and I'm glad that I'm involved in taking care of you."

A huge smile spread across Aunt Edna's face and she looked at me as if she was going to say something, but nothing came out. Then she threw her head back into the pillow and began to laugh. In the middle of her laughter, she said, "Well, I just wanted to ask you to quit being such a baby and now you've turned it around on me. Well done, Joe, well done!" I was the one who had to laugh now. With the air officially cleared I poured Aunt Edna a drink and we talked until she grew tired.

A few weeks later Edna was admitted to the hospital. Her breathing had become extremely labored and the doctor wanted to keep a close eye on her. I called Mark and asked if I could go see her. He told me afternoons were the best and that I could come down the next day. When I walked into her room, she smiled and said, "Look at me, I must be a sight?"

"I don't know what you're talking about," I said. "You look as pretty as ever!"

"Thanks Joe, but you're a crappy liar."

At that moment Mark walked in, said hello to the two of us and asked his mother, "How are you feeling today?"

"I'd feel better if I had a drink so . . ."

Right then the doctor walked into the room. "Hello Mrs. McAlister, how are we feeling today?"

Edna shifted her eyes towards the doctor. "We? *I* feel like shit, doc. How about you?"

"Sorry to hear that," he said not sure if he should laugh. "I'll see what I can do to make you more comfortable."

Apparently I wasn't the only one she was straight up with! It seems that being politically correct wasn't in her DNA. She told you how she felt and let you have it. For me, there's a comfort in always knowing where you stand with someone, someone who doesn't put a mask over their personality. And her personality was certainly fiery. But I began to appreciate the grace in which she was dealing with her own mortality. I had seen this before and it had always amazed me. Hers was a generation of hardworking individuals who didn't know the meaning of quit. If they wanted something, they put a plan in place to move forward and get it. I love and respect those qualities as much as I loved and respected Aunt Edna.

A conversation started up between Mark, who was standing on the left of Edna's bed, and Edna's doctor, who was on the right. I was sitting at the foot of the bed and watched the conversation like a tennis match, with Aunt Edna trying to get a word in between them.

Mark started off. "Is there any chance Mom can go home in the next day or so?"

The doctor returned the serve. "We'll have to see how she progresses."

"Okay, but do you think it's possible?"

"Maybe."

"Doc, I know you have to hedge a little, but seriously she really wants to go home."

"It's too early to say."

"Okay, but . . . ,"

Edna interrupted. "Dammit Mark, he doesn't want to say, because he doesn't know. Give the guy a break! Now will you please . . ."

"Mom, I'm just watching out for you."

"I know son, but let's take this one day at a time and if I die right here in this hospital then that's okay. Now please . . ."

"Uhhh, okay. Well Doctor, there's something else I wanted to ask you. Mom is used to having a cocktail every night and I think if she could continue doing that it would bring her some comfort. Is it okay if Mom has a drink?"

"Hmm, I don't know, let me think . . . ," the Doctor said rubbing his jaw. "Well, I guess it'd be okay if she had a drink. I can't think of any reason why she shouldn't."

"Okay doc, that's great, I appreciate it. Mom, I'm going to run up to the liquor store down the road. I'll be back in about thirty minutes."

He turned to leave when Edna called out. "You don't have to go anywhere. That's what I've been trying to tell you. I really appreciate all of the attention, but if you men are through talking, will one of you reach into my purse and hand me that bottle of Dewar's I brought with me?"

Mark reached in and pulled out the bottle, holding it up for us to see. The doctor looked amazed by this turn of events so Edna said, "I'm dying doc. I didn't assume it'd feel good so I figured a little swig now and then may help knock the edge off."

As everyone laughed at another Edna-ism, something struck me about her appearance. She looked grey. I'm not a doctor, but I knew this wasn't a good sign. I couldn't help but think it meant the end was probably near. Quite near. The doctor soon excused himself and I went in search of some ice. When I returned, Mark poured some Scotch into paper cups and we all toasted to Aunt Edna's health. I stayed for a while longer, listening to a few great stories about her life.

Two days later Mark called me at the office and said his mother had died. She never did get to go home. Mark thanked me for everything and told me about the plans for her service. I sat there for a moment after we'd hung up. To my surprise, I wasn't sad. Our frank conversations about life and death had somehow prepared me for her passing.

Her service was beautiful and extremely uplifting. Edna was eulogized by her closest family members and the stories they told brought down the house. It seemed that everyone there had a funny, or at least memorable, story. As I left the church Mark ran up and thanked me again for everything. I looked at him and said, "Mark, caring for your mother was one of the great honors of my life. She was a wonderful lady. I know where she is at this very moment and it's a better place than here."

Mark smiled and said, "Yeah, I'll bet right now Dad is sitting at his card game and he's just heard the two scariest words possible . . . *she's here!*"

I am thankful for many things in my life but I am especially thankful that I didn't "screw up" Aunt Edna's case.

16

After being with my company's service for more than four years, Mrs. Harrison, the one whose birthday I forgot and brought flowers to, died at the age of ninety-seven. The case had gone well and I was pleased to hear from the family that they thought my staff had made the end of her life better. Shortly after her death, I ran into her son-in-law at the health club we both belonged to early one morning. Even though we saw each other after our workouts over the years, we'd rarely spoken with each other. Not only did we work out in different parts of the club, but it was his wife who'd taken care of all of her mother's affairs (including our service). I didn't even see him at the funeral. During the rare times that we did run into each other, I never mentioned the case involving his mother-in-law—it seemed inappropriate to me to speak about our cases in public settings. Most of the things we talked about during our few conversations were trivial, such as the weather or sports. He was nice enough and we weren't solving any of the world's problems, just having casual conversations. That's as far as our relationship had gotten.

I gave him my usual greeting and received the same friendly reply. Then I thought I'd offer my condolences. Her obituary had been in the paper and several of the other members of the club had already told him how sorry they were about her death, so I felt more comfortable speaking openly to him about her. His reaction to my statement of sympathy surprised me a great deal. He was Italian and since I have no interest in revealing his real name, I'll call him Mr. Avido. Here's how it went:

"Mr. Avido I want you to know that I'm sorry for your loss. I attended the funeral of your mother-in-law. She was a lovely lady and she will be missed."

Mr. Avido tilted his head to one side, "You knew my mother-in-law? How did you know her?"

Smiling, I said, "Well, I own the home care company that provided help to her over the last several years. I looked for you at the funeral but . . ."

Instantly his face darkened. "You mean that you own the company that provided those people that were in her house all that time?"

Still smiling a little less enthusiastically, I said, "Yes sir."

Mr. Avido stepped away from me. "I think you're despicable! You take advantage of people in their weakest moments! I'm disgusted to learn this."

Not smiling, I said, "Uh, sorry but keep in mind that my company offers a private service. Your wife called me about providing care for her mother. I've never forced my company's services on anyone."

Mr. Avido began pointing at me as spit formed at the corners of his mouth. "That doesn't matter! You're a bottom feeder. When people are at their most fragile moment, you sweep in and make your money off their pain and suffering."

Holding my hands up, I replied, "Sir, I don't think you understand. I'm not an ambulance chaser. My company offers a service for people who wish to have help for themselves or their loved ones. It's not mandatory. In fact, many families choose to handle situations like your mother-in-law's themselves and not use a service like mine. That's their prerogative."

Mr. Avido's engines were lit and blast off was seconds away. "What are you saying? That we should've taken care of her ourselves? That we are bad people because we didn't do this? Is that what you're saying?"

I lowered my hands and began to get agitated myself. "Mr. Avido, I'm not saying that your family did anything wrong at all. I'm simply defending what I do for a living. We provide a service for those who wish to utilize it. I believe your family did a great job caring for your mother-in-law. She received around-the-clock care during her last years. Your family committed substantial resources to make sure she was well-cared for and as comfortable as possible."

"Yes," he said with and evil smirk. "And you made a heap of money from her failing condition, didn't you?"

I nodded. "Yes, I do need to make money in order to stay in business."

Pointing again, he said, "Then that makes you despicable!"

"What about her doctors?" I asked.

"What about them?"

"They made money from her failing condition. Are they despicable too?"

"That's different."

"Why?"

"Because they're highly educated and they must be paid for their services."

I decided it was time to jump off this crazy train, so I started looking for an exit. "Sir, I respect your opinion, but the reality is that everyone needs to make a living no matter how highly educated or completely uneducated they are. If you don't mind me asking, what do you do for a living?"

He pointed to himself with pride. "I'm an attorney."

"What?" I said laughing hard. "You guys invented making money off pain and suffering. Aren't attorneys the ones 'ambulance chaser' refers too? Ha Ha Ha Ha . . ."

Mr. Avido moved in closer, as if for some physical contact. "How dare you laugh at me."

I was still laughing as I said, "Have a nice workout, sir." I walked away, not sure if he was going to come after me. Fortunately, he didn't.

As I drove away, I wondered if we simply had had a cultural difference or if we had unexpectedly depleted some of the assets he was planning to get his hands on. When presented with a legal injustice, I wonder if Mr. Avido simply jumped in to help with no regard for how he would be paid? I doubt, it since the health cub we belonged to didn't take I.O.U.'s.

Almost all of our clients wanted us to provide home care in their home. However, home care can take place anywhere the elderly live: hospitals, nursing homes, and even assisted living centers. One of our patients, Harold Smith, was residing in an assisted living community near my health club, so after my workout, I decided to stop in for visit with him and see how he was getting along.

As I walked into the facility, there was a large commotion going on in the common area. I couldn't tell what it was about and was about to walk past it when I heard my name called out. "Well Mr. Smith, there's the owner of the company, so why don't you take it up with him."

I stopped and looked at the director of the facility, who was now pointing at me. Mr. Smith turned and began to stare a hole through me. Seeing how tense everyone was, I began in a tone that I hoped would diffuse the situation. "Hello Mr. Smith, how are you doing? Would you like to . . ."

He cut me off in midsentence. "Who authorized *you* to send *your* people into my room?"

I shook my head trying to understand what he was saying. "Gosh, I'm not sure." Seeing the director, who was a friend of mine, motion for me to come with him, I added, "Let me discuss this with the director and get back with you. Okay?"

He was still fuming as I walked away to the director's office. "Cesar, what did I just step into?"

Cesar chuckled. "Just another normal problem in the life of caring for the elderly. Here's what happened. Mr. Smith's daughter called your agency yesterday and wanted someone to check on him during the night. Your caregiver knocked on his door twice, then walked in to find Ms. Leggett on top of him in bed. Your caregiver quickly excused herself, backed out and closed the door. Mr. Smith stormed out of his room—after dressing I presume—and found the night manager, demanding an explanation for the intrusion. I'd already gone home for the day, so he wasn't able to let me have it until this morning. And you just happened to walk straight into it. How's that for good timing?"

I shook my head, chuckling. "Yeah, and apparently we had good timing last night, too. We're the *good timing* company."

"That's right, and Mr. Smith is just looking for a good time. That's makes him a perfect fit for your company."

"Thanks. I guess we made the mess, so we have to clean it up."

Cesar followed me back out to the common area and I stood directly in front of Mr. Smith looking as sincere as I could. "Mr. Smith, I'm very sorry for what happened and I take full responsibility for the intrusion. Your daughter called and had instructed us to check on you at night. We were just doing what she wanted."

"Oh yeah? What about what *I* want?!" he said loudly.

Frankly, he had a point, even though his daughter was his power of attorney. I was just about to say something when his lady friend spoke up. "You know, I wasn't going to let him go all the way."

I was processing what this statement entailed and trying not to visualize its full ramifications when Mr. Smith, who'd now been inadvertently redirected, said, "What do I have to do before you'll go all the way?"

She looked at him as if the answer were obvious. "Marry me, of course."

They were married the next day in the activities room of the assisted living center.

Unfortunately, I wasn't invited to the service. But, I did begin regular visits with a now far more agreeable man. He actually began to be a bright spot for me, especially since he was a twenty-year veteran of the Navy and told me many stories of his days as an airplane mechanic during both WW II and the Korean War. He was a great man and it saddened me when Mr. Smith's health finally took a turn for the worst.

Sarah went to see him one day and called me from the facility to say that he was in bad shape. It seemed that all of the minor issues he'd been dealing with had suddenly became major issues and his time was drawing near. Prior to this downturn, his family paid us privately for intermittent custodial care, but now he would need insurance to help pay the bills. In Mr. Smith's case, he'd paid for health insurance from a large, reputable company for years and now he needed that coverage to pay for my company's clinical services.

Getting paid by insurance companies for services rendered can sometimes be a challenge in the world of health care. Private pay clients are usually pretty reliable, since they simply cut a check and mail it to you. Insurance companies, on the other hand, can sometimes be so difficult, that it can threaten a business financially. They're like casinos or bookies—they like taking your money, but when the bet goes the wrong way and it's time to pay, it gets hard for them to let loose of the chips. To prevent this, we called to pre-authorize Mr. Smith's care and gave the insurance company the bare minimum of what we'd have to charge. They tried to negotiate with us, but we didn't budge (mainly because we couldn't). Eventually, they agreed. After all, we *are* cheaper than a hospital or long term care facility.

Once we had approval, we oriented our staff for Mr. Smith's care. We made it abundantly clear to them that their clinical paperwork needed to flawless for the insurance company. We knew we needed to be very thorough regarding all of their requirements so there would be no unnecessary delay in receiving our payments. This case was going to cost us a lot of money long before the insurance company began paying us.

We started the care and of course, it was expensive. Mr. Smith required a lot of services and around-the-clock attention as we tried to make him as comfortable as possible. Forty-five days passed without payment from the insurance company. This was right on the limit of acceptable. When we reached the sixty-day mark and there was still no payment, I knew we were in trouble.

We made numerous calls to the insurance company, which of course resulted in multiple promises of payment, but none ever came. When we questioned their intent to pay, they assured us they wanted to pay, but insisted we'd submitted our claims on the wrong forms. Of course. they were the forms they had given to us to use, but still, we redid all the claims on the new forms and had these new submissions sent via FedEx to the insurance company. After a few days of runaround, they told us that they'd never received the claims. FedEx had the name of the person who had signed for the claims, but we were told that that person didn't work for the insurance company.

This type of back and forth went on for weeks until we were finally forced to give Mr. Smith's family a five-day notice of discharge due to non-payment of all claims. Mr. Smith was despondent when he heard the news, so I went to go see him myself to explain what was going on. He didn't blame me for the problem with his insurance company, but I still felt horrible about letting down my friend. Without the care we were providing, he'd be forced to go back into the hospital. If this happened it was going to be bad for the patient and (surprise) very bad for the insurance company because of the massive increase in cost.

When I began to look at the financial hit I was facing, I went to talk to my mentor and investor Tom Terry. He was sympathetic and just as frustrated. We game-planned some alternative actions and just before I left, he said, "Joe, you can do this. Never quit!"

It was a sad state of affairs for everyone involved. After talking with Tom, I asked the family to place a call to the insurance company and see if they could convince them to stop giving us the runaround and pay us for the services we'd provided. They placed a number of calls to the insurance company, but received the same treatment that we did. And calling that place was a nightmare. Every caller would have to navigate a complicated automated system, eventually being routed to the customer service department. Once the system determined the caller actually wanted to speak with a person, the caller was placed on hold for at least thirty minutes. When an operator finally appeared, the caller would have to educate the customer service rep on every little detail that had occurred since the case began. This process took at least ten minutes, at which time the customer service rep would place the caller on hold while they went and researched the claims. If they came back on the line (which was a big if, since half the time they released the call), they'd tell the caller they would have to put a request in to have the case reviewed and a supervisor would call them back within a week. Between our office and the family, we must have logged at least twenty-five to thirty requests, but never received one callback from a supervisor. It was terrible.

Four days into the five-day discharge notice, Mr. Smith's daughter showed up at our offices and asked to speak with me. I sat across from her for thirty minutes while she sobbed uncontrollably and begged me not to discharge her father. She knew if he were placed in the hospital, he'd lose the will to live. To her, she was twenty-four hours from losing her father. I knew she was right, but I also knew I was close to going out of business.

Finally I'd had enough. We'd done everything we'd been asked to do and yet were getting nowhere. I decided to go straight to the top. I wrote a blistering letter to the CEO of the insurance company and told him what had transpired. In the letter I informed him that if the issue wasn't resolved in its entirety within twenty-four hours, I was going to alert the state board of insurance and the media about his company's complete disregard for one of their very sick beneficiaries and for their fiscal responsibilities.

I signed the letter and I faxed it to his office. Within an hour, I received a call from the man's secretary. She said that the CEO was very concerned about this issue and was looking into it personally. Within an hour after that first call, she called me back and said that a check for all services rendered to date would be waiting for me at the security desk of their building in Dallas at 10:00 a.m. the next morning. The total amount of the check was over one hundred thousand dollars. The next morning the check was there. After that, checks arrived at our office every two weeks like clockwork. I was underwhelmed that the CEO had not called me himself. It was his company and I think he should have stepped up and made the call, but nevertheless I was happy we could continue helping my friend.

I went back to see Mr. Smith and he was as chipper as he'd been since he got married. He said, "I don't know what you did, but I'm very thankful you did it."

Harold Smith lived another six months before succumbing to his ailments. At his funeral, my company was personally thanked in front of the congregation. As I listened to his daughter speak, eulogizing her father, I thought about what we had gone through with that insurance company.

Even though we had eventually figured out how to get paid, we'd put a lot of unnecessary stress on Mr. Smith in the process. It occurred to me that caring for the elderly certainly can have its challenges.

The day after Mr. Smith's funeral, I was about to call Tom and to take him to lunch when a call came in from his son. "Mike, what's happening buddy? It's good to hear from you."

"Joe, it's Dad. An hour ago he was diagnosed with brain cancer. He's having surgery tomorrow morning. The doctors say there's no time to wait. They have to go in and try to remove the tumor right away. He may not make it."

I almost dropped the phone. "What?! Oh God no! Can I come see him?"

"Not now, just pray. I'll call and let you know what happens."

Mike said they would know more a few days after the surgery, but the doctors were being very guarded with their prognosis. We talked for a few more minutes before he had to attend to some last minute details.

When I hung up the phone, I felt like I'd just been punched in the gut. Tom was more than just a mentor, he was the closest thing I now had to a Dad. He'd worked very hard and achieved a great deal. And he gave back so much to people like me, people he thought needed to be pointed in the right direction. When I had serious problems, he was the one I turned to, the voice of reason when the walls seemed to be closing in on me. Sometimes I just needed a mature friend to listen and tell me everything was going to be okay. I can't count the times Tom had snapped me out of a funk with his common sense advice on life. He was levelheaded and sincere and I trusted him completely.

I stayed in touch with the Mike during the surgery, but stayed out of the way so the family could have time to grasp the situation. The Terry's had already lost their daughter, Erika, to cancer in 1997. She was only 35. Before her death, Erika had become quite a celebrity by writing a book about the process of dying and even appeared on several talk shows to discuss her fight with cancer. When she died, her death had been widely reported. Although this wasn't a new fight for the Terry's, it was their leader who now needed help. I prayed Tom would make it through it all.

Two days after surgery word came back that, while they had been able to remove a good bit of the tumor, they hadn't been able to get it all. The surgery had lengthened his life by only a handful of months - he was terminal. I waited a few days for the shock of the news to have abated with the family and for Tom to have some time to recover from the surgery before visiting. When I finally went by the house to see him, he was wearing one of those surgical socks over his head to hide the scar that had been left by the surgery, but otherwise seemed as chipper as ever.

He immediately did what every great communicator I've ever known does: he began asking me about my life. Despite all that had just happened to him, he wasn't going to allow the conversation to center around him. It wasn't his way. He launched into a barrage of questions about my company, my family and about all other aspects of my life. As usual, I felt as if the universe revolved around me and the questions he was asking were of real interest to him. In the middle of our conversation, he asked me a question that took me off guard. "Hey Joe, have you been to see your father lately?" Seeing the look on my face, he followed up with, "I mean his grave. They didn't remove my whole brain."

I smiled and said, "I'd love to, but we buried him in Connecticut and I haven't been there in a while."

He nodded and said, "Go see him, Joe. It might sound crazy, but go see him. Don't take anyone with you, just go and sit and talk to him about things. I did that when I lost my own father and I've done it lots of times with Erika. It helps." I didn't know where this was coming from, but I assume that, like Aunt Edna, he knew I'd had a hard time coping with my father's loss, even after all of these years.

After an awkward silence, I worked in a question of my own, "How are you?"

He stretched a grin across his face and pointed to his head. "It's nothing but a small bump in the road. Nothing to be worried about."

I loved witnessing his spirit, how, even in the face of brain cancer, he could be so remarkably upbeat and positive. At that moment I was overcome by a wave of optimism and it occurred to me that if anyone could beat the odds then surely this was the guy.

However, a few months later, Tom began to decline. Slowly at first, then more rapidly as the cancer began spreading throughout his brain. His family rallied and tried to care for him, but eventually it became too much. That's when they called me.

His wife Loraine was also a wonderful person and I was amazed to witness the stoic dignity and grace in which she was handling this situation. We met so she could explain what her husband was currently going through so that I could better understand what type of care he needed. At one point she stopped and asked, "Joe, have you ever thought about the circle of life?"

A little surprised I asked, "What do you mean?"

"Well," she said, "he helps you get established in the business world. He invests with you and helps you start a company that takes care of people in their time of need and then you take that knowledge and that company and you take care of him in his time of need."

I thought about it for a moment before saying, "Yes ma'am, I guess so, but I've never been this sad about signing up a new patient."

"Sad would be not having someone like you to care for him until the end." I gotta tell you, the Terry's sure had a way with words.

We admitted Tom the next day. He was deteriorating very quickly, so I asked Mrs. Terry if I could come by to see him. She said that would be fine, so we scheduled a visit for the next afternoon. He was very weak, but as usual, his spirits were high. I sat on the side of his bed as Tom started in with his usual questions about me, which I succinctly answered. Then I said, "Can I ask you a question?"

Tom stopped, looked at me, and said, "Of course, Joe, you know you can ask me anything."

"I want to know about you and your success in life. Every time we talk it's always about me and how I can do better. I've learned so much from you, but you've never told me any stories from your own past. Tell me about your success."

"Alright," Tom said. He stared at the ceiling for a few seconds before launching into a story.

"When I began working at Ford in 1963, I was placed on a new project headed up by Lee Iacocca and Carol Shelby. My job was public relations. We worked tirelessly for months on that project, before it was ready to be introduced to the public. That project was the new Ford Mustang. We were all quite proud of that car and wanted it to make a big splash, so I suggested we introduce it in the spring of 1964 instead of at the end of the year as is customary in the auto industry. The result was that we had one of the most dynamic releases in automotive history, all because we thought outside of the box. Lee wanted to give me a lot of credit for that idea, but I wouldn't have it. I told him, "Lee, you and the boys designed one hell of a car and the people love it. That it was my idea to show it to them in the spring instead of the fall matters not a whit. The point is that we came together as a team and together we succeeded.

"You see, Joe, very few people are successful solely because of their own actions. I believe that anyone can be a success as long as they don't care who gets the credit. My success has always come from working together with others. You haven't heard me speak much about my past successes, because I don't think of them as mine and mine alone. For me to tell you about something that I did and couch it as my success would, to me, be a little misleading. Does that make sense to you?"

"Yes," I said, chuckling. "And you've just told me more in fewer words that many people have told me after hours of conversation."

"Good," Tom said. "Brevity is sometimes important. But now I've got to tell you Joe, you've turned out to be a fine young man."

I gazed at Tom and said, "If that's true, then I'm giving you some credit whether you like it or not."

This brought a large smile to his face. "Okay, just this once I'll accept it." Then he patted my leg and laid his head down to rest.

I sat for a moment staring down at him as he appeared to fall asleep, then suddenly he opened his eyes and looked at me. Without lifting his head from the pillow he said, "Do you get it yet?"

"What do you mean?" I said confused.

"Your father."

"What about him?" I asked.

"He meant a great deal to you and since his death you've spent a lot of time agonizing over his loss. The thing is, he's never actually been gone. His energy and influence have been channeled through all of the people who've guided you and given you inspiration these last few years. That's why I told you to stay close to your patients and it's why God has tested you—He's made you appreciate us more. As long as you continue to seek the counsel of others like us, your father will never truly be gone. You have many fathers, Joe. You've had us all along and when one dies another will take his place. It's up to you to find them. You've done a great job so far."

With that Tom closed his eyes and began dozing. I wiped my eyes as the impact of his words hit me. Then I stood up and quietly left the room.

A week later I stopped by for another visit, but by this time he was unconscious and in a coma. I took the opportunity to hold his hand and thank him for all he had done for me. I don't know if he could hear me, but it made me feel better to say 'thanks' one more time.

He died the next day.

Sarah came into my office with tears in her eyes and closed the door, knowing how the news would hit me. And yes, it hit hard. Very hard. Tom Terry, like his daughter before him, was too young to die. He was only sixty-nine years old.

17

After losing Tom, I spent a lot of time thinking about where I was and what I'd do next. I was used to talking with one of my father figures when I was restless like this, but I currently didn't have any handy. I needed something, but I wasn't sure what it was. Then it hit me. After my wife and the kids were in bed, I went to my dresser drawer and found the second letter my father had left for me. Quietly I made my way to our back porch and looked out at the night sky, which was filled with stars. I clicked on a dim overhead light, one bright enough to read by, but otherwise still bathing me in darkness. Holding the envelope up to the light, I saw the word 'Faith' scrawled on the outside. I opened it up, pulled out the letter, and began to read.

Dear Joe,

In the spring of '45 I was assigned the task of escorting a damaged torpedo bomber to Luzon for maintenance. The plane could fly okay, but it needed a major overhaul on its weapons systems, which had been damaged on one of its previous flights. The maintenance facility on Luzon was more comprehensive than what was available on the carrier, so that's where we took planes that needed extensive repairs. Although we rarely saw Japs in this controlled area, the Navy was still skittish about sending a plane that couldn't defend itself out alone, so my job was to make sure it made it to the island in one piece.

We took off in the morning and the flight to Luzon was uneventful. The plan was for me to wait with the plane and its pilot until the repairs were finished and then fly back together the next day. While we were waiting, a call came in from the carrier that there were reports of enemy activity in the area, and I was asked to cut my stay short and head back to the Ticonderoga. The captain wanted all available planes to be ready in case there was any trouble. It was 4 p.m. when I took off for the two and a half hour flight back. I settled in at a fairly high altitude and was cruising without incident when the carrier radioed me to say they believed my course would take me right by a Japanese destroyer. A spotter plane had seen what they thought was a destroyer, but they'd been low on fuel so it had been ordered back to base before they could confirm the sighting. And now I was scheduled to fly right by the location in question.

I lowered my altitude and flew towards the coordinates I'd been given. The spotter plane had been correct about the type of ship, but incorrect about its location and heading. Based on what I'd been told, my plan had been to pop out of the clouds a safe distance away, identify it quickly, and then call it in. But when I came out of the clouds I found myself right on top of the Jap ship. They'd heard me coming and before I knew it I was being pounded by their antiaircraft guns. The shells were showering me with flak, so I shot back up into the clouds and confirmed the sighting with the Ticonderoga. I kept getting hammered as I got the heck out of there.

Once I was out of harm's way, I assessed my plane. In no time it was clear that my Corsair had sustained extensive damage. There was a hole in my right wing, a small amount of smoke coming from the engine and some type of rear stabilizer damage. I couldn't see the stabilizer, but I assumed it was damaged because my plane was now noticeably more difficult to fly. The engine smoke was my primary concern, though. It didn't sound any different, but I knew if I didn't land soon I was going to be in trouble.

Since I was beyond the halfway point, I decided to continue on to the carrier. That was the closest place to land and I certainly wanted to land that damaged plane as quickly as possible. Still, not knowing what was wrong with the engine, I had to back off the throttle so it wouldn't have to work so hard. When I radioed the Ticonderoga to report my problem I received no reply. I tried again to no avail. It was then I realized that my radio had been damaged after my last transmission.

With no way to communicate, it became even more important that I get to the ship as soon as I possibly could. The sun was low in the sky, but at my current speed I figured I should be able to safely get back and land before dark. I continued on my course to the location of the Ticonderoga and when I arrived, I was amazed my plane was still in one piece. There was only one problem: the carrier wasn't there. I did one wide turn over the last known location, hoping it had just moved a couple of miles away, but there was no sight of the big ship. After a quick assessment of the situation I realized that now, on top of the damaged airplane, I had a fuel problem as well. I wasn't running on fumes yet, but I had no idea where the ship was and conducting a proper search for it would require more fuel than I currently had.

I kicked myself for choosing to continue on to the carrier. Using hindsight, I now knew that if I'd turned around I'd be close to approaching the coastline of Luzon. Even if I couldn't have made it all the way back to the base, at least I could've ditched the plane and walked home on dry land. Instead, I was in the middle of the South Pacific in a damaged plane that was low on fuel with no place to land and no way to find my ship.

If fuel hadn't been a problem, I would've simply continued making wider and wider circles over the last known location of the Ticonderoga, but in my current predicament I didn't have that luxury. I thought about all that had happened since I'd received the radio call on Luzon and decided that my only option was to make an educated guess of the carrier's location.

I assumed the carrier would be maneuvering itself for an attack against the Japanese destroyer. If this were the case, then my next assumption was that the captain would steer the ship southwest of its previous location. I was basing this guess on the fact that the captain would want to get closer to Luzon, so that our ship-based air force could be complimented by other aircraft located at our base on the island. I also assumed that the captain would want to cut off any attempted retreat back to mainland Japan, since the Japanese captain now knew he had been spotted. If I was wrong, I'd eventually have to ditch into the Pacific at night, which was tricky indeed. On top of that, no one would have the slightest idea where I was, a fact that would be most likely fatal.

All I could see for miles and miles in any direction was water, so I set my course, then did the only thing I could do under the circumstances: I prayed. Before long it was completely dark. I couldn't see anything in any direction except east, where a sliver of moon was rising. Flying along in total darkness with almost no fuel in a damaged plane and not even sure if I was flying in the right direction was one of the most frightening experiences I'd ever had. Never in my life have I ever felt so vulnerable. As the minutes ticked away, I continued praying that I would see the Ticonderoga. And I continued to see nothing.

Now my fuel situation was a big problem. I'd had other situations where I'd been low on fuel, but I'd never pushed my luck more than at that moment. Approximately one and a half hours after I began my search for the Ticonderoga I looked down and saw that my fuel gage was dead empty. Having no previous experience in a situation like this, I didn't know if that meant I had five more minutes or half an hour. Lowering my air speed had certainly bought me some time, but I was now to the point that if I didn't see the carrier soon I was going to have to ditch.

I was scared. I was really scared.

Even so, at one point I remember looking down at my empty gauge and then looking up through the canopy at the beautiful, clear night sky. There were so many stars overhead and the sliver of moon over my shoulder, and I thought how blessed I was to witness something so beautiful. While I looked up at the amazing night sky, I told God I would respect whatever path he had planned out for me. When I finished my prayer, I looked from the brightly lit night sky back down towards the black ocean hoping to see something that would reveal a ship. But there was still a whole lot of nothing.

Then something caught my eye on the left side of the plane. It was a very subtle change in the ocean's surface and it was illuminated by that tiny sliver of a moon, which was now almost directly behind me. I carefully altered my course to the south so I could use the moon's light to see a little better. When I did this the anomaly became clearer to me; it definitely appeared to be a ship's wake.

I was hoping beyond hope that it was Ticonderoga and I changed my course to head straight towards whatever ship was making the wake. I then began fiddling with my constant wave radio hoping that my rusty Morse code would be adequate enough to let the ship know I was an American who desperately needed to land. CW radio was a low frequency device that was separate from the plane's main radio. It was not strong enough to carry voice communications, and was only really good for sending simple codes, but it was better than nothing.

I began sending a signal that said:

SOS. Stop. MA.5. Stop. SOS. Stop. Lynch. Stop. SOS. Stop. Must Land. Stop. SOS

I sent some variation of this message as many times as I could while I flew towards the ship I hoped was my aircraft carrier and not the enemy. I would've typically used my call sign, Big Swede, for communications with the carrier, but I knew if they saw I was using my identifier, that would mean this situation was anything but typical. MA.5 was my plane's identifier while I was in it. Any plane I flew was identified by the Navy as Maltress Angelo .5, so this was another way to alert them it was me and not some Jap kamikaze trying to trick them.

When I thought I should be close enough to see the carrier, I steered my plane just a bit out to the south so that I could once again use the moonlight to my advantage and hopefully get a visual of the ship. When I did, I saw a sight that was as beautiful as anything I'd ever seen. There before me was a huge ship that could only be an aircraft carrier. I didn't have a clear view of it, but the outline was clear enough. Since it was now around 8 p.m. I knew the deck would be clear. Back in those days the only flight operations that commenced in darkness were takeoffs in the predawn hours. It was extremely rare to land any plane on a carrier at night. The only time it ever happened was at times like this, an emergency.

As I repositioned the plane to align it with the short carrier runway, I said one more prayer, sent one more SOS call, then began preparing for a very rough landing. If the Ticonderoga didn't believe that I was who I said I was, my plane would be shot from the sky at any moment. Since I could send a signal, but not receive one, I had to assume they believed me and just hope for the best. I did have one thing going for me and that was the moon—it was directly behind me. This was good because anyone looking through binoculars at my plane would be able to clearly distinguish the distinctive gull wing design on my corsair. I wasn't worried about hitting a sailor out for a nighttime walk on the deck, because by now the whole ship knew I was coming even if they didn't know who I was.

At about a half mile out I received confirmation they did indeed believe I was one of the good guys. I saw they had turned on the ship's dustpan lights around the edge of the deck. I could also see a very dim set of centerline red lights running down the runway. These two beacons were my only point of reference. During a typical daytime landing there would've been a signalman with colored paddles directing me in, but since it was nighttime I was on my own.

It had been twenty minutes since my fuel gage had registered empty. I hadn't been thinking of my fuel situation in the last few minutes as I prepared to land, but it shot to the front of my mind when my engine sputtered for the first time a quarter mile out. How cruel would it be, I thought, to have made such a gamble and won, only to crash into the ocean a few hundred feet behind the carrier. I raised my altitude just a little higher to compensate for the fuel situation. I figured if the plane died, then at least I may have the ability to glide in the last little bit.

At around two hundred yards out the engine sputtered again, but by this point I knew I wasn't going to come up short. The real problem now that I was close enough to clearly see the ship, was that I was way too high. If I didn't correct immediately, I could overshoot the runway altogether. I had been through way too much to fail now. As I could plainly see the edge of the carrier's deck, I quickly cut the engine then made a dramatic adjustment to my altitude. The resulting nose-first landing caused my plane to hit the deck hard and I lost all control. The wing that had been shot up broke off and the plane slid sideways into the metal netting that had been erected to catch out-of-control planes like mine.

The ground crew opened my hatch and began frantically trying to release my harnesses to extract me from the broken plane, but I was dazed. I remember looking at one young sailor and telling him, "Don't worry about a fire, she doesn't have a drop of fuel left in her." Then I chuckled, thinking that I had said something really funny.

Once out of the cockpit, the sailors put me down on the deck away from the plane until I could be taken to the ship's infirmary. There in the cool night air the cobwebs began to recede. They ran me down to sickbay where the docs determined I was perfectly fine except for being tired, hungry, and a little shaken by my rough landing. When they were done with me I was allowed to leave and get some food.

As I walked into the cafeteria, I was greeted by the commanding officer, "Hello Vince. The Doc said I would find you here. How are you feeling?"

"I'm fine sir, thank you, but it's been a long day."

"I'm sure it has. You know you're damned lucky to find us with no working radio."

"Yes sir, I know. I prayed a lot up there. If I hadn't found you when I did I would've had to ditch due to lack of fuel."

"Someone was watching out for you tonight, that's for sure. It looks like your prayers were answered."

The CO looked at me for a moment longer then said, "Something else kept you alive. That plane should've fallen apart underneath you a long time ago with the damage you sustained. I don't know what kept that thing in the air. Why don't you grab something to eat then head up to the deck so you can give her a proper send off."

I was confused. "Send off, sir?"

"It's damaged beyond repair. We're going to push it over the edge and give it a proper Navy burial."

I felt a genuine sense of loss at this news. The captain had been right, that plane had served me well and I owed that war machine and the people who made it my thanks.

When I made my way back to the deck, I saw the deck hands were maneuvering the plane onto a series of dollies that would be used to move it to the edge. I looked at the plane and saw for the first time that the rear stabilizer was almost completely gone. It had been blown apart by the Japanese anti-aircraft guns and was hanging together by a few very small pieces of metal. I didn't know how it had stayed together for as long as it did, but I now knew exactly what the captain had been talking about when he said the plane had saved my life.

When the sailors had the plane positioned correctly, they began pushing her to the edge and started cranking on a large jack. Suddenly, I was struck by the moment and I screamed. "Stop"!

The men all stopped what they were doing and looked at me, curiously. I looked back at them and said, "Sorry guys, but will you give me a minute?"

The chief in charge of the project seemed to understand what was happening and said, "Take five, boys."

The men walked away looking somewhat bemused. Then I approached the plane and stood next to her for a moment. I touched the outer skin and admired her as she shined in the moonlight. Then I said one more prayer while looking upward at that beautiful night sky—a prayer of thanks. I think I was thanking God, the plane, the workers who built the plane and anyone else who had a part in allowing me to safely land on that ship. Then, one last time, I patted the plane as if she were a wounded thoroughbred that was about to be put down.

The men had a job to do, so I motioned to the chief to carry on. As he approached me he said, "I know how you feel, lieutenant. It's hard to say goodbye to an old friend, isn't it?"

I smiled and said, "Yes it is, especially one who just saved your ass the way this one did mine."

He smiled back, turned to his men and said, "Get on that jack and let's get this done!"

I watched as the plane groaned and then slid over the side of the Ticonderoga, splashing into the ocean. Then we all stood there waiting for the ship's forward progress to bring it beyond the plane so that we could see her sink. As the ship passed by and we had a clear view of my corsair, we could see the plane had already sunk up to the cockpit and her damaged tail was sticking up into the air. It almost looked like the plane was giving us one final salute. In the spur of the moment I snapped to attention and saluted the plane as she slid below the waves. Since I was the only commissioned officer standing there, all of the non-commissioned officers followed suit. And there we stood, one officer and twelve enlisted men saluting an airplane—my airplane, as she sank in the deep water of the South Pacific. That must have been a sight to see.

I had no right surviving that ordeal. The only reason I lived to write you this letter is that God had a plan for me. I had faith that night and you should always have faith as well. God does have a plan and as mere mortals we have no idea what it is, so we just have to trust Him. Maybe the plan He had for me involved fathering you kids or maybe there was another reason He spared me that night, but whatever the reason, I've tried my best to live honorably. Please remember this story and know that no matter how tough your life becomes, there is a plan for you and if you have faith you will be rewarded.

I was rewarded with you, your brothers and your sister. My life is complete.

Love, Dad

I clicked off the light and sat there for a while, reflecting on what I'd just read. I tried to imagine the fear my father had felt that night. Then I thought of what I'd been through, once again comparing my life to his. If my father could have faith in a situation like that, then I could learn to have more faith in dealing with his loss, the loss of Tom and all of the other fathers who had provided me with so much knowledge and inspiration. Sure, I'd had a few challenges in my career, but having those amazing people to offset the challenges had provided my life with balance. Caring for them must've been part of God's plan for me.

It suddenly became clear. Yes, I had lost many people who had meant a lot to me, but there would be other mentors, there would *always* be others. I just needed to find them. And then, God willing, one day I'll be a mentor. And then I'll go. This is the process that binds all generations...the real circle of life.

In that moment of clarity I realized that I had done it—I had finally found Dad, and a lot more.

Then, just like he had done all those years ago when he was lost in the South Pacific, I looked up to the beautiful stars above and I said a simple prayer of thanks.

Epilogue

Two months later I was in New York for a business meeting, so I carved out a few hours one afternoon for a long overdue trip. I hadn't forgotten Tom's advice and desperately wanted to have that chat with Dad.

When I arrived at the cemetery, it took me only moments to reach the gravestone, sit down next to it and begin talking. It was a little awkward at first, but when I found my groove I really opened up and let it all go. I talked to Dad in a way that I had never been able to when he was alive. First, I told him that I loved him and that I missed him a great deal. Then I told him about his beautiful grandchildren and about all that had gone right and wrong in my life since he'd left. I sat there on that sunny day and I talked and talked for two hours. It was the most natural thing I'd ever done. And as usual, Tom was right again. I felt so much better getting my feelings out, even if I was only talking to a gravestone.

As I was wrapping up, I heard the low grumble of a piston engine airplane flying overhead. Unlike my father, I couldn't determine the type of plane just by hearing its engine, but I thought it sounded exactly like a World War II fighter plane. The cemetery was located in a heavily treed lot, so it was difficult to see much of the sky, and even though I craned my neck looking upward, I still couldn't see the plane. It was most likely from a local air show or perhaps a collector out for a joyride. But who knows? Maybe there was another possibility . . . perhaps it was my dad taking his heavenly corsair out for one more spin. That's how I chose to think about it, anyway. I stopped looking for the plane and lay down on the cool grass.

Closing my eyes, I imagined Dad sitting in that cockpit and flying for the sheer joy of flying. In my mind's eye he had a huge smile on his face and was laughing his slow, infectious laugh.

I smiled at the image painted so clearly in my mind and then I said to him, "Have a great flight Dad."

Afterward

M y father was not without his demons, but he was a good man and he taught me a lot. His stories helped teach me to respect the accomplishments of those that came before me. My profession allowed me to come face to face with a good many more people like him and that further enhanced my respect for his generation.

I loved the time I spent face to face with these remarkable people but after twenty-four years the grind caught up with me and I decided it was time to sell my business. Home care at the operational level can be extremely taxing. On top of the usual issues, a business owner must continually scale the mountainous regulatory side, which has become overly burdensome for small operators. Once committed to the decision to sell, I hoped the process would move quickly. It did not. A buyer popped up right away but the process took a year and a half—one year longer than it should have. The endless delays were very frustrating. I couldn't understand why it was taking so long.

Then one day, I received another gut wrenching call from my friend Mike Terry. This time he was calling to tell me that his mother Lorraine had been diagnosed with esophageal cancer. Like her husband Tom (my second father and mentor) and daughter before her, she had been told that her condition was terminal and to prepare for the worst. I was floored. Why was such a good family being put through so much pain and heartache? I was beside myself and simply didn't know what to say except, "What can I do?"

Mike said that his mother wanted to meet with me to discuss admitting her to our service so we set a time for the following Saturday morning. When I arrived Lorraine was all smiles. She hugged and thanked me profusely for coming over on a Saturday. We sat down and she began asking me about everything that was going on in my life. She wanted to know about my kids, my wife, my job, my dogs and even my golf game. Sound familiar? When there was a break in the conversation I said, "So Mrs. Terry, how do you feel?"

For the first time since I had arrived I saw the slightest bit of angst on her face, but only for a moment. Then she said, "I am fine, but pretty soon I'm going to need some help so let's talk about what that looks like."

When her husband was going through the end stages of his life I had been amazed at how strong she had been. Now I was witnessing that same dignity as she dealt with the final act of her own life. We discussed how the process would work, then she peppered me with questions. Of course she remembered how things had gone when we took care of Tom but on top of that she had done research on the subject so that she could be as prepared as possible for our meeting. She said she didn't know when we would be needed but wanted to go ahead and schedule the admission for the following week.

Unfortunately, we began care almost immediately as Mrs. Terry's condition quickly began to deteriorate. Within two months she was gone. Once again I found myself sitting in a church listening while someone who had meant a great deal to me was eulogized. Loraine Terry was special. She was beautiful and she was strong. I knew all of this already but hearing it in that church caused me to think about my personal relationship with her and what she and her husband had meant to me. I guess that is the purpose of a funeral service like that—to pray for the soul of the departed and to remember. I did remember and I always will.

I also thought about my personal situation. It had been well over a year since we'd agreed to sell our company to a buyer who was capable of writing a check anytime, ending the monotony of our never-ending transaction. Then something occurred to me. As Tom had so eloquently pointed out, there was a reason God had led me to this profession. Perhaps the delays were His way of ensuring that I took care of one more very important senior citizen. Evidently that was the case because we closed the transaction one month after Loraine Terry's death.

I learned a lot during my twenty-four years of caring for amazing people like the Terry's. Through my company, I have taken care of movie stars, motivational speakers, politicians, titans of business, and even one Nobel Laureate. It was an honor to be associated with each and every one of them, famous or not. If my story encourages just one young person to spend more time with an important senior citizen in their life, then writing this story will have accomplished its goal.

We can learn a lot from the elderly—all we have to do is listen.

To the reader

Several characters described at the beginning of this book are a combination of multiple individuals encountered in my professional career. I pushed several interesting characters together for the purpose of brevity and to make the story more interesting.

Regarding my father, he told me a lot of stories in the last ten years of his life, but the ones that always interested me the most were the war stories from World War II. I have always been fascinated by that time in our nation's history and most importantly what his generation overcame to win twin fights against Germany and Japan. As I state numerous times in this work, these stories helped me connect with him at a time when I needed direction, however I never assumed every word of what he told me was straight out of the history books. As they relate to this book, these stories were a means to an end - connecting a father and son. Because I cannot verify the accuracy of all of these stories I have called this book a novel instead of a memoir. My intention was to tell the story of how I was able to communicate with my ailing father through these stories, not to pass them off as fact or him as an unheralded hero of the second world war. He did serve, he did fly Hellcat's and Corsair's and he was involved in numerous battles with the enemy and for that he will always be a hero to me. But this book is about the relationship we formed, under difficult circumstances, through less than traditional means.

Acknowledgments

Having never served in the military it was necessary to consult with men who had to help me authenticate my military terminology and descriptions. I am lucky to have two good friends who took the time to help me with that process. Major Christopher Alpert USMC, Retired, who combed through this story with the thoroughness of a high school English teacher. And Laird Doctor USN, Retired, who, when I called, just happened to have an operations manual for a 1945 F4U Corsair on the desk in front of him. Your knowledge and insight was a tremendous help and I want to extend my deepest thanks to you both.

Joseph Lynch spent twenty four years in the health care industry working for public and private companies. He founded a private pay and Medicare reimbursed home care company in 1997 and sold it in 2014. He lives in Dallas with his wife and three children.

Made in the USA
Middletown, DE
12 October 2015